# *the* Passion *of* Perfection

*Gertrude Hitz Burton's Modern Victorian Life*

# June Vail

*The Passion of Perfection*
*Gertrude Hitz Burton's Modern Victorian Life*

©2017 June Vail

ISBN 13: 978-1-63381-115-7

*Cover:* portrait by Cornelia Fassett (1831-1898)

*Photo credits*
Except where noted, all illustrations and photographs
are from family collections and are courtesy of the author.

*Designed and produced by*
Maine Authors Publishing
12 High Street, Thomaston, Maine 04861
www.maineauthorspublishing.com

Printed in the United States of America

"But the effect of her being on those around her was incalculably diffusive: for the growing good of the world is partly dependent on unhistoric acts…"

—George Eliot, *Middlemarch*

# CONTENTS

*the* Passion *of* Perfection

# *Preface*

SOME YEARS AGO MY AGING PARENTS HAULED THREE DUSTY CARD-
board cartons through a trap door, down a rickety wooden lad-
der to the second floor, and into my sister's childhood bedroom. In
their uninsulated attic, the forgotten boxes had weathered decades
of Cleveland's frigid winters and humid summers. My parents suggested I have a look at them: they'd be pleased if I'd take them off
their hands.

The cartons contained treasures. Five generations had assem-
bled the raw materials for a family chronicle that spanned nearly 250
years. When I examined them more closely, I encountered Anna Gertrude Hitz Burton, my maternal great-grandmother. My first impression was of a loving young mother, writing to her two small sons, one
of whom—my grandfather—was six years old. In a rounded, fluid
script, she signed her messages with "twenty kisses" or "20,000 kisses
and fifty special hugs." The letters had been bound in two leather
volumes stamped in gold: "Gertrude Hitz Burton to Felix Arnold
Burton 1891-96" and "Gertrude Hitz Burton to Harold Hitz Burton
1894-96." As I began to read Gertrude's letters, I knew I needed to
investigate more thoroughly. I repacked the bits and pieces—diaries,
early daguerreotypes and later photographs, scrapbooks, and loose
sheets—into four hefty packages, and Fed-Exed them to my home in
Maine.

When they arrived, I began to sort through the nineteenth- and
twentieth-century materials. They revealed many untold family stories, and Gertrude's, especially, beckoned. Through her prolific correspondence, and the allusions to people, places, and events in her
father's journals, I began to piece together Gertrude's forgotten life

3

story, her links to well-known public figures and to the women's movement known as the Purity Crusade. Her unique experiences embodied broad themes connected with the rapidly industrializing Gilded Age: beauty and morality, spirituality and sexuality, illness and death.

My goal was to come to know Gertrude Hitz Burton: an ardent, ambitious young woman with a promising future, who was hindered and frustrated—and finally transformed—by her own ideals and an incurable illness.

❧

Anna Gertrude Hitz was born in Washington, DC, in May 1861, just after the outbreak of the Civil War. I followed her journeys across years and miles to the places she lived and worked during her peripatetic life: from Washington to Switzerland and back to Washington; then Boston; Maine; Florence, Italy; and upstate New York, before she arrived again, finally, in Switzerland, her father's native land. As an adult, Gertrude hardly alighted anywhere for longer than a year. Even as a wife and mother, she was never mistress of her own home. She became an outspoken advocate for sex education, marriage equality, and women's rights. Her eventful, but sadly brief, life was ended by tuberculosis. She died in a Swiss sanatorium in 1896, just months before her thirty-fifth birthday. The more details I gathered from family archives and the collections preserved in libraries here and abroad, the more I was persuaded that Gertrude's story was worth sharing beyond the family circle.

Some initial discoveries proved thrilling. During her short lifetime, a network of friends and colleagues respected and supported her, and she, in turn, influenced them. Many of them were renowned. I found personal letters from Clara Barton, American Red Cross founder and Hitz family friend, and from Mabel Gardiner Hubbard Bell, the wife of Gertrude's first employer and mentor, Alexander Graham Bell. Arctic explorer Robert E. Peary's daughter, Marie, had sent a note to Gertrude's sons explaining that her father's diaries included a first-hand account of their mother's courtship by Peary's college roommate, Alfred Edgar Burton. Naturally I wanted to find those diaries! I discovered them in Peary's collected papers in the National Archives.

Gertrude maintained lifelong friendships begun in her late teens and early twenties. I eagerly inspected a cache of letters to her college chum, Frances Haldeman Sidwell, written when they were students in the 1870s and '80s and kept for over fifty years. Gertrude's handwriting crisscrossed her square, onion-skin stationery to save space. Sidwell, who co-directed the prestigious Sidwell Friends School in Washington, DC, sent them to Gertrude's sons in the 1930s, with selected lines discreetly snipped out.

I also excavated personal correspondence between Gertrude and her young friends, Mary Whitall Smith and Bernard Berenson, who later became internationally known art historians and connoisseurs. I traced more of their exchanges to the Berenson Library archive at I Tatti, the Harvard Center for Renaissance Studies, near Florence, Italy.

Gertrude's intimate friend and her most prolific and captivating correspondent was William Bliss Carman, a Harvard-educated author and editor, later acclaimed as Canada's poet laureate. Their letters (many housed at Queen's University in Kingston, Ontario) and Carman's poetry introduced me to his bohemian Boston cohort, which included poets Richard Hovey and Louise Imogen Guiney, architect Ralph Adams Cram, and photographer F. Holland Day. The group called themselves "The Visionists." Cram described the years from 1880 to 1900, the verging-on-modern Gilded Age, as a time when for their idealistic generation, "There was nothing static in life: all was in motion, and the movement was, we believed...inevitably forward...."

In her poem, "The Knight Errant," Louise Imogen Guiney called a generation to action. I chose it as this book's epigraph for its hopeful message: though a worthy goal may remain out of reach, the quest itself can redeem flawed choices and "faulty ways." An uncompromising passion for perfection can mature into tolerance for human imperfection. Even an unsung life's fears and triumphs, struggles and scars, like the Knight Errant's, merit "honour at eventide."

Fascinated by the era, I began to grasp a late nineteenth-century cast of mind that rejected Gilded Age greed, ugliness, and inequality, yet remained optimistic about humankind's progress. Gertrude and her friends considered themselves innovative and forward-looking, even revolutionary. Women discarded corsets, embraced science, cultivated artistic and intellectual abilities, and pursued careers outside the domestic sphere. They adopted more flexible definitions of sexuality, religion, and gender roles, and worked together for social change and women's rights. They nurtured independent, unique personalities, or "performing selves," to cite cultural historian Warren Susman's term. Yet Gertrude's generation still cherished the Victorian virtues of "good character"—moral integrity, loyalty, and self-discipline. Humankind's moral perfectibility was the grand idea that inspired Gertrude's life's work.

To twenty-first-century observers, these Gilded Age women appear modern in the sense that a century and a half ago, they confronted difficulties that remain unresolved. Women today share similar struggles for unrealized social and personal goals, among them educating children and adults about sexuality, asserting marriage equality and women's right to choose, and eliminating double standards underlying domestic abuse and job discrimination.

"Passion" implies intense desires and ambitions—exciting, messy, sometimes overwhelming feelings. Yet "perfection" suggests calm and consistent self-mastery. Gertrude embodied the contradictory impulses of her transitional times. The passion for perfection sometimes paralyzed her attempts to balance career and family.

Gertrude kept reproductions of two favorite works of art, a classical sculpture and a painting, representing dual aspects of womanhood—one liberated, the other nurturing. The first was of Nike, the striding, striving, *Winged Victory of Samothrace*, personifying woman's natural beauty, physical strength, and forward momentum. The second was a tender *Madonna and Child* by Giovanni Battista Sassoferrato. To Gertrude, altruistic motherhood was a potent moral and social force.

⁊

Learning about Gertrude's life affected my own. I became acquainted with my extended family on my mother's side, across geographic borders and generations: a hundred distant cousins living in this country and abroad. I delved into Gilded Age cultural, literary, artistic, and scientific movements that formed Gertrude's world view. I traveled to far-flung cities to find the streets and houses where she lived. From the very room where she died, I shared Gertrude's view of snowcapped mountain peaks.

Personal keepsakes buried in the dusty cartons connected me to the past: a small silver heart engraved with the initials of Christina Brosi Hitz, the matriarch who emigrated from Switzerland with her husband, children, and grandchildren; and Gertrude's worn, pocket-sized letter opener, its handle carved with delicate oak leaves and tiny acorns, bundled with letters sealed with a thousand kisses.

In an era when handwritten messages have all but disappeared from our lives, I felt genuine pleasure as I opened envelopes long ago postmarked Boston, Deer Isle, Washington, and Lausanne, and removed thin sheets covered in familiar scrawls. I read (and reread) "my" correspondents' self-critical reflections, irreverent jokes, and helpful advice. After more than a century, their eloquent exchanges about loyalty and love, art and beauty, sex and death told Gertrude's profoundly human and remarkably modern story.

Brunswick, Maine

*December, 2016*

# THE KNIGHT ERRANT.

Spirits of old that bore me,
And set me, meek of mind,
Between great dreams before me
And deeds as great behind,
Knowing humanity my star
As first abroad I ride,
Shall help me wear, with every scar,
Honour at eventide.

Let claws of lightning clutch me,
From summer's groaning cloud,
Or ever malice touch me
And glory make me proud.
O give my faith, my youth, my sword,
Choice of the heart's desire :
A short life in the saddle, LORD!
Not long life by the fire.

Forethought and recollection
Rivet mine armour gay!
The passion of perfection
Redeem my faulty way!
The outer fray in the sun shall be
The inner beneath the moon;
And may Our Lady lend to me
Sight of the Dragon soon!

LOUISE IMOGEN GUINEY.

"The Knight Errant", Volume I, Number 1, April, 1892.
Courtesy of JSTOR. JSTOR is a digital library of academic
journals, books, and primary source objects.

# PART I

*Knowing humanity my star/As first abroad I ride*

CHAPTER 1

## Family Prologue

ANNA GERTRUDE HITZ, IMPELLED BY HER MOTHER'S VIGOROUS cough, arrived six weeks sooner than expected, early on the morning of May 29th. But "everything passed off much better than they all had feared," according to her father. The child's grandmother and namesake, Anna Kohler Hitz, attended the surprise birth, and Dr. Gaburi reached the Hitz home only after the commotion had quieted down.

The bourgeois Hitz family lived among other bureaucrats, storekeepers, and legislators in the Capitol Hill neighborhood. In 1861, Washington City was America's crowded, smelly, mosquito-ridden capital, with just over 63,000 residents. At the outbreak of the Civil War, a few imposing government buildings rose along the spoke-like cobblestone avenues that connected future circles and squares, but tenements and weedy empty lots, small boarding houses, churches, and bordellos surrounded these official edifices. From a hot air balloon, you could survey the landscape: a single railroad track leading into the center of town; rutted roads, rural farmlands, and the swampy Potomac just blocks from the White House; the Capitol building's half-completed cast-iron dome, surmounted by winches and derricks. Capitol Hill, to the east and south, encompassed a dense collection of houses and small businesses, taverns, markets, workshops, and stables.

The premature baby's parents—John Hitz, thirty-three years old, and Jane Catherine Shanks, twenty-four, called Kate—represented two established, but dissimilar, Washington castes. Kate's father, Michael Shanks, was a prosperous real estate developer with a home and valuable holdings in the center of Washington City. Shanks suspected his daughter's suitor, John Hitz, was after his money, and refused Hitz's request for Kate's hand in marriage. But Kate, an only child, was strongly attracted to him. He was nine years her senior, recently returned from panning for gold in California, and musically talented. She was a willful nineteen-year-old with a contrary streak, and in 1856 the daring couple eloped to Maryland.

The Shanks family's wariness and wealth contrasted with the Hitz family's geniality and modest means. Three generations of Hitzes had immigrated together to America from Switzerland in 1831. The family had successfully owned and managed a mining concern near the town of Davos, in the canton of Graubünden, until a disastrous economic collapse in 1830. Eventually, Hans Landammann Hitz and his wife Christina Brosi, with their son Johannes, a mining engineer, and his wife Anna Kohler, settled in Washington with their thirteen children. There they benefitted from connections with an already large, prosperous German and Swiss immigrant community: dairy farmers, candy makers, shopkeepers, hotel and restaurant owners, and government employees. Most Hitz relatives and friends lived near one another and communicated in Swiss German among themselves. The adults spoke heavily accented English.

John Hitz was three years old when the clan arrived in America. He became a jack of many trades, but master of few. When his father, Johannes, assumed the position of Swiss Consul in Washington in 1853, John assisted him in his official duties, without pay. As a young man, he was trained as a piano maker, and after his marriage, he supported himself and his young wife as a music teacher, piano tuner and repairman, and composer of waltzes. He later became a marginally successful music store owner, but was bankrupted by a cheating partner.

After four years in Maryland, the married couple returned to Washington with their first child, three-year-old Johanna, and reconciled with Kate's parents in 1860. They moved in with the elder

Hitzes at 29 South A Street, where, the following year, four-year-old Johanna died, and daughter Gertrude was born.

Later, in 1864, John, Kate and Gertrude moved to a white clapboard cottage with a large garden at the intersection of Pennsylvania Avenue and Sixth Street, SE. This Cape Cod-style house, where Gertrude spent her childhood, appeared more suited to a country lane than Pennsylvania Avenue. Two large, parallel brick chimneys gave the place a solid look. Low additions with separate entrances probably housed a cook and hired servant. All in all, it was an informal, inviting, and spacious dwelling, with four large dormer windows that expanded the attic space above the second-floor bedrooms. On the first floor were living and dining rooms, parlor and kitchen. Dark, formal furnishings downstairs and massive, carved Shanks family beds and armoires upstairs created a comfortable, prosperous atmosphere. As a girl, Gertrude admired her father's flair for creating and tending the fenced front and back gardens, filling them with roses and hollyhocks as well as wildflowers, ferns, and mosses. She loved the fragrant wisteria vines that encircled the porch's wooden pillars.

The property was a legacy from Michael Shanks. Both John's and Kate's fathers, Michael Shanks and Johannes Hitz, died in 1864. Michael Shanks left his daughter a fortune in real estate, rental properties, and cash. The elder Hitz bestowed on his son his sterling reputation. In his capacity as Swiss Consul, he had been a staunch Union supporter, a trusted procurer and distributor of government supplies and conveyor of information. President Abraham Lincoln and Secretary of State William H. Seward attended Johannes Hitz's burial in the Congressional Cemetery.

Although he was unqualified to do so, John Hitz cheerfully shouldered the legal responsibility for handling Kate's and both of their mothers' financial affairs that fell upon him after 1864. By law, married women were not allowed to own property in their own names. Managing his wife's inheritance, John collected rents, bought and sold properties, and oversaw building improvements. As a child, Gertrude often accompanied him around the town, waiting while he penciled complicated calculations into pocket-sized leather notebooks. Hitz often accepted partial payments and good-naturedly postponed due dates. John Hitz's great gift was for helping people: his diaries reveal a tender-hearted, intellectually curious, and profoundly spiritual man. But these positive qualities were offset by a sometimes dangerous naiveté and a hopeless head for business, which would eventually have disastrous consequences for the family, and particularly for Gertrude, as she navigated growing tensions between her parents.

On his father's death, Hitz also assumed the consular duties with which he was already familiar. The position cemented John Hitz's personal and professional ties to Switzerland and allowed his small family to travel there regularly. Kate and Gertrude made three separate, extended European visits between 1866 and 1877. Madame Hitz's Swiss passport described her as five feet, five inches tall, with blond hair and blue eyes, and a stature *bien developpée*.

Kate was accustomed to living well, and prolonged sojourns in Switzerland with her husband, and sometimes with Gertrude alone, afforded more refined and less expensive living conditions than those in chaotic post-Civil War Washington. Kate favored the mild climate of Lausanne, a picturesque city of 25,000 French speakers and a considerable Anglo-American expatriate community, located on the northern shore of Lake Geneva. Terraced vineyards surrounded the Old Town's university, cathedrals, and elegant parks and homes. Sweeping vistas to the south and west encompassed Lake Geneva, the Rhône River valley, the spectacular peaks of the Dents du Midi, and, in the distance, on the clearest days, France's regal Mont Blanc.

During the month of *le vendange*—the grape harvest—children were excused from school to roam the streets or help in the vineyards surrounding the upper town. Picture nine-year-old Anna Gertrude Hitz reveling in the warm sunshine of early October, running from the train station up the steep rue du Petit Chêne, passing by the wall of Monsieur Vulliemin's old home, the entrance to the Hôtel Richemont, and the gardens of the Hôtel Gibbon, then turning the corner at the coiffeur's onto the rue du Grand Chêne, at the Place Saint-François. When Gertrude arrived home near the formal gardens of the Montbenon Esplanade, she hurried up the front steps clasping a small bunch of wild myrtle blossoms. As a child, she was happy whenever she found a way to please her often-critical mother. She continued upstairs to her parents' bedroom with her offering, and there in the dark, curtained chamber, her mother "revealed a wondrous mystery:" a wee, soft, and very red baby sister, Jeanne Pauline. Gertrude cherished that memory.

In a photograph taken in Paris when she was about ten, Gertrude's dreamy brown eyes and strong jaw suggest thoughtfulness and determination. Her fashionable clothing reveals her family's tasteful affluence. By age sixteen, Gertrude had lived in Europe intermittently for five years. She spoke fluent French and valued her unique upbringing, but also yearned for a proper education.

Back in America in the fall of 1877, her parents enrolled her in Wilson College, located in Chambersburg, Pennsylvania, about a hundred miles from Washington. Wilson's handsome new buildings, on twenty-five acres of landscaped grounds, had opened their doors in 1870 to seventy-five female students and a faculty of eight. The founders' goal was to build "a first-class institution offering a college education for girls equal to the instruction for boys in elite East Coast schools." Wilson College aimed "to provide…that thorough and effective discipline which shall develop the mental faculties and secure both habits of thought and real scholarship," so that "the pupils will learn to think for themselves, and thus become leaders, instead of followers, in society." Nonsectarian religious training and an honor system would develop "the joint culture…of both intellect and heart," and call "into daily exercise the noblest principles of personal character."

In addition, the first Wilson College Bulletin assured parents that the college gave special attention to physical culture. During the summer before Gertrude's arrival, the college built a new gymnasium and required sports and gymnastic drills for all students. The catalogue emphasized the college's modern, healthful environment: "Severe illness is almost unknown at the College since the introduction of steam heat." Hygiene was becoming an important social goal.

At sixteen, Gertrude entered the school's two-year secondary academic program to prepare for the four-year Collegiate Course. Her classes included Latin, algebra, English grammar, rhetoric, American and general history, geography, and science (natural philosophy). She excelled in literature and philosophy, music and theater, and French.

But she was unable to complete her academic studies. To Gertrude's great disappointment, her father's questionable financial dealings had placed the family in a precarious economic position, and forced Gertrude to leave Wilson College one semester short of earning her prized degree. She withdrew from Wilson in February 1879, and, inaccurately quoting Victor Hugo's poem, "Crépuscule," (*"Aimez, vous qui vivez"*), wrote a wistful farewell message in her friend Mary Catherine Walker's autograph book: *"Aimez—et vous vivez!"*

The Hitz family's economic and legal troubles reached crisis proportions later that year. Gertrude was horrified when, in November 1879, a District of Columbia Grand Jury formally indicted her father, John Hitz, president of the recently incorporated German–American National Bank, together with C.E. Prentiss, the bank's treasurer, on charges of embezzlement and making false entries. Bail for each was posted at $5000, about $20,000 in today's currency. Bank failures had become commonplace during the booms and busts of the 1870s, and this scandal raised Kate's fears that her inheritance might disappear to pay the bank's—and her husband's—accumulated debts. She was determined to save her children from the consequences of their father's misjudgments. Although at first Kate was named her husband's co-defendant, she soon countersued, angrily denying any knowledge of his dealings, and charging that John Hitz intended to defraud her of her fortune.

By her lawyers' reckoning, the Shanks/Hitz's annual asset value from houses, rental properties, and commercial venues in Washington's thriving neighborhoods came to $117,000 in personal estate and $180,000 in real estate, or a total of $297,000, the equivalent of nearly $6,000,000 today.

When she learned of the German–American National Bank's default, Kate may well have recalled her father's dire prophecies about John Hitz before they eloped. During their secret courtship (in a letter smuggled to him by a mutual friend) Kate had explained to John that

> …When we were speaking of the opinions expressed by my father about the duplicity of every human being—I did not think we were so soon to have proof—but it is now proved to you by his expressions regarding your parents…he suspects everyone else in the same ways…and this universal suspicion has been held up to me since childhood as the best and highest wisdom I could attain—and I, having from the first a nature rather somber and melancholy, and prone to look at the dark side of everything, imbibed enough of it to make me doubt everyone who seemed to love me…

Now, a suspicious Kate was understandably exasperated, for there had been a forewarning. Seven years before, John Hitz had concealed from her his accumulated financial obligations, totaling $45,000. After that debacle, she had agreed to pay off his debts with Shanks income and live solely on John's consular salary of less than

$3000 a year, on his solemn promise that in the future, he would always keep her informed of their financial affairs.

Throughout the bank matter, Gertrude believed her father was sincere when he maintained his innocence. He swore that he had informed his wife of all financial dealings, pointing to Kate's signature on key transactions. But Kate countered, just as adamantly, that such issues were never fully explained. Kate vowed that John would pay dearly for betraying her trust. Beginning in 1879, their legal contests evolved into bitter, lifelong disputes.

The dissolution of the Hitz family followed. Kate had endured the deaths of three children. Their eldest, Kate Johanna, had died on Christmas Day of 1861, when Gertrude was seven months old. Anna Agnes passed away in 1865, before she was two. Jeanne Pauline, Gertrude's pet, born in Lausanne in 1870, died in Washington in 1876.

But in 1872 the family had welcomed their fifth child, William Henry Hitz, called Willie, blond and blue-eyed like his mother. Of the five, only Gertrude and Willie, the second and the last, survived, separated by eleven years and raised in vastly altered family circumstances. Gertrude was caught in the middle of her parents' feud when she reluctantly returned home from Wilson College to live with them and her younger brother in the cottage near Seward Square. In her bedroom, Gertrude wrote longingly to her best Wilson friend, Frances (Fansy) Haldeman:

> October 12, 1879
> Mine bonnie love, there is such a feeling of loneliness in my heart tonight—I long for the happy school-days and I must write just one or two love words. This afternoon I have spent a little while with dear old Grandmamma [Anna Hitz]…She offered me 25cts. but of course I would not accept it—poor dear loving woman! She lost everything through the failure. How I wish I had "the girls" and my precious Fansy here. God

bless you, my child. I feel very near you tonight. The two last years return with such vividness.

Her mother was determined not only to hang on to her inheritance but also to keep their seven-year-old son from his father's influence, at all costs. At forty years old, Kate created a new public identity by changing her own name officially from Mrs. John Hitz to Mrs. Jane C. Hitz. She no longer called herself Kate, but Jane.

Under the cloud of her father's criminal indictment, and to become independent from her mother, Gertrude felt she had to find a way to support herself. A dream of autonomy energized her, and may have eased the distress of leaving her college studies behind. She enrolled in the Washington Normal Kindergarten Institute, run by Mrs. Louise Pollock and her daughter Susie Pollock, on the corner of 8th and K Streets, NW, to train as a teacher in the progressive educational methods of Gustav Froebel.

Froebel had created the kindergarten concept in Germany in 1837 as a children's "garden" for learning-by-doing—a structured environment where the young child could freely grow and develop, under the care of a maternal teacher whose pedagogy was protective and nurturing, not directive. Through songs and games, prayers and nature study, the artful teacher would perfect young hearts, minds, and souls. The kindergarten movement in America, spearheaded by Boston's legendary educator Elizabeth Palmer Peabody, was quickly becoming popular, and was viewed as a means of moral and social reform. Gertrude Hitz became an ardent and skilled Froebel practitioner, or "kindergartner."

With characteristic passion and commitment—compensating, perhaps, for the overwhelming loss of family life, social standing and economic security—Gertrude confided to Fansy Haldeman her faith that every woman is capable of fulfilling her individual potential and making a mark in the world:

True womanhood is surely the strongest, most subtle influence in the world. It matters not so much its nature—if the type be itself the truest each woman can attain...and I am growing to find that the best training is always sure to be given us according to our needs—if we are willing to accept it—as it comes.

When the 1880 United States census taker knocked on the Hitz family's door at 601 Pennsylvania Avenue, Miss Anna Gertrude Hitz, nineteen years old, declared her occupation as "teacher."

# CHAPTER 2

## *Noblest Lives*

As Gertrude was settling into a career in education, two ambitious young men arrived in Washington. One of them would play a central role in her life. When Alfred Edgar "Burt" Burton and Robert Edwin "Bert" Peary disembarked from the Boston boat at five o'clock on the evening of July 9th, the thermometer read 107 degrees. Peary was twenty-three and Burton a year younger. Bert Peary sometimes called Burt Burton "Chum" or "Al." They had shared high school years in Portland, Maine, before winning scholarships to Bowdoin College and rooming together as Delta Kappa Epsilon fraternity brothers. Both young men graduated with bachelor's degrees in civil engineering, Peary in 1877 and Burton in '78, and then acquired practical surveying experience. Bert served as Fryeburg, Maine's town surveyor, mapmaker, and taxidermist for two years, and Burt joined him there following his own graduation. Both men emerged as top scorers on national examinations for six intern positions, at $10 a week, in the new Office of the Coast and Geodetic Survey, formerly a division of the Department of the Interior.

During the hot summer of 1879, by three in the afternoon when their office obligations were over, the two men hiked in Rock Creek Park, climbed the steep, 365-step metal staircase leading to the top of the Capitol's dome, sailed past Mount Vernon on a Potomac excursion boat, examined paintings and young ladies in the Corcoran Art Gallery, and enjoyed public band concerts, lounging on the White House lawn. Through the fall and winter, they set out from their rooming house at 405 East Capitol Street, SE, on expeditions to explore Washington City.

Much of the permanent population of government bureaucrats and shopkeepers lived near the Coast Survey offices on First Street, SE. Many small stores and the huge, red brick Eastern Market served those living in the mix of single family homes, row houses, hotels, and boarding houses in the Capitol Hill neighborhood. Fifteen years after the end of the Civil War, Washington was only gradually evolving into the nation's capital city. The wide streets were still unpaved.

Young people living on Capitol Hill gathered often for entertainments. As eligible bachelors, Peary and Burton were invited to church-affiliated gatherings and private parties called "sociables," with guitars and piano music, card playing, charades, and other parlor games. The two young men took advantage of their freedom, sometimes staying out till two in the morning, even during the week. Slim, wiry, handsome Alfred Edgar Burton tended to be the more outgoing of the two. Robert Edwin Peary was still promised to May, his girl back in Maine, although after a time, she returned the ring he sent her.

Gertrude made the acquaintance of both men on January 6, 1880, at a young people's get-together. Peary wrote in his diary, "In the evening went with Al to a card party at Addie Hay's. Miss Fox, Miss Hitz, Miss Wright and the Misses Mygatt, Seavey, and Van Rankin present. Spent a very enjoyable evening and got back to the room about midnight." The next evening, Al was out again and, on Friday, Bert "… Got a note in the morning from Addie Hay inviting Al and me to meet a little company at her Uncle's, 707 H St…"

After their six months' trial period, Peary and Burton found themselves among the fortunate final four Coast Survey interns appointed to permanent positions. By early February 1880, the men's workdays had become busier and their social obligations more demanding—frequent parties and evening visits, mostly in the neighborhood where they lived: at the Halstead's on C St, SE; the Edson's on the corner of 14th and B, SE; and the Hitz house near Seward Square. Among the young ladies, Bert and Burt both admired twenty-year-old Gertrude Hitz. They continued visiting with the local girls during that spring and summer. Peary and Burton called often on

Miss Hitz and Miss Fansy Haldeman, "by invitation." Together, the four took in the Opera House and the Planetarium. After the November elections, the chums "engaged a hand cart" and moved to nearby rooms at 402 New Jersey Ave, SE. By the Christmas holidays, Gertrude had become smitten with Burton, and during the late winter their relationship grew closer.

In February, too, Gertrude began to experience weakness and such severe discomfort in her knee that walking became difficult. The mysterious, persistent joint pain suggested underlying health problems, but doctors could find no obvious cause. She was determined to conquer the annoyance. Jane Hitz was connected with a national medical network through her work with the Washington Dispensary and the national Moral Education Society. She arranged for Gertrude's treatment by one of the "star" doctors of the time, Dr. Silas Weir Mitchell of Philadelphia, well-known for working with women's nervous maladies, as well as for his successful sideline career as a novelist. Jane accompanied Gertrude to Philadelphia and stayed intermittently with her daughter in a Quaker boarding house on Spruce Street, near Rittenhouse Square. After several weeks of treatments, featuring elaborate steaming procedures, electro-magnetic sessions, and encasement of the joint in a leg brace painted "fleshy beige," mother and daughter returned to Washington.

The trio of Gertrude, Burt, and Bert observed President James A. Garfield's inaugural parade on March 4, 1881, from convenient indoor box seats in her father's office at the Swiss Consulate in the Vernon Building, on the corner of Pennsylvania Avenue and Tenth Street, NW. With other business to attend to, Bert Peary soon left the couple alone. Later in her life, Gertrude remembered several inaugurations, and especially that one:

> I can see all the temporary stands & the arches & platforms & the staring rawness of it all, & the crude red, white, & blue, & I can feel the wind & cold, & recall the irrepressible thrills of my girlhood as band passed after band in the interminable processions.

... I was in my father's office—and I remember how wildly in love with each other a certain two people were & how they were left alone in the room crowded with [portraits of] Swiss heroes—Indeed I wonder the world still moves in rational order when one thinks of all the desperate lovers wandering at large.

The couple's strong mutual devotion grew, despite—or possibly because of—frequent forced separations.

In late April, the Coast and Geodetic Survey required additional staff in Memphis, Tennessee, on short notice. Bert Peary begged off the assignment because his widowed mother had just arrived from Maine for a visit. So Burton left by train the following evening, dismayed by an assignment that would keep him away from Washington for two months. Peary observed, "From indications last night, I am afraid Al is badly smashed"—in other words, infatuated with Miss Hitz.

Until early June, while Burton was in Memphis, Peary continued to call regularly on the Misses Fox, Mygatt, and Hitz, borrowing books and enjoying ice cream. "Passed a very pleasant evening with Miss Hitz," he noted, with "music, songs, etc., and when I came away, she filled my hands with roses and honeysuckle."

Gertrude and Bert Peary shared a fondness for Romantic poetry and Germanic myths—for example, Heinrich Heine's poem, "Die Lorelei," in which a beautiful siren, innocently sitting on a cliff above the Rhine River, distracts shipmen with her song, causing them to crash on the rocks. Gertrude also collected European songs and folk tales, and particularly liked the Swiss legend of the Queen of the Snows, the tale of a chaste queen, guarded by dwarfs armed with spears of crystal, who lures hunters and mountaineers to climb higher and higher in hopes of seeing her beautiful face. Her lookouts press her suitors backwards until they fall over a precipice. At the sight, the white lady begins to cry, and her tears flow down the mountain to the high pastures. Near the rocks, they are transformed into that rare, pale flower, the edelweiss.

Switzerland's lofty, snow-capped mountains symbolized pure "white places," just beyond reach. Gertrude may have imagined herself as a Lorelei or Queen of Snows, attainable only with great difficulty.

Early in June, Peary called on Miss Hitz to return a book. The Hitz garden had come into full flower: springtime's red tulips and yellow narcissi, Johnny-jump-ups and pansies were gone by, replaced by lush greenery, trailing vines, and tall speckled foxglove, pink and white phlox, yellow chrysanthemums, confetti-hued zinnias, and the promise of huge hydrangeas, some blue, some white. Her father's roses scented the backyard. Gertrude invited Peary to attend her up-coming commencement exercises at the Washington Kindergarten Normal Institute, and played some tunes for him on her guitar. When he left, she again filled his arms with flowers. But at a certain mo-ment, when Gertrude had left the room, Peary scanned her shelves and found, with disappointment, "… a little picture of Al with a cou-plet on the back: 'How sad is my heart and uncertain, while awaiting the coming of Burton.'"

Even graver uncertainties pervaded the Hitz household during that summer of 1881. On June 20th, Jane Hitz informed her hus-band she intended to abandon the house and separate from him per-manently. She announced her plan just before leaving with Gertrude and Willie for a three-week vacation at a summer boarding house, The Dennis Cottage, in Atlantic City, New Jersey. On the evening before their parting, husband and wife talked over the future of their shared home, which she had inherited and maintained for over fifteen years. John Hitz proposed to stay there as long as he could and, if she would agree, to rent out most of the furnished house, retaining a room for himself. Jane Hitz consented, matter-of-factly stating that she had already paid their servant Clara in advance for half a month, but no longer.

Gertrude left with her mother and younger brother early the next morning without protesting, but Willie did not want to leave his father, and wept frequently. Contrary to his wife's wishes, Hitz accompanied them to the station. After they boarded the train, Hitz walked to Maryland Avenue to wave as the cars passed by, and then, distraught, he wandered the city aimlessly.

To make matters worse, a cable arrived that evening from Bern, the capital of the Swiss Federation, confirming the Federation's acceptance of Hitz's resignation as Consul General. Some weeks earlier, because of the growing bank scandal, the Swiss government had requested he relinquish the post. On the day John Hitz's family left him, he also lost his sole means of financial support and his diplomatic status. His life was in ruins.

Gertrude and Willie returned briefly to Washington with their mother in mid-July, then left again almost immediately for Maine. The night before they parted, Jane advised her husband that she intended to discharge their servant Clara on August 1st. She would pack her own clothing and the children's, along with a few household articles, and store them in a rented room in Vernon Row, at 10th and K, NW. In his diary Hitz noted that, "Her tone was reasonable and she said she had no fixed plan for the future. As far as she was concerned, I could now rent out the house, furnished or not, but she would no longer pay expenses of carrying it on."

The next morning, Hitz went to his wife's room to say goodbye. He was scheduled to travel to Atlanta for a National Education

Association conference, as a trustee of the Georgetown Home Industrial School. She was in bed, he wrote, and "... such feelings as pervaded me it would be impossible to describe—something akin to Othello's—for despite all, I love that woman supremely above all others—and yet, in her presence, her cold demeanor unmans me, and causes me to say and think what I constantly regret afterwards."

Half an hour later, he departed for the station.

Jane Hitz had arranged to retreat to Down East Maine, suitably distant from both her husband and the Washington heat, on the recommendation of women friends. After a long journey by train to Portland, she, Gertrude, and Willie traveled by coastal steamer to the fishing village of Stonington, on Deer Isle, and from there, by carriage, ten jarring miles over rutted coastal roads to Captain Benjamin Sylvester's lodgings. Other guests there included enough young people to keep both nine-year-old Willie and twenty-year-old Gertrude busy with sailing, tennis, and games. Jane Hitz's acquaintances—activists, teachers, artists, and intellectuals from Washington, Boston, and other cities—were summering in rental cottages on Deer Isle and the surrounding islands.

On their return from Maine, Jane Hitz left the cottage and garden at Seward Square for good. She found a house for herself and Willie at 315 New Jersey Avenue, SE, a ten minute walk away. Although the Hitz marriage remained legally intact, Jane Hitz never again spoke directly to her husband. Communicating through lawyers, she rejected every gesture of reconciliation. She also successfully kept young Willie from visiting with his father, although they sometimes chanced upon each other on the street.

To keep body and soul together, Hitz sold valuable furniture and his cherished books. Stoves and bed frames went for scrap iron. He rented out the lower floor of the cottage, and kept the upstairs and attic rooms for himself, with kitchen privileges. There was space enough for Gertrude.

Gertrude prepared to return to Philadelphia for further treatments for her lame knee, emotionally torn between loyalties to both parents. She was struggling with profound disappointment, loneliness, and guilt, intensified by the fear of looming poverty. She longed for stability.

While she was away, her devastated fifty-three-year-old father was stricken with malaria, common in the swampy capital. Bert Peary chronicled Alfred Edgar Burton's growing involvement with the family, following Gertrude's request, during the early days of Hitz' illness: "Monday, October 17, 1881: Burt was called away from Office by sickness of Mr. Hitz; Tuesday: Al away all last night and today; Wednesday: Al still in the nursing business."

Gertrude hurried to Washington to nurse her father through his illness. She wrote to Fansy Haldeman, now studying at Vassar College, about his condition:

> … Yesterday the doctors told me very decisively that there were only two things to choose from—death or the ever probable recurrence of brain disease…Burt stays right in the house and is of great help and comfort. My father seems so glad and satisfied to have him here…I feel very well and do not overwork and above all my dear child, believe that my heart is genuinely cheerful….

A month later, however, ailing again and about to return to Philadelphia with her mother's help, Gertrude wrote Fansy a long and heartfelt letter:

Washington, DC. Nov. 25—1881

Friday—before breakfast. Upper back-room.

… I got up early this morning for the express purpose of writing to you. It has seemed impossible to find any time during the day. Well—the parlor was cold—then there were the potatoes and…Burt. I believe there are a few moments left before breakfast and these are yours.…my dear child these have been such busy, cooking, responsible days for me—and yet I seem to have accomplished very little—and it still requires large brains to make the money elastic.

But now, about Christmas. I expect to go to Phila next week and will probably stay somewhere near the whereabouts of February. Whether I will come to W[ashington] for the holidays is very uncertain. My position is one so delicate that I cannot ask for one cent more than is absolutely necessary. Matters have so adjusted themselves—that I cannot…with propriety stay at my mother's (I refer of course to the laws of inner conscience) and of course I could not impose myself upon my father with even the warmest merriest Xmas cheer—he is absolutely penniless, and until I am free from the doctor's rule—I am unable to make him other-wise. You see therefore that the chances are few.

Boston I force myself to give up—of course it must be done—I often wonder why I am so selfish—then try to be happy and thankful for you. Truly Fansy—I speak rarely of this—it would be better if I never spoke—but seeing what I have lost in strictly educational book and school life—my whole soul pines in ambitious longings for you…

You are more to me than a sweet, trustful—true-loving friend—I want you to realize that thing unattained in myself—It matters not from whence it comes—so that the power for good and growth is in the whole world…The noblest lives are surely those which make the least noise doing much.

In truth, and under more favorable circumstances, Gertrude would have enjoyed not only doing great things, but also receiving attention for them, as well. She was a teacher who relished performing, and dreamed of traveling to Boston to start a school.

During the colder months, and into the spring, Burton moved into the Hitz cottage's attic rooms, paying rent of $5 a month. Meanwhile, his former roommate, Bert Peary, had become restless and bored. On October 28, Peary wrote that he had "tendered my resignation to Professor Hilgard tonight and got my month's pay." He thought a career in the Navy might offer adventure. In December, Peary was commissioned as Lieutenant in the United States Navy's Engineering Corps and immediately traveled to the tropics to plan for the construction of a proposed canal. Decades later, and more famously, as Commander Robert E. Peary, he would explore the arctic regions, in search of the North Pole.

In 1882, a half year after Peary departed, Burton also resigned from the Coast Survey Office to take up a post in Boston, as lecturer in topographical engineering at the Massachusetts Institute of Technology. George L. Vose, his former Bowdoin College professor, was now teaching at "Tech," and recommended him for the position. And Gertrude quickly devised a plan to follow him to Boston, by hook or by crook.

# CHAPTER 3

## *Impression and Expression*

AFTER SPENDING A SECOND SUMMER ON DEER ISLE WITH HER MOTHer and brother, Gertrude joined Burton in Boston in September 1882. He found them rooms in the same boarding house.

Gertrude intended to study oral expression. Gertrude's planned studies were probably made possible with her own earnings from teaching the previous spring, augmented by her mother's subsidies. A love of drama attracted her to public speaking as well as teaching. In searching out a suitable program, Gertrude met Boston University professor Alexander Melville Bell, the father of Alexander Graham Bell. The elder Bell's research on physiological phonetics had produced numerous works on speech communication.

One of A.M. Bell's associates, Samuel Silas Curry, became Gertrude's mentor. He was a professor of elocution, first at the Boston University School of Oratory and later, at his own independent School of Expression. Professor Curry's system of public speaking sprang from the idea that all expression comes from within. This premise contrasted with then current assumptions that standardized gestures and conventional turns of phrase best commanded an audience's attention. Curry maintained that vocal intonation, posture, and gesture cannot be prescribed, but must happen naturally, in response to a lecturer's or actor's genuinely felt emotion. His pedagogical system emphasized the complementarity of reception, or acquisition of knowledge, on the one hand, and production, or creation of original ideas, on the other. "We call these two phases of education Impression and Expression," said Curry. The professor's views expanded Gertrude's preparation as a teacher. She eagerly began acquiring tools for public speaking in addition to her pedagogical work, not yet thinking in terms of feminist activism.

Boston in 1882 retained a shabby colonial charm. At the corner of Tremont and School Streets the "quaint, dark and lowly" granite King's Chapel, built in the mid-eighteenth century, and the newer City Hall stood opposite the Parker House Hotel. A block to the east, at the intersection of School and Washington Streets, the Old Corner Book Store occupied the city's oldest brick building. Nearby, commercial Washington Street's retail district, bustling with horse-drawn street cars, carriages and window shoppers, was connected by a grimy subterranean passage, called the "Rat Hole," to Province Court, a narrow back alley where a cobbler, metal worker, harness maker, and other craftsmen plied their trades in small workshops. This old underground passageway was a favorite byroad of Gertrude's, and reminded her of other dark, mysterious passageways she had known as a child in Lausanne. She would "dive down a cellar-way…way up in the north-eastern corner of the Court…& then in almost absolute blackness walk fearlessly along until the light guides you once more…" exiting into Washington Street's hubbub.

The Back Bay lay on the far side of town, across the Boston Common and beyond the attractive Public Garden, where popular swan boats glided on the lagoon. The boats were inspired by the story of Lohengrin, a knight of the Grail, who was helped across a river by a swan to defend the innocence of Princess Elsa.

Recently reclaimed from marshlands along the Charles River, the Back Bay's luxury residential neighborhood was arranged on a grid of eight streets crossing the central spine of Commonwealth Avenue and named alphabetically for English nobility: Arlington, Berkeley, Clarendon, and so on. Although the area had been prepared for development, little construction was complete. However, the imposing five-story Rogers Building, home to the Massachusetts Institute of Technology, already stood at 491 Boylston Street, between Berkeley and Clarendon, near Copley Square. There, in the fall term, Burton began teaching courses at Tech, as a lecturer in topographical engineering.

Gertrude and Burton's Boston friends included Tech students as well as some at Harvard University and Boston University's School of Liberal Arts. Early on, Gertrude encountered Bernhard Berenson, four years her junior, the son of Jewish Lithuanian immigrants and a precocious student at the Boston Latin School. His exotic looks and intellectual brilliance made him a welcome newcomer to Gertrude and Burton's circle. After one year at Boston University, Berenson transferred to Harvard as a sophomore. Gertrude and he remained confidants even after he graduated from Harvard in 1887, and throughout his later European research as an aspiring art connoisseur and critic.

Gertrude and Bernhard (who spelled his first name with an "h" until the First World War), shared an enthusiasm for the flowering Aesthetic Movement. They worshipped beauty as truth—in natural and manmade environments, in persons, and in painting, literature, music, and other arts. Together, they pondered their responses to artistic expression and introspected on their subjective impressions. They agreed, after reading their idol Walter Pater's essay, "The School of Giorgione" (1877), that their goal should be to pursue the highest quality of experience, living each minute to the fullest. Pater, a countercultural guru of sorts, maintained the value of continual awareness and sensitivity, because "every moment, some form grows perfect in hand or face; some tone on the hills or the sea is choicer than the rest; some mood of passion or insight or intellectual excitement is irresistibly real and attractive for us—for that moment only." This aesthetic ideal inspired Gertrude throughout her life, even while she directed her energies to furthering social causes.

Gertrude later described her youthful relationship with Berenson to her friend Mary Whitall Smith from Germantown, Pennsylvania: "I believe that he is a genius—but I love him for his beautiful personality, and our friendship is as close as the friendship of two girls and seems to belong to another age it is so spontaneous, so lofty and so tender."

�֍

Gertrude had met Mary earlier, in Philadelphia, while being treated for her lame knee. By 1882, Mary was eighteen and a freshman at Smith College. She noted in a letter to her mother that Gertrude "is one of my interesting young friends," whose refreshing ideas and stimulating personality motivated Mary to travel from Northampton to Boston for visits.

In her 1882 diary, Mary described Gertrude's apparently immaculate bond with Mr. Burton:

> In October I paid a most interesting visit to Gertrude Hitz in Boston. She is studying at the Institute of Technology. It seemed like another land, where everything mean and petty had dropped away. Her friendship with Mr. Burton, an old friend of hers who boards in the same house with her, is the most lovely friendship I ever saw. It is real "Platonic Love." I cannot tell how much I enjoyed being with her in those days. She also was with us last week on our "Boston Bust," as we called it.

Platonic lovers, "wildly in love with each other"?

✖

Gertrude and Burton counted themselves among the growing cadre of student guests in coed boarding houses all over Boston, drawn to the many colleges and universities of "the Athens of America." They shared their generation's rich spiritual, aesthetic, and intellectual environment, inhabited by international writers and artists. They were steeped in the words and images of the British poets William Blake, John Keats, and John Ruskin. Their American influences included Ralph Waldo Emerson, Walt Whitman, Josiah Royce, and Charles Eliot Norton. Contemporary inspiration also came from Matthew Arnold, Robert Browning, George Du Maurier, Walter Pater, Robert Louis Stevenson, Rudyard Kipling, J.M.W. Turner, William Morris, and all the Pre-Raphaelites. And, after his tour of America in 1882, "the Apostle of Aestheticism," Oscar Wilde.

The peaceful and industrially developing decades of the late nineteenth century allowed young, educated Americans to appreciate wide-ranging European artistic worlds: in music, the heroic Richard Wagner, lyrical Johannes Brahms, and witty Gilbert and Sullivan; in theatre, Sarah Bernhardt, Ellen Terry, Edwin Booth; in philosophy, the German Romantics Friedrich Schiller, Wilhelm von Goethe, and Heinrich Heine. Their philosophy tutors were Immanuel Kant, Karl Marx, and Georg Wilhelm Friedrich Hegel.

Charles Darwin's theory of evolution and Herbert Spencer's adaptation to social theory provoked debate. The sudden explosion of scientific and technological advances—electricity, incandescent light bulbs, telephones—promised a future of limitless possibilities for exchanging ideas, yet also raised doubts about negative effects of progress on aesthetic as well as social values.

Bernhard Berenson's friend Ralph Adams Cram, then a design intern and later an acclaimed architect, recalled in his autobiography the "decayed gentility" of the brick row houses in Boston's South End, where he and many young scholars boarded. He described the residents as "… music students and other searchers for fame and, particularly, that phenomenon of the period, the girl students of elocution."

Gertrude was one of those "girl students of elocution." At the close of the 1883 spring term, she learned that her teachers, Professors A.M. Bell and S. S. Curry, and the Superintendent of Public Schools in Washington had recommended her for the position of head instructor at Alexander Graham Bell's proposed Private Experimental School for the Deaf. Bell intended the school to be organized according to Froebel kindergarten methods. He proposed teaching deaf children to speak, using his father's system of "Visible Speech: The Science of Universal Alphabetics" and a technique called "Line Writing," curved written shorthand shapes indicating vocal physiology, or the placement of the tongue and lips, to create sounds.

Alexander Graham Bell had left his research post at Boston University, where he developed and tested his revolutionary invention, the telephone. In 1879 he moved to Washington to engage in intense patent litigation, begun in 1878. By 1880, through mergers and hard-fought legal battles, he had established the American Bell Telephone Company and amassed a fortune. Bell made his home in Washington with his wife, Mabel Hubbard Bell, who had become deaf at age five as a result of scarlet fever.

Professor Bell called at the Hitz cottage on Capitol Hill on September 3, 1883, to inquire how Gertrude could be reached and whether she would take on the responsibility of adapting the Froebel kindergarten system for deaf children. As John Hitz recorded their conversation, Bell wanted "to see her...to ascertain if her pronunciation...would answer his purpose of teaching a new system of articulation to children, which the deaf could learn and understand—proposing to try it on three deaf children whom he wanted taught in the kindergarten method in all other respects, and who were to pay each $250 for a year's instruction. The system [was] already found successful in Scotland..."

Gertrude was visiting a friend in New York City and not expected in Washington until the following week. Her initial meeting with Bell started off on a farcical note: her train was delayed, and when Bell called at the Hitz cottage as planned, she had not yet arrived. He returned home. Later that afternoon, Gertrude and her father took a hansom cab from the railroad station directly to Bell's imposing residence at 1500 Rhode Island Avenue, NW, at Scott Circle. Meanwhile, Bell had left again for the station. At last, they all converged at Bell's home, and he explained his ideas for a school and his methods for teaching deaf children to speak.

Gertrude was invited to return the next morning for a conversation with Mrs. Bell, an expert lip-reader, who would evaluate Gertrude's articulation. That afternoon, Bell engaged her as his school's first teacher, and the following day she began her own instruction in A.M. Bell's "Line Writing and Visible Speech." The position would give Gertrude, and her father, a measure of financial stability. Hitz, deeply in debt and worried over the pending court cases, commented in his diary: "Thanks be to the Lord for this—It is He that leadeth us if we will be but led."

Reluctantly, Gertrude left Burton and Boston behind, although she was delighted to find a challenging job in Washington, her former home. She immediately rekindled friendships there. She was quick to contact Fansy Haldeman, who was about to graduate from Vassar College and would soon begin teaching at Washington's newly opened Sidwell Friends School.

She also located Mary Whitall Smith, who had withdrawn from Smith College after her first year and returned to her parents' home in Germantown when her prominent father suffered financial losses from an unwise oil investment scheme. The two young women influenced each other. While Gertrude was teaching at the Bell school during the 1883-84 school year, Mary followed her example and earned a Froebel kindergarten teaching certificate. Gertrude adopted the use of the familiar *thee* in correspondence with her Quaker friend, who had been nicknamed Mariechen by a German nursemaid. Gertrude deeply admired the Quakers' tradition of equality of the sexes, and also favored the plain Quaker style of dress, a simple shift of muted gray, with a white muslin collar.

Gertrude's and Mary's literary, artistic, fashion, and societal interests reflected modernizing trends. Gertrude dared cut her hair unconventionally short. It was Gertrude who first introduced Mary to Walt Whitman's controversial verses in *Song of Myself* and *Leaves of Grass*. She saw in Whitman's poems an affirmation of sexuality as a natural aspect of human experience, recognizing spiritual bonds that transcended physical intercourse. At Gertrude's suggestion, Mary had borrowed a copy of *Leaves of Grass* from a liberal-minded English professor at Smith College, the feisty writer Kate Sanborn, despite warnings about inappropriate passages. Although initially shocked, Mary, like Gertrude, came to love Whitman's work. On her return to Philadelphia, Mary convinced her parents to invite the poet to their home, not far from his, across the Delaware River in Camden, New Jersey. Whitman, then sixty-four, and the Smiths, parents and children, became friends.

In November 1883, Gertrude and Mary conversed over dinner with Walt Whitman and his companion–biographer Richard Maurice Bucke, while they were visiting the Smith family. Several years later, in a letter to Mary, she recalled:

> ... a remark which Dr. Bucke made in Germantown on that Sunday afternoon when Walt Whitman came to dinner and we all staid so long talking around the table. He said that he believed that all boys passed through a period during which they disliked and avoided girls—that it was something natural and inevitable, as it was but the repetition in the individual of a period of similar feeling far back in the early history of the race. Perhaps thee remembers how entirely sure he felt he was right, and that I was wrong in attempting to ignore the feeling or to believe it could be overcome by any special instruction in regard to the sexual nature.

In contrast to Bucke's assertion that "ontogeny recapitulates phylogeny," Gertrude's confidence in the power of education to deepen and broaden understanding, and to guide and improve behavior, particularly in the area of sexuality, grew stronger during her year in Washington, teaching at Bell's Experimental School.

Gertrude organized the school's move into a little house at 1234 16th Street at Scott Circle, around the corner from Bell's home. A square, hand-painted sign identified the house as "Mr. Bell's Private School." Her father called the narrow, old-fashioned brick Victorian, with bay windows above and next to the front door, "a small bijou of a school." Its roof was crowned with delicate cast-iron filigree. A decorative fence surrounded the lawn with a hedge and vine-covered arbor. Children could run and play with abandon in the yard.

Inside, the downstairs accommodated a kindergarten for hearing children, including Bell's own two daughters, Daisy and Elsie, aged three and five. The deaf children shared recess play with the non-deaf students. Bell considered this arrangement "experimental" because the school created a middle ground between the extremes of isolating deaf children in a world of their own or, alternatively, placing them in regular schools with other children and relegating them to outsider status. Bell rejected the use of sign language as a separate means of communication, placing him sharply at odds with Edward Miner Gallaudet, founder of what would become Gallaudet College, now Gallaudet University.

Gertrude kept a daily classroom journal, on which she based a conference paper presented at the end of the school year. In characteristically vivid prose she described how she consciously created the school's aesthetic atmosphere, designing and outfitting it in accordance with her taste:

> As one's daily surroundings have so much to do in moulding effects and producing results... I should say a few words about our school rooms. They had morning and afternoon sunshine. The window overlooked a garden which in the spring burst into a wonder of bright colors and sweet smells. It

will always be a pleasure to recall the memory of those rooms with the air of the nursery and a touch of the home; the walls, with their pictures of happy children; the open fireplace; the pretty little chairs and tables, the curtained shelves full of kindergarten materials, the other toys, the horse with real hair, the steam cars, the beautiful doll with her own chair and crib and trunk full of clothes.

On opening day, October first, a *Washington Evening Star* reporter published his impressions of the deaf children's upstairs school room, saying that "it did not look like any school room I had ever seen: it could have been a parlor." The doorways and windows were hung with handsome portières and curtains, and the floor was covered with a soft rug. There were no desks or maps, and in the recess formed by the bay window was "a cute little divan that ran all around it, just high enough for the little ones to climb up on the soft cushion." There were pictures on the walls, and ornaments on the mantel and in the cabinets.

In this setting, Gertrude and Professor Bell devised ways to use Froebel's method of learning-by-doing for deaf children. They created

> ... a museum of common things—a collection of as many every day, ordinary things as we thought of. These were put into bottles and labeled on one side in line-writing, and on the other side, in script.
>
> At first, everything was labeled—the doors, the walls, the windows, the table, the chairs, and the playthings. In order to give the children the idea that these pictures or written words were the names of the objects...we established what we called "the shop system." We had racks filled with cards. On these cards were written the names of the objects. When the horse was wanted we would lead the horse to the card rack and hunt the card which bore the same word-picture as the label on the horse. Having found it, I would speak the word *horse*, place the child's hand at my throat, and after the child

made an effort to reproduce the word in speech, the card was handed to me and the child received the horse.

    … By and by as the words became familiar we did not need the cards with their written symbols…instead of hunting a card, the children came to me directly and spoke the words.

    We have had kindergarten principles in our play, in our school government, and in our general work…The chief object of this school has been the development of speech. Therefore all kindergarten methods have been subservient to that end.

She concluded:

    … We have learned that deaf children do not use signs if they can have words…We have learned that departments for deaf children should be established in connection with free kindergartens…Language is to be developed naturally…In our special work upstairs we began by playing, and have been playing ever since, as much and as hard as we could.

Gertrude's effective approach to teaching, and running the classroom in close collaboration with Professor Bell, bolstered her confidence that she might pursue a meaningful career.

    As an added benefit, Gertrude was able to help her father secure his first employment since the bank scandal. Professor Bell hired John Hitz to research and record data for a massive project on inherited deafness in the population of Martha's Vineyard. Hitz began by transcribing information from Census Bureau documents to note cards and, with the help of five women from the Bureau, completed the daunting project in record time. He collected a paycheck of $36.53, and a $20.00 reimbursement for the cost of the cards.

    Gertrude was trying to balance financial and emotional support for her father with increasing interaction with her mother, who remained estranged from John Hitz. Now financially independent and on more equal terms, Gertrude became an active member of the Washington Moral Education Society. By joining Jane Hitz in the Society's crusade to promote women's health and equal rights, Gertrude discovered her own life's work.

# CHAPTER 4

## *The Sexual Nature*

GERTRUDE WANTED TO MAINTAIN A POSITIVE RELATIONSHIP WITH her mother, who inspired a mix of respect and anxiety, while her closer bond was with her father, who offered unconditional love. Father and mother seemed to have reversed conventional parental roles. To complicate their family dynamics further, Gertrude, at twenty-two, found herself playing parent to her father, while remaining eager for her mother's approval.

Jane Hitz had chosen separation from her husband, rather than divorce, because it offered fewer legal and social disadvantages. Five years after Michael Shanks' death, the 1869 Married Women's Property Act for the District of Columbia allowed Jane the legal right to her inherited wealth and property. However, that law still gave her husband control over her father's fortune. But John Hitz voluntarily relinquished this conjugal right in 1879, after the bank scandal broke, acknowledging his moral responsibility to his wife. Consequently, Jane Shanks Hitz managed to retain most of her father's estate, although one valuable lot at 9th and G Streets, NW, was confiscated as partial restitution for the German–American Bank's debts. She stubbornly disputed this loss in the courts for decades, until her death.

Gertrude admired her mother's strength of character. Together with other influential Washington matrons, and the majority of the city's pioneer women homeopaths, Jane Hitz had founded the Washington Moral Education Society ten years earlier. Jane Hitz also was an incorporator, with numerous women from the upper echelons of Washington society, of the Women's Dispensary, the Washington Training School for Nurses, and the Washington Labor Exchange. Financially independent at forty-five, Jane Hitz continued working with advocates for women's equal opportunities in education, professional training, and employment. Her energy and entrepreneurship found expression through leadership in women's organizations, and Gertrude followed her mother's example.

Believing that childbearing was the root of women's oppression, the Moral Education Society's members held that women should have the right to determine when—and whether—to bear children. The group vigorously promoted the concept of "voluntary motherhood" or Alphaism, asserting boldly that sexual union should be for procreation only. The Society's motto was, *Every child a wanted child!* Alphaism celebrated the maternal role and emphasized the importance of the domestic sphere. But at the same time, it provided a rationale, and a means, to liberate women from some restrictions of traditional gender roles.

Just as Gertrude returned to Washington in 1883, the Moral Education Society's nationwide membership was peaking. Gertrude eagerly supported the group's far-reaching social agenda, and their shared dedication to the Society's goals united mother and daughter.

The Society's homeopathic physicians had been among the first women admitted to progressive Eastern medical schools such as Boston University, Howard University, and the University of Pennsylvania. Women homeopaths were largely barred from male-dominated allopathic medical schools. Even after earning a degree, they were regarded skeptically by the practitioners of "regular" or "heroic" medicine, who prescribed drugs to counteract symptoms of disease. In Washington, these women created for themselves a legitimate community of mutual support.

The president of the national Moral Education Society, Dr. Caroline Brown Winslow, was educated at the Western College of Homeopathic Medicine in Cleveland, Ohio, and moved to Washington in 1864 to start her practice based on natural remedies. Until the end of the Civil War, she worked in military hospitals. Besides providing covert homeopathic care (prescribing minute quantities of natural substances to stimulate the body's immune system), she offered comfort to sick and wounded soldiers, writing letters and attending to their personal affairs. (Gertrude's grandmother, Anna Hitz, who had improvised at Gertrude's unexpected birth, had similarly nursed and supported wounded soldiers. The Hessian soldiers who fought for the Union, and whose native language was German, called her "Mother Ann.")

After the Civil War, Dr. Winslow remained in the capital and practiced homeopathy, with attention to diseases of women and children. In 1869, with Dr. Susan Edson, she established the National Woman Suffrage Association. Subsequently, the two physicians became leaders of the active community whose work focused on the Homeopathic Free Dispensary, of which Jane Hitz was a co-founder and treasurer.

Dr. Winslow also edited and published the *ALPHA*, the Society's national journal, from her home at 1 Grant Place, on Capitol Hill. The *ALPHA*'s 1882 issues offered articles, reprints from other magazines, book reviews, letters, and editorial comments, including: "Marriage—Its Dangers and Duties" by Harriet Shattuck, a paper read before the Washington Society for Moral Education at their public meeting January 22, 1882; "Race Deterioration," a review of an article in the *American Journal of Obstetrics and Diseases of Women and Children* on "The Effect on Women of Imperfect Hygiene of the Sexual Function" by Dr. Charles Fayette Taylor; "Honesty in the Family" by May Wright Sewall; and "To the Friends of Froebel," a letter signed by Elizabeth Peabody and others regarding the 1882 National Froebel Kindergarten convention in Detroit.

❧

The Society's motto, *Every child a wanted child!* confused some people. Political activist and *ALPHA* spokeswoman Dr. Ellen H. Sheldon explained, in reply to a reader's letter to the editor, that "The name *ALPHA* was given to this journal as it proposed to begin with the first letter of the alphabet of life, to study and advocate the best mode of life growing out of the rights of children....In my opinion it is a crime equal with murder to unintentionally and recklessly incarnate a life..."

To do away with the tragedy of unwanted children, the Alphaists proposed a radical method, "continence except for procreation." To achieve their goal, they promoted the idea that "... Continence is the highest moral standard ever presented to mankind, equally applicable to the married and unmarried, and makes of virtue and morality a living principle..."

They maintained however, that "continence except for procreation" did not demand abstinence from sexual relations. Continent love-making (mutual *coitus reservatus*) elevated the sexual act to a higher spiritual plane, beyond physical union. By prolonging penetration, with both partners mutually controlling orgasm and avoiding seminal emission, the couple remained at the plateau phase of intercourse for as long as possible. Alphaists emphasized that such continence rescues sex from degradation: "The idea that the affection existing between the sexes is...impure has acted as a poisonous miasma upon the race... It must be purified from the dross of such association and endow love with life—a soul—and it will then result in the highest good for all."

Alphaists denied any resemblance of their preferred method (later called *Karezza* by its primary advocate, Dr. Alice B. Stockham) to the "free-love" ideology (interestingly, called "perfectionism") of John H. Noyes, leader of the utopian Oneida community in central New York. In his 1872 book, *Male Continence*, Noyes described discovering "a natural method of controlling propagation." He encouraged withdrawal, or *coitus interruptus*, a fundamentally different means of birth control. He and his followers advocated the practice of "free love," separating the "amative" from the "reproductive" function. They promoted frequent intercourse among consenting partners. In this way they succeeded in "nailing marriage to the cross," as he put it.

Miss Sheldon disdained Noyes' idea of "free love" or "complex marriage:"

> The Oneida Community...is merely a masculine institution controlled by masculine opinion and, as I understand its workings, merely controlling natural results...[it advocates] indulgence of sensuality, which...cannot fail to bring disease and degradation...In this latter part of the nineteenth century woman claims a position above what mere sex has heretofore allowed her—that of an individual, independent life, and intellectual companionship with men.

By uniting love and procreation, Gertrude and the women of the Moral Education Society intended to revolutionize popular attitudes toward sex. They wanted to eliminate the double standard and eradicate the societal evils that dishonored women: drink, violence, prostitution, rape, poverty, and sexually transmitted disease. The Alphaist solution was to educate all boys, girls, and adults, male and female, about sexuality and, above all, to develop the idea that by self-discipline, sexual expression could be controlled and elevated to a spiritual level.

They maintained that "reserved force" or "sedular absorption" created a deeply satisfying communion, mystical and ecstatic, achieved through "carefully choosing extended moments of union" and "emphasizing stillness, calm and tenderness, to eliminate force and ignorant, 'primitive' copulation." The reciprocal nature of this "conservation of power" was vital. Beyond improving individuals and marriages, the Moral Education Society aimed to perfect the human race, one child at a time. *Every child a wanted child!*

❧

No reliable techniques for controlling conception existed at the end of the nineteenth century. The most common methods were withdrawal, the vaginal sponge, the pessary (a forerunner of the diaphragm), expensive condoms, spermicidal douche, and the rhythm method of abstinence. However, most, if not all, of these devices were widely considered unnatural and deviant by the Moral Education Society's supporters, as well as the general public. The Alphaists' sweeping model of mutual, restrained sexual pleasure, enhancing spiritual union, and eliminating fear of "random propagation," provided a radical, natural, yet scarcely practical means of elevating women's status.

The Society campaigned against many conventional Victorian attitudes, and introduced the taboo subject of sexuality through literature and "books for every woman." The *ALPHA*'s July 1882 Book List included articles and essays explaining basic physiology and human sexual functions, and encouraging frank communication between men and women. A long catalog of suggested readings included: "A Private Letter to Parents, Physicians and Men Principals of Schools," by Saxon; "The Relation of the Sexes," by Frederick A. Hinckley; "Antenatal Infanticide," by Mrs. Mary L. Griffiths; "Vital Forces," by Dr. E. P. Miller; "The Relation of Maternal Function to the Woman Intellect," by Augusta Cooper Bristol; and "The Duties of the Medical Profession Concerning Prostitution and Its Allied Vices," by Dr. Frederic Henry Gerrish, Maine General Hospital.

For Gertrude, looking ahead to marriage, one influential volume on the list was *Tokology: A Book for Every Woman* by Alice B. Stockham, MD—"Teaches Positively Painless Pregnancy and Parturition. Gives Certain Cure for Dyspepsia, Neuralgia, Constipation, Headache, Change of Life, &c." Stockham's book was dedicated "To all women who, following the lessons herein taught, will be saved the sufferings peculiar to their sex." It became Gertrude's most trusted companion and guide.

❧

During the year Gertrude joined the Society, she formed a club to recruit younger women to the Alphaist cause. Dr. Winslow encouraged Gertrude to write about women's bodies, marital relations, and the roles of hygiene and sex education in raising healthy children, despite her apparent inexperience. Both Gertrude and Jane believed in the righteousness of the cause for women's equality. Jane's perspective was based on her own marital trials, and Gertrude's on youthful idealism and hopes for a marriage of equals. She was still strongly connected to Burton, who remained in Boston.

Gertrude produced a thirty-two-page pamphlet titled *The Importance of Knowledge Concerning The Sexual Nature: A Suggestive Essay*. She equated the "Sexual Nature" with other fundamental human "Natures:" the Spiritual, Intellectual, Physical, and Emotional. Although Gertrude's own applied knowledge was presumably limited, and she presented little scientific evidence for the ideas she expressed, the twenty-two-year-old confidently offered guidance on developing a love for beauty; avoiding self-abuse; teaching truthfully about sexuality; and dressing naturally and simply, liberated from the confining corset. She also advocated egalitarian marriages through mutually-agreed continence; attending to hygiene, diet, and exercise to ensure a strong and pure family life; and eliminating the scourge of prostitution by offering women alternative training and employment. This last objective paralleled her mother's efforts as a founder of the Training School for Nurses and the Labor Exchange, as well as her work on the Board of the Home Industrial School.

Gertrude's *Essay* envisioned a world where love and sensuality are appreciated as a natural part of life. However, will-power and self-discipline assure that sexuality's "vital force" does not dominate. Instead, through "clear standards based on sound knowledge" and a "truer, healthier understanding of sex," energy is conserved and available for diversion to higher creative activities, so that every life is lived more fully, and every child is truly cherished.

For the *Essay's* cover, Gertrude chose a quotation attributed to J.F. Millet, the French painter already well-known in America: "All is proper to be expressed if our aim is only high enough." The choice may have been metaphorical: Millet was beloved for paintings such as *The Sower*, which hung in the Boston Museum of Fine Arts, depicting a peasant scattering seed on his field. His depictions of workers at their daily labors were unexpectedly earthy subjects for works of art.

Gertrude began by explaining, "It is my purpose...to suggest some thoughts concerning the sexual nature which my observation and life have made true to me." She divided her discussion into four parts: Childhood, Youth, Prostitution, and Marriage. Each section interwove advice about proper practices for health, education, and sexual relations, as ways toward the ultimate goal of perfecting human life. The *Essay* rather freely incorporated quotations from works by poets, teachers, doctors, and philosophers. The *Essay's* third section took up the social evil of prostitution, destructive not only for the women driven to it, but also for the families of men who frequented prostitutes. It introduced, too, the notion of prostitution, or rape, within marriage, addressing the concerns of women whose husbands treated them as sexual property, which, as then legally defined, they were. Gertrude had heard this subject discussed in a Boston sermon by the Unitarian minister Cyrus A. Bartol, who maintained that: "... It is this degradation which has unconsciously brought a sense of shame in connection with the sexual organs. And it accounts quite sufficiently for the feeling of disgust felt by so many women for the sexual act..."

Her *Essay's* exhortatory conclusion borrowed from a pamphlet titled "The Cancer at the Heart," by Frederic Hinckley: "Oh yes, friends, there is an ideal womanhood, and ideal manhood, an ideal love...It is where two hearts draw together in love and freedom, and go through life serving each other's highest needs; it is where continence is the established law of being; it is where children come as the sound, loving, divine offspring of reason and affection." She envisioned sharing this ideal love with Burton.

Jane Hitz and many Society members served as Gertrude's models—for example, Dr. Grace Roberts, with whom, in later years, Jane Hitz shared a home. Many were social activists with professional careers who were unafraid to live outside conventional patterns of marriage and motherhood, yet nevertheless regarded maternal influence and women's domestic roles central to society's progress. The Society's ideals, mingling Victorian ethical standards, progressive values, and radical methods, emboldened Gertrude. She began to define her life's mission more clearly: public discourse could stir others to action. Using her skills as a teacher and her recently developed abilities as a public speaker, she would promote voluntary motherhood, health, and hygiene to all who would listen. And she would become a living example of a perfect wife and mother.

Immediately after completing the spring term at Bell's school, Gertrude had an opportunity to test her *Essay's* theories: she and Alfred Edgar Burton married in June 1884. Burton had been promoted to assistant professor after two years in the rank of lecturer at Tech. At the semester's end, he traveled to Washington to collect his belongings, still stored in the Hitz attic, and escort Gertrude north to their new, joint adventure. The couple anticipated a union combining love, friendship, and mutual support for each one's chosen work. Their vision of human perfectibility, exemplified in an egalitarian marriage, did not then take account of possible frustrations or disappointments. Some things can only be learned from experience.

In mid-June, the printing firm Brentano's published three thousand copies of Gertrude's pamphlet. *The Importance of Knowledge Concerning the Sexual Nature: A Suggestive Essay* joined the Moral Education Society's book list, on sale for twenty-five cents a copy. Excerpts appeared as a lengthy article in the August 1884 number of the *ALPHA*. Mr. Beresford, the printer, estimated Gertrude's pamphlet might sell at least those three thousand copies, and possibly up to twenty-five thousand.

# CHAPTER 5

## *Was There Ever a Greater Miracle?*

AFTER THE HECTIC PACE OF THE PRECEDING YEARS, AND TRAVEL from Philadelphia to Maine, Boston to Washington, Gertrude eagerly anticipated the permanence of marriage, but she felt uncomfortable leaving her father behind. On June 13, 1884, she was up late packing. John Hitz seemed agitated by her preparations, so she decided to present him then with her going away present, a check for $100, the savings from her salary at Professor Bell's school. Her gesture both relieved and upset him. He had little to offer in return. After a fitful sleep he rose early the next morning, and was "much affected, in spite of myself—Extremely painful to be unable to give Gertrude a better material dowry—literally no present, but the contrary—to be made the recipient from her of the net earnings of last year's work…"

They promised to remain close, through letters and visits.

Saturday the 14th was rainy, so Gertrude and Burton departed by carriage to catch the morning train north. After they left, John Hitz cashed her check, deposited a small amount in savings, and paid various bills and accounts owed.

Anna Gertrude Hitz and Alfred Edgar Burton chose the austere Old West Church in Boston's West End for their wedding ceremony. The first church on the site had been built in 1737. The cry of "No taxation without representation!" was coined there in an early Congregational pastor's sermon. By the nineteenth century, the church had become Unitarian. The building and its eminent minister, Cyrus

Augustus Bartol, were well-known to the couple from Sunday services the year before. Dr. Bartol sought to simplify and revitalize Unitarianism and liberate it from formal ritual. He lectured frequently on Transcendentalism at Bronson Alcott's Concord Summer School of Philosophy—his address the preceding summer was titled "Emerson's Religion."

The pair asked Reverend Bartol, whose views on marriage Gertrude had included in her *Essay*, to perform the ceremony, with no family present. Burton's father, Alfred Merrill Burton, a bank treasurer in Portland, Maine, had died during Burton's senior year at college. After his death, Martha Jane Larrabee Burton, his mother, and Mary Agnes Larrabee Burton, his redoubtable older sister, moved to the Larrabee family's home in Brunswick, where Alfred Edgar attended Bowdoin College. They regarded Gertrude's unconventional ideas about voluntary motherhood as outlandish. They did not look favorably on the marriage.

The bridal pair honored individual conscience above all, like Dr. Bartol and Ralph Waldo Emerson, and accordingly, the Hitz-Burton vows omitted the traditional promise "to obey." Prizing simplicity and purity, the couple barred wedding photographs and discouraged gifts. To emphasize the spiritual dimension of their bonds, they also resolved not to exchange material gifts on future anniversaries or holidays. The couple was married on the same day that Gertrude's *Essay on the Importance of Knowledge of the Sexual Nature* appeared in print, a coincidence that might be seen as portending tensions between theory and practice.

After the ceremony on Monday, June 16th, Gertrude sent her father a brief telegram, which he received the next morning: "Married at noon in Boston. Leave for New York this evening by boat—Good night—Gertrude."

On their wedding day, in the early afternoon, John Hitz had paused in his room to read over the marriage service and passages from the Bible. His daughter's nuptials reminded him of his own elopement in 1856, when the bride's parents and the groom's family were also absent. John Hitz sent congratulations to the honeymooners at Heather House in Schooley's Mountain, New Jersey, about forty-five miles west of New York City. Some days later, feeling "dull and inert," he spent a morning addressing and sending off their wedding announcements. The delicate engraved script on small ivory cards perfectly matched the couple's understated aesthetic.

The following week, as they had planned, the newlyweds traveled to New York City for international meetings at the Institute for Improved Instruction for the Deaf, attended by Professors Alexander Graham Bell and Edward Miner Gallaudet, together with articulation teachers from England and Germany. Gertrude's presentation followed Bell's address on "Line Writing, or Shorthand for Universal Use, including the Deaf." Her paper described the instruction of very young deaf children by means of the line writing system—the phonetic writing she had employed, using Froebel kindergarten methods, at Bell's Experimental School.

The Burtons had booked rooms at the Astor Hotel and dined together with John Hitz that evening. The next day, the three rode in a horse drawn streetcar to Sunday services at the Swedenborgian Church in Brooklyn. Crossing John A. Roebling's spectacular new suspension bridge, which had opened just a year before, they admired its combination of robust engineering and delicate design. Later they traveled back to Manhattan by ferry.

Gertrude and Alfred Edgar journeyed on to Boston, to take up married life. She missed the professional status and personal connections she had enjoyed in Washington, and quickly moved to establish ties with Boston women's groups, including the Women's Educational and Industrial Union, the New England Women's Club, and the Home Club. This last group was led by Mrs. Ada H. Spaulding, wife of Dr. Ebenezer Farrington Spaulding, a prominent homeopathic physician active in the evangelical Maverick Congregational Church of East Boston. The Home Club sponsored lectures and raised money for charitable causes, such as a day nursery for working women and a women's scholarship for study at MIT.

Mrs. Spaulding became another of Gertrude's older mentors, a respected model and a friend, partly on the basis of their shared admiration for the poetry of Walt Whitman. When Whitman's *Leaves of Grass* was banned in Boston five years earlier, Mrs. Spaulding publicly defended his work, including the "Children of Adam" section which contained most of the offending passages. She corresponded with Whitman from 1887 to 1891, and through her public defense of his art and ideas, she converted a circle of influential Boston friends to more open-minded views on sexuality. As president of the Home Club, Ada Spaulding invited Gertrude to speak to members about hygiene, dress reform, and voluntary motherhood. Gertrude enlisted her new husband, a precise draftsman and amateur artist, to contribute anatomical charts and illustrations. Unfortunately, no examples of this handiwork survive.

Gertrude described Mrs. Spaulding as "… a little woman with a slight, graceful body, and…gray hair which lies in beautiful simplicity about her forehead and has the effect of a benediction—it is so soft in its undulation, so smooth to the touch. Her face is essentially spiritual—and her eyes have the inner light of the saints. I marvel at her constantly—for she is as open-hearted as a child—she a woman… whose life and position have given her wide knowledge of the world."

At the New Year, Gertrude made good her promise to remain connected with her family in Washington. She returned for three weeks, accompanying her father to dinner and plays, staying overnight occasionally at her mother's, and entertaining her brother Willie, now twelve. She also traveled to Martinsburg, West Virginia to call on her friend Fansy Haldeman, at home with her family for the holidays.

On January 20, 1885, Gertrude attended the annual three-day National Woman Suffrage Association convention at Washington's 16th Street Universalist Church, with her mother. The two women discussed the meeting's importance—especially the keynote address by pioneer women's rights advocate, Elizabeth Cady Stanton. Some of Stanton's listeners were shocked by her bold assertion that women should be able to vote not only in state, but also in federal elections. Gertrude and her mother supported full political equality. She attended other sessions with her father, a long-standing advocate for women's rights, in the egalitarian tradition of his native Switzerland.

Early on the morning of Gertrude's departure, John Hitz accompanied her to the station, but then, unwilling to part from her so soon, he rode along as far as Baltimore, returning to Washington by the next train. On their way, he remarked on his own increasingly complicated legal and financial situation, and especially his concern over the dispersal of family furnishings. If the worst happened, he said, and he had to break up the household as a result of the pending criminal trial, she and Willie would have to divide his pictures, books, and remaining furniture.

Everything in the house evoked memories, but Gertrude was particularly interested in the Swiss books and artifacts. She had begun to prize her family's history more, now that there might be a new generation on the way. She must have guessed already that she was pregnant. She may even have confided in her father, because on the train they conversed about the right of children to be wellborn, "… holding that the first success in life was to be conceived in wisdom— the first failure in life to be conceived in ignorance."

During the spring and early summer months, Gertrude followed to the letter the regimen suggested in Dr. Alice B. Stockham's childbirth handbook, *Tokology*. The prescribed prenatal program, Dr. Stockham promised, would produce not only a healthy child but also, in the long run, contribute to a more perfect human race. Gertrude ate a diet of mostly grains and fruits, enjoyed as much fresh air as possible, and took care to assure pleasant surroundings, nonbinding clothing, moderate exercise, daily baths, abstinence from sexual relations, and, above all, positive thoughts.

Dr. Stockham warned against negativity in the book's concluding chapter: "In following the teachings of *Tokology*, care must be taken that the mind is not directed to watching for and fostering morbid symptoms." She stated that "The mind, the real self, controls all the functions pertaining to life, and its supremacy can be directed toward removing morbid tendencies. One can train the mind to this end…It is simply the conquest of self and sin…" And, she advised her readers, "Cheerfully, hopefully bring the soul into harmony with the good in the universe…Learn to subordinate the body."

Gertrude shared Dr. Stockham's firm belief in the mind's power to regulate the body. With her troublesome knee apparently cured, she did not, at this point, suppose that she lacked sufficient self-discipline; nor did she consider that Dr. Stockham's mind-over-matter views implied that an insubordinate body might signal not only moral weakness, but wickedness.

In late May, Gertrude arranged to leave their rooms at 105 Myrtle Street, on Beacon Hill, to lodge for the summer in Mr. and Mrs. Putnam R. Clark's large house, situated in the sunny fields of East Medway (now the town of Millis), twenty miles west of Boston. The nearby rail station made an easy commute for Burton, who remained in town working. Gertrude often sat beneath the old apple tree in the yard, reading or playing the guitar to inspire and soothe the infant they expected in early August.

John Hitz arrived at the Clark farm for a two-week visit in July, sharing meals with Gertrude and several young lodgers sponsored by the Christian Association's Country Week sojourn for needy city children. She welcomed his company, and he was overjoyed to see his daughter again. He strolled through the woods by the Great Black Swamp, read aloud to Gertrude, lying in the shade of the apple tree, and listened as she read him excerpts from the book *Parturition without Pain* and favorite passages from George Eliot's novels and essays. They passed the time writing letters, taking leisurely rides in the country-side, and visiting friends in nearby Brookline. During the second week of her father's visit, Burton left Boston for Maine, to visit his mother. Fortunately, he returned to the Clark farm on August 4th, in time for his son's arrival the following day.

Gertrude's young doctor–midwife, Kate Sanborn, an 1883 graduate of Boston University Medical School, had established her homeopathic practice in the town of Medway, five miles west of the Clark farm. John Hitz accompanied Gertrude on visits to Dr. Sanborn as her time drew near. He described the young physician as a "fine, energetic and earnest young woman." At their second meeting, he found her "splendid, natural, strong and sensible." Gertrude willingly placed herself in Dr. Sanborn's hands, regarding her as a trusted friend as well as her doctor. Curiously, Dr. Sanborn shared her name with the teacher and journalist Kate Sanborn, Mary Whitall Smith's English professor at Smith College, who, by another strange coincidence, also lived in Medway.

Dr. Sanborn proved both capable and resilient, guiding Gertrude's long labor and complicated delivery at the Clark homestead. Following Dr. Stockham's tokological advice, Gertrude refused pain-killing drugs during her eighteen-hour effort. She described this intense experience to her old Philadelphia friend, Mariechen, Mary Whitall Smith, who, by this time, was married to an Irish barrister, Benjamin Francis Conn "Frank" Costelloe, and living in London. Gertrude wrote that

… My faith in the possibility of painless parturition was so strong that I approached labor without a single fear. I followed the directions in *Tokology* to an extreme—that is, very, very strictly—and as I have told thee the whole pregnancy had been a glorious season of most perfect physical unconsciousness. The word "agony" was so utterly unimagined that the realization of it was like the first introduction to hell. But my mind was so clear and I was so anxious to be brave, that I endured the worst, until towards the long, long, long last hours, and then it did seem useless, nay cruel—to endure the torture any longer.

I did not ask for ether…But I did ask for something to help me to produce contraction—as all effort of my own, for the last sixteen hours, had been so seemingly fruitless. The doctor mixed something in a glass—but she told me afterwards it was only to soothe me…As I look back now it is impossible to recall the agony of those eighteen hours. It is absolutely impossible to imagine such pain—and so it has faded away entirely, and I see only the dramatic quality…

The delivery itself was traumatic and transformative:

… the presentation was not normal. The breach presented first, so that the hips had to be expelled before the legs could be freed from their bent position, and allow the body and shoulders to be expelled. The head was thus caught and retained, and the danger of strangling was very great. The doctor said the placenta was unusually large, and that perhaps the child had been so closely packed that it could not turn to the normal position.

… When I see thee I want to tell thee the details of the day—the terrible storm—during all that dark, fearful night, and then the glad burst of sunshine and the clear calm sky and the little child saved from its pitiful death—(think of choking one's first child within one's own body at the moment of birth!) and the wonderful triumph of it all—as I lay so comfortable and serene upon my bed and saw the beautiful fresh body—complete + living! Was there ever a greater miracle?

The birth experience was anguished and ecstatic, horrific and beautiful, and as life-changing as Gertrude had imagined. She and Burton named their son Felix Arnold Burton, with hopes for his happy future: *Felix* is Latin for *fortunate*.

But in the succeeding months, Gertrude recognized her own growing sensitivity to noise and intolerance for commotion. She confided to Mary: "… although I know Arnold has been a remarkably good baby, I also know that his crying—that is to say his inability to definitely express his needs, has disturbed my whole nervous system. It almost drives me insane." This was Gertrude's first acknowledgement of her inability to master her own physical and emotional reactions.

During the following winter and spring, her family's legal and financial troubles in Washington challenged Gertrude with a vexing quandary: who needed her attention and guidance more, her infant son or her beleaguered father?

# CHAPTER 6

# *A Most Trying Experience*

THE LEGAL SYSTEM, MOVING AT A SLUGGISH PACE, HAD ENTANGLED John Hitz and his wife in multiple lawsuits involving the German–American National Bank's failure, beginning in 1879. Finally, in May 1886, their troubles were coming to a head: the original indictments of fifteen bank trustees were reduced to just two, John Hitz, bank president, and Charles E. Prentiss, cashier, for "making false entries in the books." Between the earliest stage of the bank difficulties and the looming jury trial in the Supreme Court of the District of Columbia (since 1936, called the United States District Court of the District of Columbia), Hitz's lawyers continuously fought charges of fraud and misappropriation.

Despite his clouded reputation and meager income (a regular salary would have been confiscated to pay outstanding debts), John Hitz actively engaged in social life and community service. He busied himself on the Board of the Washington Home Industrial School, administered New Church (Swedenborgian) activities and taught Sunday school classes, presented papers at National Education Association conferences, managed Swiss Benevolent Society doings, and coordinated some Red Cross projects. He volunteered his services to Clara Barton, a family friend whom Jane Hitz and Gertrude had met while "taking the waters" in Dansville, New York, in the early 1870s. In 1881, John Hitz worked closely with Clara Barton to win Congressional approval for an American Red Cross, equivalent to the international organization based in Geneva.

Gertrude and most who knew Hitz believed that he had been foolish, but not malicious, in the bank matter. His typically soft-hearted and soft-headed behavior inspired an affectionate tolerance among friends. Most thought that Hitz never should have been involved with banking in the first place. In revealing testimony, John Hitz's friend and associate, W. G. Metzerott, blurted out his view, under questioning by Jane Hitz's lawyer, Mr. Enoch Totten:

Q: Mr. Metzerott, was not the reason of your condemnation of this savings and national bank enterprise the fact of Mr. Hitz's unfitness for the management of such a concern?

A: I have known Mr. Hitz for many years; we have been brothers almost. (Pausing).

Q: Well, speak it out, Mr. Metzerott.

A: One moment…He is too much a philanthropist for a bank president.

❧

Months before the 1886 trial, John Hitz had signed over the deed to his residence of nearly twenty years to a court-appointed receiver, B.U. Keyser. He had already sold or given away most of his remaining books, furniture, and household belongings. He placed a newspaper advertisement for a room near Clara Barton's residence and workplace, at 947 T Street: "Wanted by a single gentleman: A good sized, cheerfully located, unfurnished room in the vicinity of Vermont Ave and T St NW." He found rooms at 1310 V Street for $5 a month. On April 30th, he slept at the cottage for the last time and noted in his diary, "I part with it as I would part with my body that had served its purpose—reluctantly in one sense, because seemingly it had served me well—Gladly in another because it will sever the love from a body of which the soul is gone." On Saturday, May 1st, he loaded his wagon and left the house. The first item the mail carrier brought him at the new residence was a cheerful, sympathetic postcard from Gertrude.

ৡৢ

The trial began on the morning of May 3rd. The next day, in Boston, Gertrude received her father's unsettling telegram. He had spent a suspense-filled day in court as the jury was selected and sworn in. He had been warned that the prosecutor would attack him and his co-defendant mercilessly, "imputing the basest motives and implying criminal intent." Indeed, the government's special counsel, Ronald Ross Perry, opened the case with aggressive, no-holds-barred arguments. When court adjourned at three in the afternoon, the judge ordered the printing of pleas.

Gertrude responded on the same day that she would come immediately, although she could not bring Arnold along, because of the expense. Hitz spent the next day in court. On returning home at ten o'clock in the evening, he found a telegram announcing Gertrude's arrival by train at 10:47. Relieved, he rushed to the station, then delivered her to the home of their friend Mrs. Kappeler to spend the night. For the remaining days of the trial, Gertrude stayed in his V Street front room and accompanied her father to the courthouse.

The German–American Bank cases against John Hitz and Charles E. Prentiss were concluded at 12:30 p.m., on May 13th. The jury members, instructed by Judge Arthur MacArthur, returned their verdict swiftly, at 3:30 that afternoon. To widespread amazement in the courtroom and in the press, the jury found the defendants guilty as indicted. The headline in *The Republican*, on May 14th read "A Surprising Verdict." The article explained, "The verdict caused much surprise, as it was generally believed there would be an acquittal." The accused were immediately taken into custody and ordered to jail to await sentencing,

ৡৢ

Gertrude and a guard accompanied Hitz in a herdic—a small, two-wheeled, horse-drawn carriage, equivalent to a taxicab—from the white courthouse at Judiciary Square to the "New Jail" overlooking the

Anacostia River, at the eastern end of Capitol Hill. The red sandstone building, at 19th and B St, SE, had been completed in 1875.

As they entered the building, Gertrude was stunned by the absurdity of her father's trial and imprisonment, which was becoming as pivotal a chapter in her life story as in his. She signed in at the concierge's heavy oak desk in the spacious reception hall, its large windows covered by metal mesh. Twin stairways, also enclosed by metal screening, led to several levels of cell blocks. The jail's population of about two hundred inmates included white and black, males and females, adults and children: murderers, drunks, prostitutes, pickpockets, and two convicted embezzlers.

Although Gertrude was disturbed by her father's incarceration, she was favorably impressed with the accommodations. Cells were regularly "blue-washed," or disinfected and thoroughly cleaned, the bedsteads and chairs steamed, and the mattresses changed. Good food was provided and supplemented with generous donations from Hitz's many callers. On the first morning, Hitz was served a breakfast of shad and fried potatoes in a tin box. Dinner included veal cutlet, collard greens, potatoes, asparagus, lettuce, bread and coffee. Throughout the spring, summer, and fall, Gertrude and friends brought him strawberries, butter, cake, and apples along with chairs, sheets, towels, socks, candy, brushes, and flowers for his cell. Hitz paid the prison cook about $1.50 every two weeks to prepare the additional bounty for his own meals and to offer extras to the other prisoners.

The jail's warden, John S. Crocker, was a former brigadier general in the Union Army. General Crocker's experiences as a prisoner during the Civil War motivated his policy of rehabilitation, rather than punishment. Nevertheless, his humanitarian approach caused one skeptical newspaper account to refer to the Washington Jail as the "Hôtel de Crocker." Warden Crocker's philosophy explains the remarkably civilized conditions of Hitz' and Prentiss' seven-month confinement. The Report of the Attorney General for 1886 detailed:

"The discipline of the Jail has been kept up…by the practice of humane treatment towards all the inmates, and without the infliction of severe penalties…This encouraging condition may be attributed to proper classification, separate cells, kind treatment, plenty of good substantial food, good beds, clean and comfortable quarters, skillful medical treatment, and the judicious and efficient manner in which the officers of the institution have discharged their duties."

At first, Hitz and Prentiss shared cell Number 67, but the men found sleeping difficult, so after a month, Dr. Prentiss' bed was moved to cell 65, while Hitz remained in the original space. Gertrude arranged for a local cabinet maker to install a two-drawer writing table for him there. Bookshelves, a small library, writing paper, pens, and ink brought by visitors made the cell's southeast corner a comfortable work space.

Most days, Hitz's cell door was left unlocked and open. Periodically, however, the facility's relative peace was broken by the transfer of gangs of eight or ten prisoners to the dreaded Albany Penitentiary. Hitz called the treatment of those penitentiary-bound inmates "… a disgrace to the American people: two by two, handcuffed and shackled together all fastened to a chain running along the line—" Their humiliation was a reminder of Gertrude's greatest fear: potential penitentiary sentences for Hitz and Prentiss themselves.

Gertrude usually called in twice each day, in the early morning and late afternoon, traveling on foot or by herdic, and often accompanied by friends or Mrs. Kappeler's children, Jessie, eleven, and Freddie, nine. She collected and delivered laundry, mail, and city gossip about the trial, as well as newspapers and books of interest. From Burton in Boston, she passed along a short story, "The Third Category," by her friend Bernhard Berenson, now in his senior year and editor of the undergraduate *Harvard Monthly*. She wrote her father personal letters and encouraging messages, and reported on her own lobbying efforts on his behalf.

Hitz's visitors numbered upwards of twenty on Sundays, and on average days, six to eight. But often, when they were alone, father and daughter conversed frankly about family matters, political issues, and the subject of sex. Hitz had long meditated on Emmanuel Swedenborg's theories in the *Delights of Wisdom Pertaining to Conjugal Love.* Gertrude shared her ambition of becoming a public lecturer and sex educator, and proudly showed him Burton's large, skillfully drawn anatomical charts. She described her ambitious plan for a two-volume set on reproduction in plants, animals, and human beings—an aesthetically pleasing, yet accessible, work on sexual relations. She proposed, "First, a small and plentifully and well-illustrated book, entitled *The Story of Reproduction*—for children, commencing with the wonders of reproduction in a grain of corn—its rootlets and gradual development into the stalk—and process of reproduction by the tassels and wind—then on to animals and finally the human being...," and a second book, "also well-illustrated—more scientific and intended for adults and parents, showing reproductions from the simplest forms of vegetable life up to animals and human reproduction—All to be gotten up in the best typographical order and style..."

In June, Hitz's lawyer General R.D. Mussey's motion for a new trial was denied, so he requested the defendants be allowed to post bail. However, prosecutor Perry insisted the defendants be sentenced immediately. In a three-page letter, American Red Cross founder Clara Barton appealed personally to Judge MacArthur not to condemn John Hitz to the grim Albany Penitentiary, but "at worst, to place him in a prison where he might continue to serve society by writing up Reformatory and Child-saving work, the Red Cross, etc."

When the two defendants rose in the courtroom for the judge's pronouncement, Gertrude stood with her father. To their horror and dismay, Judge MacArthur imposed sentences of five years in the Albany Penitentiary. The headline in the *Washington Evening Star,* on June 5, 1886, read:

## FIVE YEARS IN THE PENITENTIARY
Messrs. Hitz and Prentiss Sentenced Today—A Motion for
Suspension of Execution of the Sentence Granted

For scheduling reasons, the defense's formal request to delay
implementation could not be heard before the summer recess, so an
appeal could not be taken up until after the start of the court's general term in October. Later on, in mid-July, the court denied a second
motion for release on bail. The two prisoners then had to remain at
the "Hôtel de Crocker" during the long, hot summer months.

This shocking turn of events stiffened Gertrude's determination to exonerate her father. She weighed her family loyalties and
decided to remain in Washington for the duration, separated from
her husband and son, even though she had already been absent from
Boston for over a month, and Arnold was not yet a year old. She
would have preferred to have the baby with her, but Jane Hitz was not
amenable to taking Gertrude and Arnold into her home and helping
with child care. She was unsympathetic with Gertrude's loyalty to
her father, and she was unwilling to upset her own routines. Their
disagreements caused scenes.

However, Gertrude happily welcomed her husband and son
to Washington, along with Arnold's nurse, red-haired Ida Brophy,
on June 16th, the couple's second wedding anniversary. Burton
sported a fashionable moustache. The family remained together for
a week. Gertrude decided that staying with her father was the right
thing to do. So that her son might not forget her, Gertrude had her
photograph made in a large and lifelike format. John Hitz thought
the resulting portrait was "not as good a likeness as I would like to

have. Gives her a more strong and thoughtful inner expression—but not that more habitual cheerful and bright one."

When John Hitz suggested Gertrude spend August in Maine with Burton's family, and then visit her mother on Deer Isle ("thinking it would be less expensive, and do them all good"), she argued against it. She reasoned that Arnold would not miss his mother as much as Hitz would miss his daughter. Gertrude expressed her opinion that, now that her mother had built her own summer cottage on Deer Isle, accepting her hospitality would "… only gratify…her [mother's] worldly vanity." Justifying the morality of her decision, she theorized that by *not* visiting, "… Willie and her mother would eventually see there were even higher purposes and duties of life on the spiritual plane than possessing, and living snugly in, a cottage at the seaside." Consequently, in service to "higher purposes and duties," Gertrude continued her daily visits to the jail during the stifling summer months. In a sense, she was constructing a prison of her own.

The number of Hitz's callers dwindled: many Washington friends retreated to the mountains of Virginia, West Virginia, or Pennsylvania. Near the end of July, Gertrude escorted young Freddie Kappeler for a week's respite at Mrs. Ida Hummer's boarding house near Berkeley Springs, a spa in the eastern panhandle of West Virginia, about a hundred miles away. During Gertrude's absence, Mrs. Kappeler delivered Hitz's daily mail. But on July 31st, Gertrude and the boy returned sooner than expected, carrying a basket of fresh berries picked in the Blue Ridge Mountains. She and Freddie had left before the end of their stay because Gertrude could not put up with the crowded boarding house's "… too many summer lodgers, and of the wrong kind." She explained to her father "her ungovernable dislike for the sphere of people there, and could not overcome these feelings." Guests "had sampled her lemonade—and arose late, not stirring out until after 4 PM." For the sake of her fraying nerves, she required calmer, more orderly surroundings. She decided to remain in the city, at Mrs. Kappeler's.

Hitz may not have perceived Gertrude's growing emotional turmoil. The two reinforced each other's belief in the importance of self-discipline. Knowing it would lift her father's spirits, Gertrude copied out William Ernest Henley's poem "Invictus" to post on his cell wall: "I am the master of my fate; I am the captain of my soul…" Father and daughter also continued their "long conferences in regard to sexual matters—continence and absolute restriction of sexual acts to procreation…." Invoking scientific theory and moral law, Hitz recorded that "[She] gave me her experience with her women physicians who agreed…that the very fact of man having been given mind and free will, made it incumbent upon him to exercise his functions only for their legitimate purpose—whereas the animal, having no mind, was given natural instinct and periodicity to regulate it…"

However, by the end of August Gertrude confessed she was exhausted. The heat and strain became unbearable, even for such an exceptionally high-minded daughter. She decided to go Down East for a couple of weeks, after all. She left on the evening of September 14th, her father's fifty-eighth birthday, after presenting him with a leather-bound portfolio of Burton's sketches documenting Arnold's first year. She had been away from her husband and young son for four and a half months.

Gertrude's plan for a two-week break evolved into a six-week stay. She was delighted to be with her family again, yet still anxious about her father. She returned to Washington with Arnold and his nurse Ida on October 28th, and resumed daily visits to the jail, often bringing the baby along. They stayed, at first, with Jane Hitz, but soon Gertrude reported friction and decided to take rooms elsewhere, "owing to her mother's deportment in regard to her being there with Ida and Arnold." The tensions between mother and daughter seemed always near the surface, particularly since Gertrude's reason for visiting was so closely linked to her father's predicament.

Gertrude secured rooms on the corner of 8th and A Streets, SE, including meals, with a Mrs. Worthington, who, strangely enough, was related to the US District Attorney, Augustus S. Worthington, and a family friend of the aggressive government prosecutor in her father's trial, Ronald Ross Perry. Through them, Gertrude learned that Counsel Perry would continue his fanatical pursuit.

The defendants' lawyers estimated the case would be scheduled shortly after the middle of October. However, it was postponed until November 10th, and then again, twice. Finally, Hitz's attorney General R.D. Mussey announced on Monday, November 22nd that they expected to commence argument the following day. He did not speak encouragingly, but nevertheless pinned some hope on a new presiding judge, Judge David Kellogg Cartter. Gertrude thought Cartter might be less impressed than his predecessor by Mr. Perry's abusive, dramatic tirades. Clara Barton wrote another impassioned plea for leniency.

Arguments continued for ten days, pausing only for Thursday's Thanksgiving holiday. On December 6th, with the court still unready to announce its opinion, Gertrude and Hitz allowed themselves to consider the delay a favorable sign, signifying "… either only partial agreement [with] the indictments, or rejection of them, requiring carefully written opinions to sustain the judgment—otherwise an opinion would [already] have been delivered." Hitz found himself feeling "much brighter and calmer."

On December 11th, Hitz again received positive reports of the proceedings from witnesses in court. On the 12th, he welcomed the usual flock of Sunday callers.

❧

Monday, December 13, 1886: The morning was quiet. John Hitz was editing an article on military ethics when the guard on duty at the concierge's desk came up to cell 67. Guard Linkenback brought news from the wife of Hitz's co-defendant, Mrs. Prentiss, who had just arrived in the visitor's rotunda downstairs. She had come directly from the post office, where she met Mr. Dickerson Hoover, to whom Mr. Walter D. Davidge, Dr. Prentiss' lawyer, had announced, "The indictments were quashed!"

Hitz felt a kind of electric tremor and suddenly knelt where he stood, fervently reciting the Lord's Prayer. He rose, still shaking, and hurried down the staircase behind Mr. Linkenback to talk with Mrs. Prentiss. His mind slowly grasped the meaning of Counsel Davidge's words. He conferred with Mrs. Prentiss for half an hour, and then returned to his cell, where he took a little lunch.

Gertrude arrived not long afterwards, bringing confirmation straight from the courthouse. She was allowed to come directly to his cell. In her arms she carried roses for the guards. She reported that Judge Walter Smith Cox, substituting for the ailing Judge Cartter, delivered the opinion, sustaining the demurrers and remanding the case on the basis of a Supreme Court precedent. At court, she said, everyone was greatly pleased—bailiffs, marshals, office clerks, lawyers, and surprisingly even Judge MacArthur, who had first sentenced Hitz and Prentiss to the federal penitentiary. At the prison, the guards, wardens, and other prisoners rejoiced. John Hitz ate dinner in his cell, and then received his counsel, General R.D. Mussey, who arrived with a copy of the official release. Gertrude and her father rode off with General Mussey and the newly freed Dr. Prentiss to see Arnold and Ida. Then they hired a carriage and visited other exultant friends. Later, they ordered flowers to be sent to the lawyers, took tea at the Musseys' home, and finally rode to Mrs. Kappeler's house, where Gertrude, exhilarated, stayed the night.

Her father returned alone to his room in V Street. He was too overwhelmed to make plans for the future, though he reckoned on returning to the jail to collect his things. In the days following their release, Hitz and Prentiss delighted in a barrage of telegrams and visits from friends. On the street, Gertrude and her father chanced upon Jane Hitz, who bowed to Gertrude, but not to her husband. She was stouter than when he had last seen her, but at forty-nine, Jane Hitz stood as erect as ever. He felt overcome by feelings of love, anger, regret, and, quite probably, vindication.

In Boston, Burton had been without Gertrude for many months. But whatever the consequences for their marriage, Gertrude now decided to stay on with her father during his reentry to civilian life. She feared Hitz would struggle emotionally without her moral support, and financially without a steady income. She looked for new lodgings for herself, Arnold, and Ida near his V Street rooms, and settled on Mrs. Calvert's house, 1351 U Street. She took up the task of cataloguing data from the Department of the Interior on marriages and births, for Alexander Graham Bell's Martha's Vineyard project.

John Hitz resumed taking breakfast at Clara Barton's T Street house. One morning, Clara Barton suggested he consider devoting his life to Red Cross work, and offered him a monthly salary of $30 to cover his costs. He was grateful for the opportunity to work with the organization he had helped establish—and even more grateful for the paycheck. On December 22nd, he began catching up on Red Cross correspondence and arranging supplies for relief transports.

Gertrude welcomed her father to her rooms on Christmas day, just in time for Arnold's first look at a holiday tree. While her father took dinner at lawyer Mussey's, Gertrude and Arnold shared Christmas with her mother and Willie, now a handsome, blue-eyed fourteen-year-old. Although it rained continuously during the holidays, Hitz concluded his 1886 diary with the comment that "… materially

[and] spiritually [the year] opened with all manner of forebodings—
[but] passed out in spiritual peace and joy."

However, personality conflicts flared up between John Hitz and
Clara Barton's close associate at the Red Cross office, Dr. Julian Hub-
bell. Hitz was paid only until March 12th. Hoping to salvage the situation, Gertrude approached Dr. Bell, who was happy to have her father take up the Martha's Vineyard statistical tasks again. On March
24, 1887, John Hitz began working with Alexander Graham Bell on
a permanent basis. With her father's employment secured, Gertrude
departed at the end of March, after nearly a year in Washington.
John Hitz wrote: "Thus closed a most eventful period of our mutual
lives—A most trying experience since May last..."

In May, Gertrude received the latest Washington news: Hitz
was weathering ongoing legal disputes with his wife; helping Mrs.
Kappeler bury her husband in the Prospect Hill Cemetery, after
his shocking suicide; and attending Fansy Haldeman's wedding to
Thomas W. Sidwell, director at Sidwell Friends School, where Willie
was now a student.

Hitz sent Gertrude's personal effects to suburban Jamaica Plain,
outside of Boston, along with a writing desk and child's wagon. The
Burtons were renting a tidy new house just off Lamartine Street, at 3
Glenvale Terrace, a short walk from a commuter railway stop. Pink
roses, in a special delivery box, arrived from her father on May 29th,
Gertrude's twenty-sixth birthday.

# CHAPTER 7

## *A Sea of Uncertainty*

FOR OVER TEN YEARS GERTRUDE HAD EAGERLY ACQUIRED NEW SKILLS and welcomed new challenges—at Wilson College, the Froebel kindergarten training school, and Boston University. She had devised a curriculum and taught at Bell's school for deaf children while lecturing and writing for the Moral Education Society. She had met the challenges of marriage, pregnancy, and childbirth. And she had played a crucial role as her father's advocate and ardent supporter during the legal proceedings that ended, finally, in his exoneration. She relished those tests and took pride in her hard-won accomplishments as an independent woman.

Returning to suburban Boston seemed something of an anticlimax. Though Gertrude welcomed the chance to settle into family life after being active in the wider world, she was unaccustomed to the tedious and strenuous routines of housekeeping and childcare. She approached her maternal responsibilities and wifely duties less enthusiastically than before, and sensed uneasily that her absence had fundamentally changed her relationship with her husband.

Yet they sometimes found time to be together. A July heat wave and a bout with mumps left the usually industrious Burton uncharacteristically weak, idle, and homebound. But on the brighter side, Gertrude wrote to Mary on August 25th, his quarantine gave them "delightful long days together all alone reading and talking and relaxing." She confessed:

> … We both enjoy mere existence so intensely and are impressionists by temperament and habit—and so we absorb our philosophy and do very little hard thinking. Whenever we

do yield to the enjoyment of each other it seems quite enough to be.

Yet signs of trouble were becoming more obvious:

> O dear! There is a great deal to force me to believe in purely evolutionary theories. I find that I grow more and more sensitive to my environment every year of my life—Indeed, there are moments when I seem to be simply a mass of sensibilities, and I feel as if the mere strain which the daily life brings with it would crush me utterly! Some days I am sorry—deeply sorry—that I have no way of expressing all that I see and feel.

There was little time in ordinary life for creative pleasures, although she began to practice again on her guitar—old songs and some Spanish melodies her mother had transcribed for her from memory.

In mid-August, having recovered from his illness, Burton set out with two summer session Tech students to map sections of New Hampshire's White Mountains around Mt. Moosilauke, a bald, 4,500-foot peak west of Franconia Notch. Their expedition ended badly. On August 18th, the Lewiston, Maine, *Evening Journal* ran a short article about their misadventure, describing their intended day trip, leaving from the Tip-Top House and following the rough bed of Baker's River to Breezy Point in East Warren, about six miles away. But before they had gone three miles, fog closed in, and darkness fell. Stranded overnight without food or warm clothing, "they resumed the journey at first light and reached their destination at eight o'clock, greatly fatigued and dangerously chilled." Burton was frustrated and embarrassed by this escapade, which seemed to undermine his reputation as a competent outdoorsman and topographer. He sent both student assistants packing and, after a brief return home to Jamaica Plain, departed again to finish the New Hampshire survey work himself.

When he left, Gertrude and Arnold traveled to her mother's cottage on Deer Isle, which she had declined to visit the previous summer, citing her moral obligation to her father. Jane Hitz had acquired a two-acre point of land from the Sylvester family three years before, in 1884, for $25, after vacationing for several summers at Captain Benjamin Sylvester's boarding house. Jane had selected the house site by viewing the coastline from a boat, a method of choosing real estate that locals considered quite odd. By 1886, local builders, who referred to her as "Madame Hitz," had completed a two-storied bungalow, the first private cottage in the area built by a summer visitor. The unpretentious cedar shingle-style house was trimmed in dark red, and commanded stunning ocean views from its wraparound porch. Wide wooden steps led from the generous verandah to rocky, wind-swept Hitz Point. Jane Hitz was known for leaving a lamp burning in a seaward window, so mariners could get their bearings from the steady light.

Gertrude wrote, "There is no more beautiful sight than sunset from the porch." Viewed from a wooden rocking chair, Sylvester Cove and Dunham Point dominated the foreground, and beyond them, on the western horizon, the silhouetted outlines of Mt. Battie, Mt. Megunticook, and the gentle, lower Camden Hills, called by Native Americans "the swells from the sea."

Inside, the cottage's mullioned windows faced west and south, toward Butter, Eagle, and Great Spruce Head Islands, and the vast, shining Penobscot Bay. To the southeast, a Mill Pond sandbar connected Hitz Point to Mill Island at low tide. The kitchen windows faced northeast, into the woods. The sitting and dining rooms flanked two sides of a large central chimney. Each room had a generous fieldstone fireplace and wooden mantel intricately hand-carved with flowers and grasses.

Gertrude delighted in the island's natural beauty, but during that summer visit she became painfully aware, again, of her mother's implacable hostility toward her father. During the long months of the trial, Gertrude had become a sounding board for each of her parents, and she agonized over her deeply divided loyalties. Helpless to change the situation, she confided to Mary: "And what are we all? Struggle—struggle—struggle—some succeed (in what?), others fail—each pursues his phantom of happiness. Yet, surely the world progresses and man was born to be noble and brave and free. Ah! But Life is so short—so short—and that troubles me!"

Was she, too, struggling to find freedom?

Writing to Mariechen helped Gertrude put her feelings into words. Mary Costelloe had given birth to her own first child, Rachel, called Ray, in June. She wrote asking about Gertrude's pregnancy, Arnold's birth, and baby care. Gertrude responded to each of Mary's questions, with time on her hands and an uneasy mind. Over the course of several days, she filled sixty-five sheets of writing paper before mailing them to England, exclaiming, "I never wrote a longer letter in my life…seems a long time to give to an absent friend. But O what would we not give to have the friend really with us…And then who would count the hours?"

Gertrude was eager to debate philosophical notions, exchange gossip, and give advice about childrearing. She still addressed Mary using the Quaker "thee," though neither woman considered herself a Quaker. On marrying her Irish barrister husband, Frank Costelloe, Mary had converted to Catholicism. The two young mothers eagerly shared their experiences with first-borns. Arnold's short life had been full of illnesses and separations, while Ray seemed a model child. Gertrude wrote: "I am glad for thee that Ray does not cry—'never cries?!'…It rests me even to think of thee really having a 'delicious rest.' I do not seem to have rested for two years…but I feel that rest will come and I am not discouraged…"

She was still awed by having given birth: "… it is so mysterious and wonderful this calling of a new life from nowhere to our own flesh and blood, and then waiting a few brief months and suddenly seeing and touching a completed human being…And yet all the while being ourselves—quite the same, according to all outward appearances…"

Shifting her focus from childbirth to childrearing, Gertrude expanded on her approach to hygiene and her Froebel-inspired conception of an ideal mother as non-interfering, a helpful yet firm teacher:

> Thee wants to have me send thee some of my maternal wisdom…my belief in the power of hygiene is immensely great—quite gigantic…I have always made a sunny large airy nursery the first condition of existence. In cold or bad weather I would open all the windows and dress him up in his warm outdoor clothing and so give him exercise in the fresh air without danger of sudden changes. The sun-bath is an excellent idea, I think.

Yet Gertrude was becoming aware of the growing contradictions between her maternal ideals and her professional ambitions: her life's duties and desires, *shoulds* and *wants*. She aspired to perfection in her chosen roles as wife and mother, yet could not deny her appetite for adventure and public acclaim. To navigate her existential confusions, at twenty-six, she relied on passion, courage, and her aesthetic sensibility:

> … my sea is a sea of uncertainty. I have a life-preserver, however, which always brings me safely to the surface and grants me large glimpses of a sunny sky. My life preserver is my passion for the beautiful. Of God, of Death, of Immortality I know little. But I shall swim with unfaltering courage, however thick the fog! I am often bewildered, Mariechen, and then I take hope because I think I can realize that I am young and surely I will understand all these great questions sometime. The principal thing is to be sincere and to feel the nobleness of living.

This "passion for the beautiful" included not only the truth of art, poetry, music, and drama but also the aesthetic pleasures of fashionable clothing. For all her sober rationality on some topics—for example, sexual continence—Gertrude harbored romantic yearnings for poetry in her life, as she had recognized in her Boston days through her friendship with Bernhard Berenson. Knowing that Mary was mingling socially with prominent literary and artistic personalities in Anglo–American intellectual circles, she was curious to learn more about England's Aesthetic Movement. As a barrister's wife, Mary would have access to the latest London news. Gertrude wrote:

> Does thee really dress in aesthetic ways?—In gowns lovely and simple which I imagine can be worn in England without appearance of affectation? O I am desperately interested in beautiful dressing! I never dressed more poorly than I do now but my circumstances force me just at present. But O the vision of myself sometimes after I go to bed + lie awake like a child the night before Christmas tasting in imagination all the sweetness+ glory that may come!
>
> What does thee know of the aesthetic circle in London? Hast thee met William Morris? And does thee know people who are earnestly devoting themselves to the cultivation of the beautiful? Does thee know anything of Walter Pater?

These thoughts, particularly about Walter Pater, the idol she and Bernhard Berenson had worshipped five years earlier, inspired her to suggest a meeting in England between Mary and

> … my friend Bernhard Berenson, of whom I am sure I have spoken. He is now in Paris having been presented with a five year private scholarship, as he graduated from Harvard this June…I am hoping that you may meet each other before the five years are over. He is to study Art and Literature in France, Spain, and Italy.

Gertrude's casual but heartfelt suggestion would have dramatic consequences in years to come—for Mary, Frank, and Bernhard, and herself. She loved bringing together favorite friends from her wide, though now shrinking, circle of acquaintances, and imagined herself a magnetic force, drawing together likeminded comrades. She would not have predicted that, sometimes, by bringing others together she might find herself excluded.

Gertrude's "passion for the beautiful" in life and art also informed her message as a sex educator, through lecturing and writing:

> I know I have a definite work through which I can do great good + for which I feel especially fitted. Every time that I speak I learn more what is needed + more of my weakness and my power. I realize fully that no great change in sexual life can take place until the whole subject is raised to a higher plane of feeling. Mere knowledge is helpless without all appreciation of the deeply poetic and sacred sides of this subject. I always try to appeal to the aesthetic and religious natures and so uplift the imagination...

Mrs. Ada Spaulding, Boston Home Club president, and Gertrude's mentor, was a summer resident of Deer Isle. She invited Gertrude to speak at the Deer Isle Village Congregational Church, up the hill from the post office, town hall, and several small, clapboard storefronts along the village's single, unpaved street. Gertrude's audience consisted mostly of mothers, wives, and daughters of the island's fishermen and quarrymen. She described to Mary her initial trepidation and the group's unexpected response: "... I dreaded the undertaking, fearing that I would not find any bridge to lead my spirit to the door of their hearts. Imagine how delighted I have been, since I was able to bring them all to tears. And to have had evidence of a sincere appreciation of the purity of sexuality."

After this success, Gertrude was invited to speak a second time, but postponed another lecture until the following summer:

The interest and enthusiasm aroused by the few words I uttered (so falteringly and almost hopelessly) have been so great that the minister sent me word that the church was at my service. And the lady who owns the large town hall also offered to open the doors wide…I have been touched to the heart with a stirring faith.

I really found that these country women—notwithstanding their narrow material lives—were more easily awakened than women of wider intelligence + finer culture. Of course surprise and curiosity enter in as important factors and perhaps more ignorant and unworldly women realize but little of the vast importance of sexual purification. Yet it is hopeful to see women accept so eagerly suggestions which in most cases must revolutionize their whole attitude of mind.

Her goal was to transform behavior, and elevate sexuality from the merely physical to the spiritual sphere.

Yet, Gertrude was struggling in her own marriage, and Mary, too, was becoming disenchanted with her circumscribed life as a mother and politician's wife. The two women shared the dilemmas of many socially progressive women in England and America. Their intimate exchanges became mutually reinforcing. In search of strategies to sort out their contradictory feelings about marriage, motherhood and careers, they discussed literature, including George Eliot's novels and Mrs. Anne Gilchrist's recently published letters. Gertrude concluded one note:

I want to send thee the extract from one of Anne Gilchrist's letters and then I will say goodnight and good bye. She expresses what I am growing to feel in regards to the possibility of doing the individual work of a student, and at the same time devoting one's attention to the care of young children—

and also in regard to the absolute need of solitude of a quiet oasis in the midst of a day's responsibilities.

Anne Gilchrist wrote:

> I find it such a harassing strain to attempt two things… [But] After all they will not always be children and if I have it in me to do anything worth doing with my pen, why, I can do it ten years hence if I live, when I shall have completed my task so far as direct instruction of the children goes. I shall only be forty-six then, not in my dotage. A divided aim is not only most harassing to a conscientious disposition but quite fatal to success—to doing one's very best in either…

However, Gertrude remained ambivalent about postponing her professional ambitions, and prefiguring Virginia Woolf's requirement for a "room of one's own," declared that:

> … This winter…[I will] try to have an hour at least for solid undisturbed work, if I have to hire a room in the neighborhood outside our own domains. Speaking occasionally is an easy matter and a delight and inspiration. But to find time to write a book—every year of delay a seeming wrong to the work—this is a hard question.

She then contradicted herself, though, adopting Gilchrist's argument:

> But after all what are twelve months or twenty four in the endless march of years?! And Arnold needs me most before the "school age"—after his own life can be regulated, my own will be easier to arrange. But I do not intend to wait until I am "forty six"!! Do not fear my accepting Mrs. Gilchrist to the letter and date!

Gertrude had copied out Gilchrist's words without guessing that, sadly, she would not live to the age of forty-six.

Around this time, Gertrude confessed to her father, on a post-card, in German, *"Es thut mir immer weh!"* (I am always in pain!). Whether referring to physical afflictions or emotional woes, or both, she certainly felt anxious and confused about her future path. Gertrude also shared Mariechen's increasingly restless letters with her father. John Hitz responded sympathetically about the women's troubles, and his own:

> What lives we lead?! How unsatisfactory in many ways. Surely there must be a condition of peacefulness—a state where one can live out their real inner lives on this earth— alas, it seems continual struggle or war—anxieties—cares. Where is our foundation?

At sixty, he felt depressed in spirit. Impulsively, and without comment, he sent copies of Henrik Ibsen's play, *A Doll's House*, re-cently translated into English, to both Gertrude and his wife, finding in its themes of female roles and marital revolt strong parallels with their lives, and his.

By mid-month, however, John Hitz's situation began to look more promising. In early November, Professor Bell, with Hitz as his assistant, left for Edgartown, on Martha's Vineyard, via Boston, for two months of data collection. Gertrude wrote to him there regu-larly—she had a cold, she was lecturing, she was discouraged that Ida had given notice and was leaving for the winter. And, longing for a change, dreaming of Europe, she wrote about Switzerland, the per-fect alpine country she had adored as a girl: pure and calm and white.

Just as Gertrude was putting Arnold to bed, on the last day of 1887, John Hitz returned to the mainland from Martha's Vineyard and arrived in Jamaica Plain. He planned to stay for a week or two, helping the Burton family settle into yet another new home, at 50 Green Street. Gertrude missed the great double-trunked maple on Glendale Terrace whose leaves had glowed yellow in the fall, but she preferred their spacious, new, three-story duplex, named The Malvern, close to the shops on Centre Street and more suitable for a growing family. The Burtons were expecting a second child, due in late June.

## CHAPTER 8

## *Change Above All Things*

GERTRUDE LEFT 50 GREEN STREET EARLY ON THE FINE, COLD MORN-ing of January 3, 1888, for Chelsea, a manufacturing and ship-building city directly across the Mystic River from Boston. On arriving at the meeting of the Women's Educational and Industrial Union, she presented a lecture entitled "The Children's Right." The Union had been founded a decade earlier to respond to miserable labor conditions, crowded housing, poor sanitation, and the exploitation of women and children, resulting from increasing industrialization, immigration, and unregulated Gilded Age capitalism. Gertrude's talk was included in a winter series with a presentation by prominent reformer and philanthropist Ednah Dow Cheney, on "Censorious-ness," and another on "Hygiene for Young Women," by medical pio-neer Dr. Marie E. Zakrzewska, founder of the New England Hospital for Women and Children.

Meanwhile, Burton was absorbed by his teaching, and often set off for Tech before breakfast and worked on after dinner, at home. When John Hitz retired at nine o'clock one evening during his New Year's visit, he left his son-in-law still lettering a sectional city plan. Gertrude and Arnold spent much of the visit with her father in their new home. He laid carpets in the dining room, living room, and hall. In the bathroom he installed shelves, towel racks, and a ledge for a small gas hot water heater. He played with Arnold, whom he consid-ered "the veritable embodiment of wholesome child life," visited old Boston friends, and one day, met Burton for a tour of the Massachu-setts Institute of Technology.

After supper, the family often gathered to talk and read aloud to one another. Sometimes Gertrude shared Mary's latest letter from

London. The intellectually frustrated Mary wrote in exasperation about her relentless duties as a mother, women's rights activist, and politician's wife. She commented ironically (giving voice to Gertrude's own thoughts, perhaps) that: "My own greatest trouble in life is that...spirit of individualism which leads me to keep thinking about my rights instead of my duties...rights are a sort of legal fiction..."

Gertrude gave another public talk the following week. In the late afternoon, with Burton and her father, she left for East Boston, a neighborhood of immigrants, where that evening she lectured to a Home Club gathering presided over by Mrs. Ada Spaulding, in the Grand Army of the Republic Hall. Her talk addressed a new demand in teaching, the subject of procreation considered from an educational standpoint. Gertrude illustrated her topic with Burton's beautiful, large-format anatomical diagrams and drawings, some of which had been modified, her father noted, "to suit the uneducated state of her prospective audience." Upwards of fifty people attended, all women except Burton, Hitz, and Professor Dudley Allen Sargent, director of physical training at Harvard's Hemenway Gymnasium, whose ideas about vigorous activity for girls and women challenged Victorian stereotypes of fainting females. Hitz noted that Gertrude's presentation was very well received, "making evidently a deep impression—12 midnight before we got to bed."

Gertrude's growing confidence as a lecturer motivated her, during this second pregnancy, to begin working on the books on reproduction in plants, animals, and humans she had mapped out for her father in the Washington Jail: the first volume for children, the second for adults. An early chapter in Volume One introduced the subject of propagation by recounting "The Story of a Fern."

The story begins:

"Come into the woods with me, where all is so sweet, and so still, and there is a beautiful silence. Looking down to the rich dark earth we find a delicate fern and listen to its quiet and wonderful story. Lift up the long, feathery leaf, turn it gently, and on the underside you may find a number of tiny black or brown dots…"

"The Story of a Fern" explains that the leaves are called *pinnae*, and the dots, *sporangia*, or spore cases. When the cases dry they burst open and the spores inside fall to the ground. These develop into *zygotes* that contain both the necessary *antheridia* (multiple spiral-shaped fertilizing spermatozoids) and the *archegonia* (ovaries containing a single ovum). The story continues anthropomorphically:

"After the…spermatozoid has reached the entrance to the ovary, it finds the ovum waiting and they both blend their life together and form the beautiful little seed from which a new fern is to be born. When the ovum is fertilized…the seed grows and grows, safely within its nest…By and by, after long quiet, for all these delicate things need much silence and patience, the door is made ready to open again; a little fern slowly comes into the world…"

The text clarifies that ferns reproduce in this way, sexually, in alternating generations. They can also reproduce non-sexually, by means of rhizomes, a method that does not rely on male and female reproductive parts.

As the story ends, Gertrude credits scientists with revealing the wonderful ways of ferns: "… men and women who have spent earnest lives searching to learn more and more." But she also promises her young readers that they can make discoveries of their own: "… if you look and listen lovingly the ferns will whisper their beauty to you…"

After Gertrude's death, John Hitz edited this unpublished manuscript and printed it as a memorial souvenir, a delicately illustrated tribute to her "life work," exemplifying her belief that "There is nothing in sexuality which forbids a fearless and open search for the highest truth concerning it; the real shame lies in neglecting this matter...."

Gertrude rekindled her interest in pedagogy early in 1888, when Arnold was nearly three. The prominent educator and Froebel kindergarten advocate Elizabeth Peabody, eighty-four years old, was living at 290 Lamartine Street, a five minute walk from the Burtons' duplex on Green Street. Gertrude consulted her often. One evening, with her father, Gertrude visited Miss Peabody, who entertained them, Hitz noted, with "an interesting disquisition on kindergarten methods." Afterward, they proceeded to the city to take supper with Gertrude's former mentor at Boston University, Professor Samuel Silas Curry, who now headed his School of Expression with his wife, Anna Baright, a respected teacher of elocution. They had expected Burton to join them, but he was busy with other commitments.

Gertrude was laid up with a cold in her eyes on the following mild, sunny Saturday, while John Hitz worked around the house, played outside with Arnold, and took a long walk through the prosperous suburb of Brookline, nearby. As Gertrude recovered, an unexpected telegram arrived from Professor Bell, recalling Hitz to Washington straightaway. After his departure, and later in her pregnancy, Gertrude sorely missed her father's practical help and emotional support. She felt unable to manage all the details of her life without regular, reliable domestic help.

No correspondence survives to suggest Gertrude's state of mind as she awaited their second child. She seldom appeared in Hitz's diary entries. In contrast to the leisurely, bucolic period leading up to Arnold's birth, Gertrude spent her time and energy during the spring of 1888 at home, meeting the exhausting demands of daily routines. She wrote her father on May 26th that she was very weary. The new baby, likely conceived the preceding August when Burton returned from his misadventure in New Hampshire, was expected in less than a month, just after the Burtons' fourth wedding anniversary.

Meanwhile, Alexander Graham Bell's longtime assistant, Dr. Radcliff, retired, and John Hitz officially became Bell's secretary. On the one hand, his tasks included the tedious sorting and recording of Martha's Vineyard data on the deaf, and, on the other, performing services and odd errands for Bell and his family. He also took on responsibilities for general correspondence and frequently met with the parents of deaf children. The pace was demanding, and Hitz, like Bell himself, was often up late, working until midnight. He was eating only sporadically—often with no dinner aside from bread or milk. His fatigue was offset in part by Bell's cordiality: "[Bell] said, among other things, 'Mr. Hitz I would like to see or get into your mind—you think so differently from me…our affections seem on the same plane—our thoughts discretely apart.'"

John Hitz could now rely on a regular salary of $75 a month. In his capacity as secretary, he also spent time at home with the Bells, sharing their family life. He described the scene one day: "Mr. B busy on his diagram of elemental energy—or conservation of energy—the principle involved being that no force is lost, only transferred in some other form—Mrs. B lying on the settee most of the time, in a beautiful heliotrope morning gown, reading *Goldelse* by Marlitt (in German)—a perfect picture—one which I greatly enjoyed."

However, domestic tranquility at the Bells' household was rare, because of the hectic schedule. On April 24th, a cablegram from London arrived from the Royal Commission on Deaf Mute Instruction, inviting Professor Bell to appear before them in June. Bell quickly accepted and asked Hitz to aid him in London. John Hitz happily agreed. Besides this heaven-sent opportunity for travel to Europe, another key event in Hitz's life occurred, a month later. On May 24th, Helen Keller, with her mother and her teacher, Anne Sullivan, stopped over in Washington to meet Dr. Bell on their way to Boston. John Hitz later became Helen Keller's "foster father."

❧

Gertrude sent a last-minute cable to the Cunard steamer wharf in New York to wish her father *bon voyage* before his departure for England, on June second. Then Bell and Hitz were off, aboard the *SS Aurania*, a ship with a reputation for rolling with heavy swells. Nevertheless, the eight-day passage proved uneventful. The two worked in close quarters at a table rigged in their cabin, collating reports and survey data. In London they continued their preparations for several days, awake until two a.m., preparing statistics and documents for the printer.

Hitz attended the session of the Royal Commission, where he assisted Professor Bell with charts, cards, and references regarding deaf classifications, hereditary patterns, the teaching of language, and appliances for testing hearing. This intense activity absorbed all Hitz's attention: his diary during the London stay records no communication with Gertrude. However, he found time to visit Mary Costelloe at her London home, at 40 Grosvenor Road.

Gertrude was delighted that the London voyage allowed her father to continue on for a three-month Swiss journey. On July 4th, Bell and Hitz proceeded from London to Paris, where they parted. Bell paid Hitz's way to Switzerland, providing a hundred francs besides. John Hitz visited family and old friends, with an eye to a permanent return to the land of his birth.

In Bern, John Hitz contacted acquaintances, had his photo taken, arranged for visiting cards, and bought books and maps for the trip. Then he quickly made his way to Lausanne, where he found countless changes since the previous decade, before the bank scandal, when he had served as Swiss Consul. He also recognized familiar landmarks that Gertrude, too, would know. She eagerly read his description of a sojourn to the nearby village of Corbeyrier and a hike overlooking the Rhone Valley, where he viewed the superb Dents du Midi and Dent du Morcles—"never have seen more inspiring scenery," he wrote to her on a postcard. He toured Lake Geneva by steamer and pronounced the sight of Mt. Blanc as "... pure and imposing, glorious in its sublimity."

Gertrude studied his letters with great interest, recalling old times. In Davos, Hitz inscribed Gertrude's name in the municipal rolls, as an honorary citizen of his own birthplace. Her father's enthusiasm reinforced her own passion for Switzerland. In her mind's eye, as in the Victorian imagination generally, Switzerland's sublime mountain landscapes symbolized purity, permanence and perfection—an escape from petty concerns and complications. A few years later, she planned her own voyage "home."

After three weeks of travel, a cousin, Conrad Hitz, welcomed John for a holiday with the extended family. Three letters from Gertrude awaited him at Conrad's house. One announced his grandson Harold Hitz Burton's arrival on June 22nd. Until then, Hitz had remained unaware that Gertrude had produced a second healthy boy. ("Hallelujah—thanks are to the Lord.") Both Arnold and Harold bore names evoking Anglo Saxon heroes, popular in the 1880s. But while Felix Arnold's name was inspired by hopes for his happiness, Harold Hitz Burton's middle name connected him intentionally with his maternal Swiss heritage.

Gertrude, looking fatigued, greeted her father on October 11th in Jamaica Plain, where Hitz traveled immediately after arriving in New York. The nursemaid, Ida, who had returned to service during the summer, also seemed "rather worn, her red hair not so bright." Otherwise all appeared normal: Hitz found Arnold alert, although "suffering an attack of dysentery," and Harold, "a strong-looking child—different from Arnold, good-natured and very well-formed." However, Gertrude seemed preoccupied, her mind "constantly fo-

cused on the proper mode of management of very young children—
what best to do to secure desirable development," and what to avoid.
Her perfectionism seemed to paralyze her. To her father, she appeared indecisive and overwhelmed, and she consulted daily with
Elizabeth Peabody.

❧

Ida gave notice that she would again take a winter's leave, so
finding a dependable replacement became urgent. Father and daughter spent some days riding about to search for domestic help while appreciating the luminous fall foliage of golden elms and russet maples.
They spent other days indoors at 50 Green Street, writing letters and
playing with the children.

Gertrude listened as Hitz confided that his tenure in Washington was uncertain for the present. He still half-believed he could
return to Switzerland and make a career there. But after a week in
Jamaica Plain, he received a letter from Professor Bell, who proposed
to devote himself now primarily to projects on behalf of the deaf.
When he assured Hitz that his help would be very welcome, Hitz
telegraphed he would leave for Washington on the coming Saturday.
On Friday, he bought his steamer ticket.

Gertrude appeared in a very nervous state during the final
hours of his visit and, to Hitz's great dismay, for the first time spoke
to him directly about her extreme anxiety. She confessed that "... she
needed better service and separation from her immediate surroundings—a change, above all things—otherwise she feared she would
surely break down."

❧

Hitz took her, with Arnold, by carriage to call on a friend in
nearby Roslindale, hoping to soothe her, and then returned home
for a meal. However, when Hitz left at six o'clock for Boston, he was
still fearful for Gertrude's emotional stability. He changed trains for

Providence, then boarded the steamer *Rhode Island* for New York City. There he made unsuccessful inquiries at Swiss House about hiring a servant for Gertrude. After his five months' absence, November and December passed in a rush of work on census charts, consultations, his usual social and church meetings, and the Christmas holidays.

❧

For Gertrude, the recurrent, frustrating searches for domestic help became a desperate pursuit. She was increasingly troubled by her own perceived failings as a mother and as an aspiring professional. Although each of her boys was "a wanted child," the responsibilities for caring for them, without dependable support, and often without her husband's company, proved more difficult than she had imagined. She had been unable to create a "quiet oasis," a room of her own, for writing. She often felt under the weather, and she was very lonely.

At the same time, Burton was awaiting MIT's decision on his promotion to the rank of associate professor. For him, this was a critical juncture, with his career hanging in the balance. He still often left Green Street early in the morning and returned after the evening meal. He reasoned, justifiably, that their marriage agreement encouraged each of them to follow separate callings. But their paths were diverging widely, leading Gertrude and Burton further and further away from the loving, companionate marriage they had anticipated, less than five years before.

Gertrude with Doll, about 1864

Gertrude with Sailor Hat, Paris, about 1873

Alfred Edgar Burton, Bowdoin College 1878
*Courtesy of Bowdoin College Archives and Special Collections, call number 239.1.*

Gertrude, about 1878

Bernhard Berenson at eighteen

Mary Whitall Smith at eighteen

John Hitz, Swiss
Consulate Office,
about 1882

The *ALPHA*, advertisements 1882

Cover of Gertrude's Essay, "The Importance of Knowledge of the Sexual Nature," 1884

Alfred E. Burton       Gertrude Hitz

Married

Monday, June 16th 1884

Marriage announcement 1884

Gertrude
about 1884

Gertrude with Arnold 1886

Alfred Edgar with Arnold 1886

The "New" Washington Jail 1880s (Library of Congress, LC-USZ62-106343)

## THE EVENING STAR.

### WASHINGTON:

**TUESDAY............December 14, 1886.**

**CROSBY S. NOYES.................Editor.**

THE RELEASE OF MESSRS. HITZ AND PRENTISS.—The news that the Court in General Term had declared the indictments against Messrs. Hitz and Prentiss, officers of the defunct German-American National band, to be defective, was taken to the jail yesterday morning, at ten o'clock, by Mrs. Prentiss. Soon afterwards Mr. Hitz' daughter arrived. The news, of course, was most welcome to the two prisoners, who have been confined in the jail for several months. During the day many friends called and joined with them in their rejoicing. The order of the court directing their release was taken to the jail at three o'clock by Gen. Mussey, counsel for Mr. Hitz, and at four o'clock Messrs. Hitz and Prentiss left the building, accompanied by their friends. This was the final scene in a case that has occupied the court and the public attention for several years.

The *Washington Evening Star*, December 14, 1886

# PART II

*A short life in the saddle, Lord! / Not long life by the fire*

# CHAPTER 9

## *Darkest Day*

N EW ENGLAND'S LATE WINTER WEATHER DARKENED GERTRUDE'S already dismal mood: letters to her father grew increasingly despondent. January 1889's 12.53-inch rainfall set a Boston record, and it rained again during the entire month of March. Gertrude had become not only disheartened but also physically weaker.

Unable to regain focus, and struggling with guilt and anger, she desperately needed help at home. She had little energy for the noble causes that had sustained her energy for nearly a decade, and she missed the many relationships that had encouraged her in her work: her mother and the women of the Moral Education Society; her teaching mentors; her employer, Alexander Graham Bell; friends Mary Costelloe and Frances Haldeman Sidwell; and finally, her husband. His own career seemed all-consuming. She felt increasingly called upon not only to support him, but also to manage the household and care singlehandedly for her sons. She felt unequal to becoming the mother and professional she aspired to be, let alone a spokeswoman for marriage equality, with "humanity her star." Her father thought she might be cheered to know that her essay, *The Importance of Knowledge Concerning the Sexual Nature*, was at Brentano's for reprinting, but days after he sent the happy news he received another "decidedly grim letter." References to Burton disappeared from their correspondence, presumably because of her unhappiness: the usually thoughtful John Hitz apparently sent no greeting for his son-in-law's birthday, March 26.

In mid-month Hitz wrote to Gertrude, inviting her to come with the children to spend a month or two in Washington—perhaps the warmer weather would be a tonic. But she responded she could not, because of the cost and disruption to their lives. Then, on April 2, she alarmed him: "Arnold ill—come on as soon as convenient—" At that, Hitz notified Bell it might be necessary to leave suddenly for Boston. However, three days later Gertrude reassured him that Arnold was better. Still, her almost daily pleas for help implied that her own situation was growing more serious. Hitz felt sick at heart. Clearly, she did need a change, above all things.

On April 7th, the first warm day of spring, Gertrude took a decisive step, renewing an acquaintance made before Harold was born. Picture her at a desk by a sunny window in the downstairs front room at 50 Green Street. Listening for Harold's cries, and only half conscious of the boys shouting and playing tag in the muddy schoolyard across the way, she fidgeted with the pen. She wrote slowly, looking absently out the window, pausing to find the right words. When writing to her women friends, Gertrude's words flowed freely, filling page after page, but now she was writing to an amiable poet, William Bliss Carman, whom she had met the year before. He was lanky, with a fine-looking face and light brown hair worn long, in the aesthetic mode. A native of New Brunswick, Canada, he descended from Loyalists who fled north during the American Revolution.

Carman first arrived in Boston in 1886 to attend Harvard, following university studies in Fredericton and later in Oxford and Edinburgh. Gertrude had encountered him among her Harvard literary friends, and not long after their meeting, Carman sent her a sheaf of poems. She had waited too long, nearly a year, to respond with the comments she had promised him. But catching up on correspondence was not the reason she chose to reconnect. She sensed that, with his poetic sensibilities, Bliss Carman could help her escape from growing depression. She wrote:

The Malvern 50 Green St.
Jamaica Plain, April 7, 1889
Dear Mr. Carman,

The sheet of verses which came to me so long ago pleased and interested me so much. I am really grieved that my word of gratitude comes to you so late!

I have been in very great trouble this winter and have felt unable to attend to the joys and graces of life. Perhaps I have thought of you a great deal more by neglecting you. When I opened the wrapper and saw what was before me I wished I might grasp your hand at once that you might [know] how glad I was you remembered me…

As he requested, she remarked briefly on his verses, appreciating especially their "reserved power" and the blending of "tenderness and severity:"

What strikes me most is a peculiar terseness and compactness—the suggestion of much more than is expressed and the consciousness of reserved power…Then there is the mystic strain, which of course you know, without the pointing of another…But I want to tell you of one thing which I feel myself and which perhaps you are not at all conscious of—and that is a blending of tenderness and severity which makes me think of the sudden blossoming of flowers in snow. I seem to feel the atmosphere of a northern country constantly about you and to be constantly reminded of the rapture of spring and the fervent glow of a warm and sensitive heart. It seems to me almost like a Wagner "motif" and runs through all the music like a distinctive song.

She concluded boldly:

I hope I may see you again and that you may wish to seek me out if you chance to be near me.

In sincerity, Gertrude Hitz Burton

She sealed and addressed the envelope. Did she then cross the room to the moss-green divan and seat herself sideways, press her right hand against the wall, and, leaning forward onto the cushions, rest her head in the crook of her left arm?

※

Gertrude's appeals spurred her father to leave for Boston a week later, on April 14th, a Sunday. He arrived in time for Monday morning's breakfast, bearing fragrant pink arbutus blossoms, an evergreen symbol of lasting love. He found Mr. Burton and the children well, "and Gertrude bright, but feeble in strength." They spent his first day at the house, basking in spring sunshine on the balcony most of the afternoon, Gertrude in a hammock and Arnold playing around them. He found Gertrude's "lethargic, listless condition very unaccountable" and he looked after the children to be sure she rested. Local women—Miss Merridew, Mrs. Bradford, and a girl, Mary, were helping with the baby and with Gertrude's needs, but neither Mrs. Bradford nor Miss Merridew could commit to a regular schedule. Hitz observed there were "attendants enough, but only makeshifts—nothing to be depended upon."

Father and daughter spent the following week either at home or house-hunting. They searched real estate offices for a suitable country rental where she and the children might be happier during the warmer months, since Burton's summer plans centered on conducting his Tech field course in surveying and cartography. They wrote inquiries for houses north of the city, by the sea, in Gloucester and Rockport, Essex and Ipswich, and in the farm country to the west, in East Medway and surrounding towns.

※

On April 23rd, the two rode the commuter line to Rockville and Millis, looking at possible rentals. Then they hired a horse to call on Dr. Kate Sanborn, Gertrude's friend and doctor, whose homeopathic practice was located on School Street in Medway. Gertrude later described this medical consultation of April 23, 1889 as "one of the darkest days of my life." Dr. Sanborn explained that Gertrude's apparent nervous condition was dangerous: in homeopathic terms, a faulty autonomic nervous system was preventing normal circulation of blood to the internal organs. She pronounced the condition life-threatening, and delivered a stunning, baffling prognosis: Gertrude, soon to be twenty-eight, might have only ten years to live.

Gertrude and John Hitz had a "brief talk...about her condition and about locating for the summer and other personal matters," which he did not record in detail. He was witnessing his formerly poised, self-confident daughter, his pillar of strength, deteriorate physically and emotionally. She seemed nearly defeated, increasingly isolated from friends and colleagues, and forced to reconsider her mission as a lecturer and a writer. Her husband was diligently pursuing his career, as they had agreed. But her life as wife and mother seemed a cycle of frustration, anger, and guilt. Her failing health left her with weakened physical resources. Gertrude confessed to Mary Costelloe that she could not relate to her children in the way she wanted unless she felt rested, yet the children themselves had become the source of nervous exhaustion and anxiety. How would she carry on? John Hitz was at a loss. He wrote to their Washington friend, Mrs. Kappeler, about Gertrude's coming back to the capital with him.

Later that day, when the two returned to 50 Green Street, they discovered an orange quarantine card tacked on the door of the adjoining apartment, warning of scarlet fever. Distressed, they decided to remove the children temporarily to Mr. Putnam R. Clark's familiar boarding house in East Medway, where Gertrude had lodged previously. Arising early the next morning, Gertrude left by train to make arrangements while her father attended to packing and sending off the baggage. He departed at ten o'clock with Mrs. Bradford, Miss Merridew, Arnold, and Harold. Gertrude met them at the Medway station with a team and wagon, and they drove to the Clark's farm, where they ate midday dinner. Afterwards, John Hitz drove the team back to Medway and sent off several telegrams and letters—one to Mr. Burton, advising him of the move. Then he walked an hour back to the Clarks', in a hard rain, east along the railroad track.

The old Clark homestead, a large, 1710 central-chimney salt-box, stood on Stoney Plain, up Farm Street at the sharp curve where it intersected Cedar. The two windows on the first floor flanked the massive front door, with three second-story windows lined up above. A summer kitchen and several outbuildings were scattered to the rear among large oak trees, with the fields beyond. The Burtons had boarded there four years earlier, when Gertrude "nested" in the country, awaiting Arnold's birth and preparing to welcome their unborn child. She wrote later that, at that time, she "… had lived in the fields from morning to night with a few poets and the story of noble lives— and my guitar—and yielded all my life for weeks and weeks to the large, sweet influences of open sky and sweeping winds, that the dear unborn life might have the calm and the joy of all, all these things."

Wistfully, Gertrude longed to enjoy a similar summer idyll. For several days, she and her father again traversed the countryside with Mr. Clark's team, looking at rental houses. They were exhausted each day when they returned to the Clarks' place, where John Hitz was uncomfortably accommodated on a pullout sofa in the parlor.

On Wednesday, the first of May, Gertrude decided simply to remain with the Clarks, renting two large rooms and a small one for herself, the two children, and a nurse, at the rate of $12.00 per week.

But almost immediately, her father noted, she became "unable to do anything," overwhelmed by headaches and dizziness. On Friday, she made out a list of articles the family required from home. Her father returned to Jamaica Plain to meet Burton and collect the necessities.

The two men gathered sheets and towels and the children's toys and clothes, seldom speaking, and avoiding each other's gaze, while attending to the tasks at hand. The reticent Burton, bit by bit, described Gertrude's gradual falling to pieces and acknowledged the unraveling of their marriage. Burton's explanation of the situation was so devastating that Hitz could not bring himself to recount the details in his diary. He summed up the awful scene:

> ... AEB[urton] revealed the cause of all Gertrude's troubles—assuming all blame—making a clear statement and ready to accept the consequence—Kept cool & so far as I can recall preserved strictly Christ's example in treatment of the matter and the responses made—feel deeply, very deeply for him—and deeply, more deeply for Gertrude—
>
> Good Lord do thou preserve them and impart strength to pass through this severe ordeal...AEB approves Gertrude's ideas in regard to her lifework—I dare not write more—stunned & spiritually struck dumb by the revelation.

The "cause of all Gertrude's troubles" remains a mystery: we can only speculate. What did Burton disclose that evening as they folded pajamas and diapers, then packed toys and blankets into boxes and baskets? He "assumed all blame." During their long separation, while Gertrude was in Washington, had he been unfaithful, finding comfort and satisfaction with other lovers? Or with prostitutes? Had he contracted syphilis and infected her with the disease? Or had Burton forced himself on her, in violation of their vows of continence except for procreation? After their youthful infatuation, had the couple found themselves sexually incompatible? Was he homosexual? Bisexual? Was she?

Was he, in her view, abandoning his paternal responsibility for shared childrearing? In his eyes, had she become cold, demanding, and difficult to live with? Was the problem partly the medical condition that plagued her body and spirit? Postpartum depression, or some variant of what was then commonly called hysteria, or neurasthenia?

During nearly five years as husband and wife, Burton had become increasingly preoccupied with his career, and Gertrude with housekeeping, childrearing, and her own fragile health. Their past expectations for lasting happiness now appeared naïve.

Hitz later discussed Gertrude's shocking situation with his closest friends in Washington. In one brief, memorable conversation, Alexander Graham Bell pointed out an obvious explanation. In Bell's opinion, the fundamental cause of Gertrude's troubles was "her adherence to the principle of voluntary motherhood." Bell asserted that "pleasure was naturally the primary motive for sexual relations, even for animals, [and] that it was a fallacy to hold it should only be for procreation," as the Alphaists maintained. In fact, Professor Bell bluntly declared, "Gertrude's views on the subject have brought about all the troubles she has to undergo."

The shaken father and stoic son-in-law spent the night at 50 Green Street. By noon the next day, Saturday, eight pieces of baggage stood ready to be collected for express delivery to the Clark homestead. Hitz and Burton traveled to Medway by train, and after supper helped bring up a portion of the articles from the station.

Hitz felt spiritually bruised. Even the following day, Sunday, he continued to be dumbfounded by Burton's revelations, and spent some time alone reading from Swedenborg's texts and the Bible, the Book of John, Chapter 20:26: "Then came Jesus, the doors being shut, and stood in the midst, and said, 'Peace be unto you.'" Burton had stated his own offenses and accepted responsibility for his actions, and now was turning the other cheek, following the Golden Rule. John Hitz wished them both peace.

They unpacked and aired their belongings in breezy sunshine. Hitz strolled with Arnold into the pinewoods and fields. When Gertrude felt poorly on Monday morning, they arranged for a Mrs. Tyler to come by train from Chelsea to help care for her and the children during the day. By afternoon Gertrude had improved enough to drive Mrs. Tyler back to the station in the buggy.

On Tuesday, father and daughter set in motion their plan to evacuate Gertrude to Washington: first, a morning visit to Dr. Sanborn to confer about Gertrude's condition, and to settle the doctor's essential role in looking after Arnold and Harold during Gertrude's absence. Then, in the afternoon, father and daughter departed by train, leaving the boys with Burton at the Clark homestead. Changing trains in Woonsocket, Rhode Island, they bought through tickets to Washington on the Pennsylvania Line.

The capital was stifling. Mrs. Kappeler regretted that she couldn't invite Gertrude to stay with her for more than a day or two; in any case, the commotion at the Kappeler house would have proven nerve-wracking. Since her husband's unexpected suicide, Mrs. Kappeler was studying to become a dentist at the Columbian Medical School. She supported her two children, Jessie and Freddie, by working at the Patent Office and renting out rooms in their home.

Jane Hitz moved Gertrude to the stately Riggs House Hotel on the corner of 15th and G Street, NW. Long talks with her mother, who sympathized with her daughter's illness and commiserated with her marital unhappiness, seemed to calm Gertrude. But Washington's humidity became oppressive, and Jane Hitz suggested they leave immediately for Maine. On short notice, they arranged for treatment at the Maine General Hospital in Portland. Dr. Frederick H. Gerrish, a prominent Maine physician and a member of the Moral Education Society, accepted Gertrude as a private patient. After she improved, Gertrude would travel to Deer Isle to recuperate.

Mother and daughter departed by train on May 14th. To help with Gertrude's expenses, John Hitz pawned his remaining valuables, a watch and a vase. He stood at the grade crossing at Second and Maryland Avenues to wave farewell, but could not catch a glimpse of them as the cars rolled by. Not long afterwards, on a May 31st picnic outing to Mount Vernon with a party of friends, sadness overwhelmed him. He became "very depressed...wandered off to the woods gathering daisies, wild briar and laurel—had several weeping spells thinking of Gertrude and my wife."

Before she left the capital, Gertrude wrote again to Bliss Carman, who had responded quickly from his home in Canada to her initial letter:

> May 14, 1889 Riggs House, Washington, DC,
> Waiting for the Northern train.
> Dear Mr. Carman:
> It may be a long while before I can really answer the delightful letter which came from you and found me out so pleasantly on one the darkest days of my life—I hope you may learn to know how peculiarly sweet that first letter from you must have been to me...For surely it will be revealed to you, when I tell you the nature of my great trial, that your fresh, trustful hand, coming to me so frankly and so unexpectedly out of the wide, wide void, is truly like a message of the Gods—Saying: "Here! See what we grant thee from out the human world—a new friend—a vision of a young, ardent, earnest Soul—and more than all, the crowning best of all—the living Soul of a poet!"

... I came here [to Washington] to seek rest and change but am forced—owing to heat and my great weakness—to return to the North...I am going to a hospital to be buried in silence and to be taken care of by those trained to woo Nature's forces back again to the dear poor body!...

... I will send you my address that you may write to me as often and as freely as you will. From me you must expect absolutely nothing—only words in pencil now & then... Gertrude Hitz Burton

Maine General Hospital's massive red brick building still stands high up on a bluff above the Fore River, on Portland's leafy Western Promenade. From there, on clear days, to the west, the peak of Mount Washington rises above New Hampshire's Presidential Range, affording the "unparalleled views" promised by the hospital's brochure. On May 15th, Gertrude was cloistered in a bright, white room on the top floor, determined to regain control over her mind and body.

# CHAPTER 10

## *Blood Tells Its Power*

G ERTRUDE'S PRIVATE HOSPITAL ROOM WAS PAINTED WHITE AND FUR-
nished with an easy chair, a dresser with a white linen scarf,
and, on the washstand, a flowered china bowl and pitcher. Instead of
an iron bedstead like those in the crowded wards on the lower floors,
her wooden bed offered a spring mattress and starched, snowy sheets.
Nurse Cready, a Canadian trained in New Brunswick, cared for her,
tidied the room, brought her books, water, meals: every comfort.

Silence.

The hospital's healing hush created a sense of order and calm.
After ten years of striving to live up to her own ideals of motherhood, family loyalty, and professional accomplishment—and to meet
others' increasing demands for support—Gertrude began to sort
through long-suppressed thoughts and feelings.

Jane Hitz's approach to her daughter's care was ahead of
the times. Jane always sought out the best doctors and most up-
to-date therapies. Although the Hitz family normally relied on homeopathic physicians, in 1881 Gertrude's mother had consulted the
legendary Silas Weir Mitchell in Philadelphia about her daughter's
inexplicable knee pain. In this crisis, Jane Hitz again entrusted Gertrude's health to an allopathic physician—a "regular" doctor—at
Maine General.

Most hospitals were slowly changing from institutions where the
poor or insane went to die, to places where the affluent might receive
expert diagnoses, skilled treatment, or surgery under the care of a

private physician. Frederick Henry Gerrish was a nationally respected surgeon specializing in gynecology at Maine General Hospital. He was one of the first American doctors to embrace Listerism, the germ theory of disease, acknowledging the importance of antiseptic techniques in the operating theater. At the time of Gertrude's stay in 1889, he was president of the Maine Board of Health and a professor at the Bowdoin College School of Medicine. He was also a member of the Moral Education Society, and widely known for his strong views on the social and medical evils of prostitution. The 1886 *ALPHA* published Dr. Gerrish's essay, "Prostitution and Its Allied Vices," as a series of featured articles. His critique emphasized the basic immorality of regulating or licensing prostitutes. Instead, he advocated a revolutionary change in society's values that would eliminate the double standard and so eradicate prostitution altogether. Like Jane Hitz and Gertrude, he believed optimistically that science and reason could, and would, eventually do away with immoral human behavior, improving and transforming the human race.

The selection of Dr. Gerrish, a gynecologist, may have indicated that Gertrude was suffering from a physical ailment requiring more than the customary rest cure for neurasthenia, or "nervousness." For uncomplicated cases, the rest cure—widely popularized by Dr. Mitchell, who was also known as "Dr. Diet and Dr. Quiet," and fictionalized by another of his patients, Charlotte Perkins Gilman, in her story "The Yellow Wallpaper"—remained the recommended treatment: a change of scene, isolation from family members, confinement to bed, and limited mental or physical stimulation.

But Gertrude's case may have been more complicated: did she suffer from lacerations of the cervix, a common occurrence? Fibroid tumors? A peritoneal tear? An ovarian cyst? Had her husband infected her with venereal disease? It is impossible to know whether she underwent treatment for these or other conditions. Common allopathic remedies included drastic astringent "cures," such as applications of nitrate of silver, sulphate of zinc, corrosive sublimate, or tannic acid to the abdomen or vulva. Alternatively, physicians introduced probes, heated white-hot or wrapped with a swab of nitric acid, to burn and scar mucus membranes. Galvanic shocks were also popular for unspecified gynecological symptoms, including fibroid tumors.

Surgical options included removal of uterine tumors, the ovaries, or complete hysterectomies. By the 1890s, women increasingly chose hysterectomies to end recurring problems, a risky operation in the era before widespread antiseptic procedures. Patients who underwent surgery were kept to recuperate in hospital for about a month. Beyond these dangerous surgical techniques for gynecological disorders, several additional "regular" therapies for "nervous exhaustion," "neurasthenia," and "irritability," were listed in the contemporary *Merck's Manual of the Materia Medica*. These remedies also give pause: for example, quantities of arsenic, cocaine, opium, cimicifuga (black cohosh), and strychnine "in small doses."

But perhaps Gertrude merely undertook a longed-for period of imposed leisure. Postpartum depression was not a common term in 1889, but Gertrude would have recognized its symptoms, codified a century later, as some of her own: loss of appetite; insomnia; intense irritability and anger; overwhelming fatigue; loss of interest in sex; lack of joy in life; feelings of shame, guilt, or inadequacy; severe mood swings; and (at least some) difficulty bonding with the baby.

Four months after Harold's birth, her father had commented that Gertrude seemed constantly worried about "the proper mode of management of very young children—what best to do to secure desirable development, and what to avoid." He had observed that she was "in a very nervous state—needs change, above all things… better service and separation from her immediate surroundings for a time—otherwise she will surely break down."

And she had broken down. Now, floating in time, she alternately slept and reflected on her grave situation.

She awoke early on her twenty-eighth birthday and responded to Bliss Carman's most recent letter in a rush of gratitude:

Wednesday, May 29/89

My friend, that was a noble, beautiful letter to send me! At first reading I was choked with tears—it was so sweet to have your gift of sympathy—so wonderful and kind and tender—and it does me good to the very soul to read such fine, lovely music in words.

Today is my birthday—it is a clear calm bright morning—I write very early scarce six o'clock.

I have always been grateful to have been born with the last lingering smile of Spring...I was so anxious to breathe the air of this earth—so impatient of my short, short life—that Nature yielded me two more whole months than She gives to most of her babes. And so I was born with many unfinished talents, and have the impulses & aspirations of all that I might have been, if my tiny body & soul had had their full ripe time. And this comforts me, you see, for much of my weakness & deficiency!...

I am gaining some good here—bodily good, I think, and mean to go to Deer Isle, Maine, about the middle of June. My mother has a charming cottage there built on the spot which is one of the most beautiful in all the world...

What "bodily good" and emotional benefits did Gertrude experience during her hospital stay? In *Tokology: A Book for Every Woman*, the exemplary Dr. Stockham advised that the body is "a reflection of the spirit," and that when one becomes ill, it is a sign that "you have not risen above error, discord, and sin..." Furthermore, she asserted that "... uterine disease is a very common cause of insanity in women..." and counseled that to prevent attacks of hysteria one must "treat the uterine affection from which they arise."

"Nervousness," or neurasthenia, was widely presumed to signal a malfunctioning reproductive system: nervous exhaustion could cause or exacerbate abdominal troubles, and, conversely, physical irregularities could produce or worsen a state of nervous irritability or hysteria. To prevent and cure women's diseases, Dr. Stockham recommended nonrestrictive clothing, a healthy diet, and exercise. Gertrude had rigorously followed these guidelines, but now she despaired of achieving the desired results. Nonetheless, she remained persuaded by Stockham's insistence that the "mind can rise superior to the body in uterine affections, as in all other bodily ailments." She believed, with Stockham, that she should be able, "by persistent argument with [her] self, to conquer or dispel the thought of pain or disease." And she trusted Stockham's claim (couched in pre-Freudian terms that equated the ego with soul) that, "By seeking to ennoble and enrich the lives of others, by ignoring a personal sense and pleasure, the soul—the ego—becomes in harmony with the spirit of the universe, and this harmony should give health of body, as well as peace of mind."

A decade earlier, Gertrude had trusted that selfless efforts—living a noble life, "accomplishing much, with the least amount of noise," would naturally ensure a healthy mind, body, and spirit. However, her experience in the year following Harold's birth contradicted this theory. Reluctantly, she began to allow that her goals of an ideal marriage and model children were more difficult to achieve than she had imagined, and even, possibly, less fulfilling. In fact, she confessed to both Mary and Bliss Carman that her husband and children caused anxieties, anger, and frustration.

In her quiet, white room, Gertrude began to envision a future path, parallel to her husband's, which would allow him to pursue his career, and she hers. She realized that for her, like her mother, divorce was not advisable—legally, financially, or emotionally. She also recognized that she and Burton would never achieve the exalted spiritual connection, the "soul blending," of true marriage. But they could maintain a mutually cordial relationship. Since her spouse was disposed to follow the Golden Rule and fulfill his obligations as husband and father, she could rely on his assistance, for the children and herself.

Several possibilities presented themselves. Gertrude was inspired by her father's trip "home" to Switzerland and his half-formed plan to return there permanently. She now wore the edelweiss brooch he had given her nearly every day. Since Burton was always eager to travel and explore, she strategized a family tour abroad for the following summer. In her mind, when her husband returned to teaching at Tech in the fall, she would remain abroad, settling in Lausanne with the children. She would need money, but with letters of introduction from her father to former colleagues and friends, and with the help of the extended family, she would open a kindergarten and become self-supporting.

For the near term, during the coming autumn, she and the children would find suitable rooms in suburban West Newton, where she would surround herself with likeminded, enlightened women. Arnold would attend kindergarten there and, with a nurse for Harold, she would finally find time to write. Burton would let an apartment in town, within walking distance to Tech, sleeping later and avoiding the hated commute. He could visit them in West Newton on weekends, or as he wished.

Shortly after June 16th, their fifth wedding anniversary, Gertrude was released from Maine General Hospital. The discharge ledger listed her unspecified disorder as having been "relieved," although not "cured." She left Portland for Stonington by steamer to convalesce on Deer Isle.

Once settled in her mother's cottage at Hitz Point, Gertrude again sought Bliss Carman's support. He was spending the summer in his hometown, Fredericton, New Brunswick, not so far from Maine, and she hoped to convince him to visit her:

June 20, 1889, Thursday evening, Sunset, Deer Isle, Maine

Whenever a letter comes from you I feel a hand has been extended to me from my home—The true inner home of the spirit.

Indeed I have been planning, hoping that I might see you here ever since the long quiet days in the hospital. I had a map by my bed among my other papers, & there one day I found Fredericton and you seemed much nearer to me ever afterward; and when your letter came telling about the view from your window, I was really able, you see, to follow your words and trace the broad river& the fields...

Deer Isle is South of Eastport, South of Mt. Desert—but is so easily accessible by steamboat from St. John (& the fares are not very expensive) & I have been wishing I might have you here in my mother's cottage.

O the Mountains in the West! They are a constant inspiration; and as I look & look & look they seem more exquisite to me every hour. The line along the sky is such a wonderfully restful, well-modulated line—and the atmospheric effects are very charming. Then the woods & the wildflowers and the sailing—and about all the absolute quiet & entire absence of people—Do you wonder I am enchanted and long to share this beauty with you?...(as I write this I hear my mother playing on the guitar—the melody floats up to me—a trembling minor strain—which plays upon the heart strings like sighs & half whispered words—)...

... Fare you well—and thank you every day for the beautiful frank way in which you have greeted me. How short, how precious life is—how strange & full & rich the human heart! Every warm grasp, every tender thought sends the blood quivering to the center of our being—and shames us because we are not more trustful, more loving—we who are all living for a brief dream in the fair round earth.

She was living each day with a keen sense of life's beauty and her own fragility.

*&*

While Gertrude's letters to Carman expressed existential com-
passion, her exchanges with Mary gave voice to their shared frustrations. From London, Mary confided that as Frank pursued his political ambitions, he demanded she fulfill twin roles: charming wife and
hostess, and political activist, delivering speeches about social justice
at meetings of Liberal Associations, Home Rule Unions, Education
Reform Leagues, and Temperance Societies. Mary concluded bitterly in her diary, "Therefore, woman, sink thyself and thy needs and
empty hopes. Join the army of those who exist to fill up the gaps in
the interesting lives of others, and learn, as most women learn, to
consider it enough interest for thee."

Mary feared a second pregnancy. She had converted to Catholicism for Frank's sake (Frank Costelloe was an Irish nationalist
and Member of Parliament), and she regarded artificial birth control
devices "unnatural." She did indeed become pregnant again. Before
the birth, she wrote in her diary, on February 21, 1889, "A woman
who is going to have a child ought to be removed from all care and
responsibility. I have had all kinds heaped on me, and Frank is too
busy to take more than a spasmodic kind of care."

Mary Costelloe's younger daughter, Karin, was born in March.
Over the following months—exactly the period when Gertrude wrote
her first desperate letter to Carman, then suffered a breakdown and
took refuge in Maine—Mary, too, descended into depression. However, Mary's situation played out in more glamorous surroundings:
she was mistress of one home, in London; another, Friday's Hill, in
the Sussex countryside, was held on long-term lease by her parents.
A nanny cared for the children. Her affluent family, who moved to
England to be near her and her brother Logan at Oxford, spirited her
to the Continent in late fall, for a respite.

Mary wrote to Gertrude from Andermatt, Switzerland, where
her mother hoped she would regain emotional balance. In her reply,
Gertrude deeply sympathized with Mary's unhappiness and described
her own precarious situation. Both women chafed at the restrictions

of marriage and motherhood, and lamented their husbands' lack of understanding. Gertrude commiserated with Mariechen's desire for a life of her own.

❧

Following her own plan, Gertrude settled with Arnold and Harold in West Newton, while Burton lodged in town "for his nerves."

> Dec 5/89 Box 15 West Newton, Mass
> My dear Mariechen,
> The letter from Andermatt came last night. I hasten to answer it early this morning long before sunrise that I might not fail of sending thee a word at once.
> Am at West Newton one half hour from Boston on Boston and Albany Road. The children are here and I have a nurse who promises to do well in general respects. Mr. Burton has a room on Tremont St opposite the Common + finds it a great relief to be free from trains and near enough to the Institute to sleep as late as he may desire. Moreover in this way he can secure absolute solitude for study + for rest—which in his present condition of overstrained nerves are absolute necessities. He comes to spend the night in West Newton twice and three times a week.
> O my poor child how well I understand that "wretched illness." I am only too glad to know that thee [finds] three or four weeks sufficient to repair the misery of a whole summer. I do trust most fervently that when brought back to the same conditions in London thy strength will not fail thee. I feel it is a matter of long years with me…
> And O my precious Mariechen…I hope that thee may find thyself once more—calm, self-possessed + high above all failure. The humiliation of such nervous weakness burns in the very soul!

In addition to the shame of her own nervousness, Gertrude confessed embarrassment over her changed physical appearance—her imperfect body failed to meet her Botticelli-like standards of beauty:

> Everyone who sees me—that is among my old acquaintances—tells me that I have grown much larger. I tell thee this in order to prepare thee. Since Harold's birth I think the upper part of my frame has really broadened + thickened and so I find myself farther away from sylph-hood than ever. Thee knows I have longings towards the tall and stately, lean + lanky-flowing drapery sort of thing. It is rather hard to concentrate all one's spirituality in the face!

The news that Mary might visit America in the spring, after a five-year absence, thrilled Gertrude. She added that she, in turn, longed for Europe and, with an urgency spurred by her acute sense of mortality, she declared:

> The possibility of seeing thee brings a feeling of such intense delight—it borders on delirium—if thee comes in May I shall try my utmost to go back to Europe with thee. America is no longer the place for me. Blood tells its power in moments of weakness or passion—the Switzer in me must have the mountain air—to stay here is but a living death…

If life were to be brief, it should be exciting. Making fresh plans for Swiss exploits revived Gertrude's appetite for adventure: in a different environment, who might she become? She anticipated new challenges in old, familiar Lausanne. Switzerland seemed the perfect antidote to disillusionment and self-doubt. Her mood was shifting.

# CHAPTER 11

## *Four Vagabonds*

GERTRUDE WAS NO LONGER CHARTING HER COURSE BY "HUMANITY'S star." She had taken a detour from the route of lecturing and writing she had envisioned. Dr. Sanborn's diagnosis of a life-threatening illness and Gertrude's emotional turmoil refocused her attention inward, and toward "the beautiful." She and her friends Mary, Berenson, and Carman, now geographically dispersed, shared a resolve to live their individual lives to the fullest. All four, in their late twenties, were weighing duties against desires. Where to live? With whom? How to live, and for what purpose?

1890 became their year for moving in new directions, along separate paths. Gertrude yearned for the chance to realize her authentic, ideal, self-sufficient self, spurred by the failure of her marriage as well as the possibility of an early death. Mary, at twenty-six, entertained the prospect of abandoning commitments to social activism, as well as marriage and motherhood, and experienced a reawakened passion for art. Berenson agonized over whether to remain in Europe and prioritize his personal ambition over his Boston family's needs and expectations.

Bliss Carman, like Gertrude, was soul-searching as he prepared to sell his family's house in Fredericton and move on to an editorial job in New York. At twenty-nine, he was in dire financial straits, but his poetry had begun to flourish. As Gertrude had observed in her first letter in the spring, his symbolist approach produced mystical verses evoking a sense of "things left unsaid." He shared, by mail from Canada, early versions of poems that echoed her awareness of life's brevity and the evanescence of things.

Gertrude and Carman corresponded throughout the fall. One

November evening, from West Newton, she wrote to him describing the constant effort to restore her shaky nerves:

> Sunday Night Nov. 24, 1889
>
> Dear Mr. Carman—how really kind you are! I never had a pleasanter letter to break a long silence and to urge the heart to ease and speech....I appreciate with an especially keen delight your generous view of a friend's letter-writing. I can write to you so frankly now.
>
> I have been much occupied and I have also been very weak. Although I write from my bed tonight, I am up and about most of the time but need to be alone a great deal and to lie down hours together. The trouble is that something has snapped in the fine mechanism which unites body and mind. At the time that I went to the Hospital I was suffering from the effects of trouble so serious that I greatly feared the loss of mental control. Now that I am spared that worst of all living deaths, I find myself incapable to meet the demands which my work as mother requires. Nothing exhausts me so utterly as my children and yet I believe this to be because they are so much to me, and the appeal they make to me goes to the vital centre of my nature. It will take a long, long while to restore calm to the shattered nerves. Meanwhile, I can only be still and wait, giving the poor precious children of my best in such pitiful ways that I dare not think of the passionate longings which must go unexpressed.

As for her objective situation, not much had been resolved, beyond Arnold's schooling:

> For the outer world—I can tell you that I have been passing through great difficulties in finding a suitable person to take charge of my children, and a suitable place in which to live. I am in West Newton because there is an excellent kindergarten. Every morning Arnold and I climb a hill and

go to a little house perched on the rocks at the very Summit. Here is a small heaven. Here I leave my child in the midst of sweet influences—and know that at least here he is treated reverently, and is not degraded. Harold—who was born about the time that I first met you—grows to be a most lovable child, with a smile that seems as natural to him as the sunshine to a summer's day. He is far more serene than Arnold, and more exuberantly glad. Yet so far, my heart draws to the first child as one whose soul will suffer more.

Carman had again asked for her comments on his poems. She hesitated, but offered frank, constructive criticism:

> What harder thing could you ask of me than to criticize your verses? I am nothing of a critic in a technical sense—of the construction and mechanism of poetry I know very little. Of its charm and power and music I know more, because it appeals to me unconsciously and so far as it touches and delights me, it becomes my own...
>
> Since you ask I must answer....What your work lacks in my eyes is directness and conciseness. I never know quite what you mean—although the quality of the music is at once superior and elevating. I am always more struck by passages than by any one piece of work as a whole. I apply this even to *Death in April* which soars high above all others—it is great and it is beautiful—but the veil obscures the spirit. I do not find you—I can only feel you.
>
> I wish you were near enough to answer all this by audible speech—I dread a misunderstanding.

She concluded with a smattering of news: Bernhard Berenson's family in Boston, with whom they both were well acquainted, had moved: "... they are living in another house. It is a pleasanter home for them and [his mother] Mrs. Berenson is full of enthusiasm." Then she added another random detail or two: "... I tore out a slip about

Mr. Aldrich's last book for you—cutting the paper with the pin of my edelweiss which I always wear as a loyal Swiss....As I say goodnight I am conscious of a feeling of gratitude which rises...asking you to believe that all you write comes as a blessing to me..."

Before Christmas, Gertrude moved with the children from her Post Road lodgings into West Newton, a village of suburban homes, generous lawns, and broad-minded citizens. Mrs. Hussey's boarding house, at the corner of Elm and Webster Streets, was situated one block from the West Newton English and Classical School, locally called the Allen School, after its founder Nathaniel Topliffe Allen. The progressive school had been co-educational and racially integrated since it opened in 1853. The Allen School's kindergarten, where Arnold was enrolled, was the nation's first, established as an experiment in 1863. Gertrude was a friend of Allen's daughter, Sarah, a teacher there.

Gertrude was exhausted, and in bed with a severe spell of headache, when John Hitz visited her toward year's end, traveling with Professor Bell for a Modern Languages Association convention at Harvard University. Gertrude's health gradually improved, but the cause of her fragile condition remained a mystery. Later during the winter, she suffered a worrisome bout of bronchitis, with coughing severe enough to produce traces of capillary blood, which she definitely considered "too insignificant to be called hemorrhages."

Encouraged by her father, she relished planning for the summer's European voyage. She hoped to rendezvous with Mary in England, and also with Berenson, who was continuing his European travels, absorbing the art of Renaissance masters. Well-heeled patrons, including Boston art collector Isabella Stewart Gardner, whom Berenson had impressed when he was a Harvard undergraduate, supported his rarified research. When Gertrude told Berenson of her proposed European visit, he replied in November from Gibraltar—in nearly unreadable, cramped handwriting—and confessed that, although he was grateful for the opportunities he had enjoyed during the past three years, he dreaded returning to America, because he feared he'd be forced to make a living there as a degraded "fifth magnitude literary person:"

> ... Of course, I have not quite wasted my time, though the gods only know in what stead all this fine dilettantism will stand me. I am getting rather anxious and even rather indifferent about my future. Had I plenty of money I should dream of nothing but continuing my study of pictures all the rest of my life—or until I tired of it...

The youthful Berenson was afraid that after "promising treasure" to the friends who had invested in him, he might turn out to be a fraud. He acknowledged that in the years since he had seen Gertrude, he had become both "more vulgar and ambitious" yet, at the same time, "finer" than he had been at Harvard. He speculated that he and she might now have grown apart since their Boston days: he had meanwhile realized that the concept of "the beautiful" (which they both had adopted as their holy grail) "is an abstraction, I fear, more fit for the Concord School of Philosophy than the frequenter of great galleries." As a disciple of the art critic Giovanni Morelli, Berenson was now more interested in discovering the nuances of individual artists' techniques than in defining or endorsing universal ideals.

Early in the summer of 1890, Berenson was pondering a future without the patronage that had bankrolled his training as a connoisseur. But he decided, finally, not to return to America, whatever the cost. He knew this would profoundly distress his family—and especially his younger sister, Senda. They were looking to him for financial and emotional support. At this juncture, by luck and chance, Berenson met a young aesthete, Enrico Costa, who asked for help in choosing paintings for his collection. By the time Berenson and Costa reached London in July, Berenson was certain he had found his life's work: he would dedicate himself to professional connoisseurship—although he was still unclear how he would support it.

Gertrude had adored Mary and Berenson separately since their student days, and each of them respected and loved her in return. They remained among her oldest, closest friends, although she had been separated from them by great distances in recent years. Gertrude had first introduced Berenson to the Costelloes in a letter to Mary three years earlier, when he was beginning his immersion in European art. Now, Gertrude again put them in contact, as she planned to visit both friends in Europe. In early August 1890, Mary and Frank Costelloe invited Bernhard Berenson to Sunday dinner at their country house in Fernhurst, Sussex.

Although Bernhard had impressed Mary positively on his earlier visit, she described their second meeting as producing "a chemical reaction" in her family life. At twenty-five, Berenson was a year younger than Mary, compact, trim, dark-eyed, and dark-haired. His looks were exotic, his presence magnetic, and his conversation supremely knowledgeable and articulate. Mary saw in him the aesthetic sensibility—and romance—that her older politician husband lacked. On renewing Berenson's acquaintance she "… felt as though [she] were a dry sponge put into water." Disillusioned by her efforts to promote women's issues and to advance her husband's career, and still mildly depressed following Karin's birth, she recognized that Berenson's world of art could become her true home. Gertrude envisioned the three of them sharing long hours of fascinating conversation.

❧

Meanwhile, Gertrude continued corresponding with Carman, who lingered in Fredericton through the fall and into late winter. He was trying to sell the family home following his parents' deaths and had already auctioned its furnishings to pay his bills. For him, it was a time of financial distress and artistic insecurity. Like Berenson, he remained rootless.

In January 1890, Carman answered a notice in *The Independent,* a distinguished New York literary review and an official organ of the Congregational Church. The weekly publication required an office editor and literary assistant. Canada's Metropolitan Bishop, John Medley, a family friend, recommended Carman for the position to *The Independent's* editor, Henry Chandler Bowen. Carman arranged for his sister to buy his share of their family home for $1000, and, flush with this money, he arrived in New York for an interview. He signed a one-year contract as office editor, took rooms in Greenwich Village's Washington Square, and applied himself to the prosaic job of assigning articles as well as reviewing manuscripts for publication.

In the spring, Carman moved to Arrochar on Staten Island, at the narrow entrance to New York harbor, for cooler temperatures near the beach. There he produced his breakthrough poem, "Pulvis et Umbra," a probe behind the veil of external realities and a confrontation with death: "There is dust upon my fingers/Pale gray dust of beaten wings/Where a great moth came and settled/From the night's blown winnowings..."

During this time, Carman also composed the first of the wanderlust poems that would popularize his name over the coming six years, in the best-selling collection, *Songs from Vagabondia.* There he explored motifs of freedom and manly comradeship with fellow poet Richard Hovey and artist Thomas Meteyard. As an added surprise, London publisher Thomas Nutt had been so impressed with Carman's first poem, "Low Tide at Grand Pré," that, unsolicited, he proposed publishing a collection of Carman's new works. The prospect both excited and dismayed Carman: Gertrude's warnings about his verses' obscurity echoed criticism offered by other trusted readers. He postponed accepting the flattering proposal, fearful of issuing a book before his work was ready.

❧

Carman was on hand in New York on July 12th to see the Burton family off on board the *SS Spaarndam*, scheduled to arrive in Rotterdam on July 24th. John Hitz helped finance their steamer tickets, and provided letters of introduction to Swiss colleagues to promote the kindergarten project in Lausanne. The family's itinerary included an extended tour of Switzerland for Burton, Gertrude, Arnold, and Harold, and a new nursemaid, twenty-four-year-old Inez Rebecca Bliss, from Middlebury, Vermont. Her family name, Bliss, may have predisposed Gertrude to engage her for the trip. Carman, whose given name was William Bliss Carman, was called Bliss after his mother's maiden name.

They planned to reach Lausanne by late August. At that point, Burton would take leave of Gertrude and their young sons, and continue to Paris to enroll in a drawing course until mid-September. Then, as a newly promoted associate professor, he would depart for Boston and his fall semester classes.

From Washington, John Hitz telegraphed to the party on the dock: "Best wishes, pleasant voyage and a hearty welcome in Helvetia!"

CHAPTER 12

# *The Spirit Beautiful*

FOR GERTRUDE, LAUSANNE'S DARK, HIDDEN PASSAGES, MEDIEVAL UNI-
versity buildings, ancient cathedral, steep cobblestone alleys, and
terraced parks with spectacular views of Lake Geneva and the Alps
were treasured memories that promised fresh discoveries. Gertrude's
old friends there—Fanny Byse, wife of English university professor
Charles Byse, along with Madame Morf and her daughter Madame
Carrard—welcomed her warmly. Their network of local acquaintances eased the transition to lodgings in the Pension Clément, 7 rue
du Grand Chêne, not far from the Montbenon esplanade where,
twenty years before, Gertrude had plucked a small offering of wild
myrtle leaves to please her mother, on the day Pauline was born.

Gertrude set about establishing a kindergarten for the children
of English-speaking expatriates. Mary, in London, wished she could
send Ray, now four, to the school. The two women had not managed a reunion. Mary had cancelled her visit to America the previous
spring, and the Burtons' summer tour did not include England. But
Mariechen promised "... Another time will come...Send me a word,
my friend, of the Swiss address..."

Meanwhile, Berenson became the Costelloes' favorite guest.
Bernhard and Mary were constant companions in the galleries in
London, and Frank sometimes accompanied them. Gertrude's and
Mary's correspondence began to include long exchanges concerning
Berenson, and their girl-talk strengthened the long-distance friend-
ship. By September, Berenson, traveling the Continent again, prom-

ised Gertrude he would visit Lausanne the following January, writing archly, "That will give you time to think me over, now that I am again an almost constant object of your thought. I too will have time… to really find out whether I am at all worth thinking about…neither sincerity nor openness are natural virtues of mine…"

Nevertheless, he sincerely asked Gertrude to write to his younger sister Senda in Boston, a great favorite of Gertrude's, with whom she already corresponded. Berenson was plagued by guilt over his decision to remain in Europe, saying, "You don't know how I feel about her, not only sorry for the bitter disappointment I have given her [by not returning to help support the family], but so anxious about her present and future." Twenty-one-year-old Senda had just refused a marriage proposal, to her father's great displeasure. With Gertrude's encouragement, she had enrolled in the Boston Normal School of Gymnastics to prepare for a teaching career in physical education and hygiene.

In October, Gertrude received Berenson's letter from Vienna: he was interested in knowing more about her project. "I hear you have got up a kindergarten at Lausanne. Tell me about it if you will. I am as much as ever interested in the education of infants—psychologically if not practically…" He was on his way to Budapest, then Siena and Florence, and wildly enthusiastic about the prospect of returning to Italy: "To be in Italy again—what a joy! It makes my blood leap up to think of it. At times I can't imagine how people find it possible to exist elsewhere…" His travels and intellectual mission inspired Gertrude and connected her to his fascinating world of history and art.

In October and November, Berenson became even more the object of Mary's and Gertrude's intense scrutiny. As Gertrude was launching her kindergarten school, Mary declared:

> I was much interested in all thee said of Bernhard. Of
> course it could be quite impossible to analyze his character
> on paper—and probably useless. I wish indeed we could talk
> about him. He has done so much…in helping me see things

at first hand, in showing me how many beautiful things there are in the world, that I cannot be grateful enough to him....It is quite extraordinary what a faculty he has of making people love him! They pardon him all his faults because he is so utterly delightful. I feel terribly worried about his future...I understand him in some ways so well, partly because I care for him so much....He has quite filled my thoughts—our thoughts— this Autumn...

The Costelloes planned to join Berenson in Florence and Rome for Christmas. Sensing Bernhard's future significance as an art critic and connoisseur, Mary began organizing his ideas: "He has been writing to me a great deal about pictures. I keep all his letters methodically numbered...For a book, later..."

However, the two "New Women" still considered Berenson's devotion to art an evasion of public duty and escape from real life. Bernhard pronounced social and political reformers absurd—"they simply can't change things..." The problem was how to reconcile the love of beauty with a moral responsibility for social progress.

While Gertrude carried on teaching in Lausanne, she explained her misgivings about his views. Mary replied from Cambridge, where she was presenting a talk on American women, "... I entirely agree with the spirit of all thee says about B. It is exceedingly painful to have to think of him in the wrong, but I do feel he ought to take thought for his future, that he is bound in honor to make some use for the world of the talents and opportunities so freely lavished on him."

She reported that Berenson believed that a few more years of study would give him "that exquisite and rare culture which only one person in a thousand could ever attain:"

Because it is so beautiful he dimly feels that it must be of some use in the world...The crux is just here: Culture is a very subtle and fine blossom—in the highest degree it is very rare upon earth. The flaw is leaving out the morals and social elements—but how to make him see this I don't know!

He thinks Art and practical life are opposed....Charming and delightful he always is—but one wants him to be useful and brave as well.

In late January 1891, Gertrude received a letter from Perugia announcing Berenson's imminent visit to Lausanne. He looked forward to their conversations, he said. However, it is likely they focused mainly on the subject of Mary. He wrote in advance:

> ... I can't tell you how grateful I feel—grateful to you not only for this friendship you have given me, but for having thought of sending me to her three years ago when I was first in England. What a difference it has made to me, more than I can tell. Dear Gertrude, you don't know at all what a wretched, worthless being I was, so you can never realize all that Mary is doing for me. Perhaps I shall be able to tell you something about it when I see you...

Shortly after visiting Gertrude, Berenson returned to London, and Mary and he became lovers. Mary confided to Gertrude that March 7th was their "special anniversary." Gertrude had not anticipated this turn of events, but still remained in close contact with each of them.

Gertrude's teaching venture eventually proved unsuccessful, although John Hitz sent a money order for $25 at Christmas to help with the kindergarten's expenses. During the spring of 1891, Gertrude reported no major health crises, although she suffered from fatigue and physical discomfort. She celebrated her thirtieth birthday quietly on the 29th of May. The following month, Mary graciously invited her to England ("What happiness to be with you again. BB will be here too I hope. Bring the children..."), but, instead, Burton joined his family in Switzerland for the summer holidays, after his own solo tramp in England and Scotland. Together after a year apart, the family visited friends and toured Switzerland again before moving on to Italy—first Venice, then Florence—in late August. There, Burton once again separated from Gertrude, Arnold and Harold, and Miss Bliss. He sailed for New York from Rotterdam, on board the *SS Spaarndam*.

Disappointed in the outcome of her Lausanne kindergarten project, Gertrude eagerly anticipated Mary and Bernhard's arrival in Florence, planned for September. The company of old friends promised the comfort of acceptance, reassurance, and encouragement. Mary had abandoned her children and husband for a passionate new love and a new life of study and writing. "Everyone who knows me disapproves," wrote Mary. But Gertrude admired them both still, and accepted their revolt against social conventions. Her European experience had apparently mellowed the rigid Alphaist ethics of her twenties. At thirty, her attitude was becoming more pragmatic and her standards more flexible.

Despite Florence's oppressive late summer heat, Gertrude settled herself, Arnold, Harold, and Miss Bliss into spare but comfortable rooms at the small Pension Pendini, 6 via Luigi Salvatore Cherubini. The quiet, leafy residential neighborhood was a healthful distance north of the River Arno. Its broad streets were paved with large, smooth, gray stone slabs. Next door to the Pension was a convalescent nursing home, the Convent of the Little Sisters of Mary, where an English Catholic sect served the ill and dying. One block west, on the via Pier Antonio Micheli, were the Botanical Gardens of Florence, founded in the sixteenth century by Grand Duke Cosimo I de' Medici. A little farther along stood the small Holy Trinity English church (Anglican Episcopal). A left turn there led to the nearby

Piazza San Marco and the handsome San Marco convent, where the fifteenth-century radical reformer Girolamo Savonarola had been cloistered, early in his career.

Gertrude had relocated to Florence to coincide with Mary's and Bernhard's travel plans. In her book of Ralph Waldo Emerson's essays, she penciled a note in the margin of the poem introducing the chapter on Friendship: "Marked for Mariechen, Florence, Italy, September 1891, after a separation of over six years." She underlined and highlighted a passage: "… And after many a year, /Glowed unexhausted kindliness/Like daily sunrise there…O friend, my bosom said,/… All things through thee take nobler form…/And look beyond the earth…/…The fountains of my hidden life/Are through thy friendship fair." Between the pages she pressed a four-leaf clover.

Gertrude was preparing to open another kindergarten for expatriate English children. Meanwhile, however, Mary and Berenson prolonged their tour of the Continent, part of a year-long plan to study art together. Frank Costelloe had agreed to Mary's art research under Berenson's tutelage, and had even financed her travels. Mary's unsuspecting husband believed she would return to him after a year, fulfilled, and ready once more to take up her family duties. Frank Costelloe's illusions began to evaporate in October, however, when Mary and Berenson reached Florence and took neighboring apartments near the Ponte Vecchio, overlooking the River Arno. During the lovers' brief autumn stopover, Mary and Gertrude located another, larger family apartment in anticipation of Mary's mother's visit in December, with daughters Ray and Karin. The elegant building was five minutes' walk from Gertrude's rooms in the Pension Pendini. It faced the extensive, centuries-old Gherardesca Gardens on via Principe Amadeo (now the Via Matteotti), a stone's throw from the English Cemetery at the Piazzale Donatello.

Before long, however, Mary and Berenson resumed their travels, promising Gertrude they would return to Florence for the winter months. Their obvious preoccupation with Italian painting—and each other—left Gertrude feeling abandoned by the very friends she hoped would share her European adventure.

❧

Gertrude suffered endless childcare complications during the warm, lingering autumn of 1891. Miss Bliss departed to visit some young Americans she had met in Venice, leaving Gertrude for a time without reliable help. As winter approached, Gertrude's health declined and the kindergarten plan remained unrealized. Mary (who, for appearance's sake, had returned briefly to London) was now not expected back in Florence with the children until late December. Distressed, Gertrude wrote to her, explaining that her British doctor, W.W. Baldwin, had determined she was too ill to remain in Florence until after Christmas.

Believing she would be forced to leave the city soon without meeting her friends, Gertrude asked for Berenson's advice about which artworks she should not miss before departing. He advised her to experience Florence's treasures—paintings and architecture—with her own eyes and, above all, not to rely on what "the experts" (including himself) judged worthwhile. Nevertheless, Berenson proceeded to counsel her in detail:

> To begin…If we were tireless or immortal I should make no distinctions in matters of art. But considering that the past has left us such wonderful things, to which the present is adding things more wonderful still; considering furthermore that we pay for our enjoyment with great fatigue, it is important not to spend our available energy on anything that is not really the greatest and the best. The only way, however, to get to know what that is, is to use one's own senses…Let me tell you that I am even more anxious that people should look with their own eyes, than that they should devote their attention only to what seems to me worthy of it.

He pointed out that painting is only one mode of Renaissance expression—and that, in his view, the greatest achievements were in architecture:

> ... and in Florence one can see that greatness. Go to the Pazzi Chapel, Brunelleschi's first work. Look at the portico, get the music of it, for it is a wonderful song. Then go to San Lorenzo. The church is beautiful, but spend all the time you can in the sacristy. This is a temple to the graces...The cloister of San Lorenzo is a charming spot in the early morning. Santo Spirito is another church to which I would have you go.

He continued, "Michelangelo's tombs attain the summit of great and surpass even the best the Greeks have left us. And Donatello is to Michelangelo what John the Baptist was to Jesus Christ...have a long look at Donatello's *Cupid* in the Bargello."

Gertrude sensed that by demonstrating her sincere interest in his knowledge of art, she had finally grabbed Berenson's attention. He advised, "Go to the Accademia. No stairs to climb. Give Botticelli's *Primavera* a fair trial and then the upper part of the altarpiece in the larger hall, *The Coronation of the Virgin*."

And in Santa Maria Novella, "Look at Filipino's frescoes in the first chapel to the right of the cloister—what decorative painters they were in 1494..."

Berenson further recommended Caravaggio's *The Rest in the Flight*, in the Tribune of the Uffizi; Botticelli's *Calumny*, and the three Giorgione's in the Venetian Room. And, "In the Pitti you must see Raphael's *Donna Velato* and his portrait of Julius II. The Titians in both galleries are good, particularly the portraits. If you see all I have mentioned you will have enjoyed all a mortal can."

Bernhard concluded on a personal note, "I would give a great deal to see you again. I fear you are puzzled about me, and certainly what you saw of me last winter was puzzling. I am very sure on the whole that you would like me more than you ever did."

❦

Gertrude's energy and self-esteem were at low ebb, but Bernhard's responsiveness motivated her. She set out to follow his suggestions, eager to impress him and Mary as a worthy comrade. After an exhausting day in the galleries, she described with hallucinatory insight her encounters with Botticelli's works, in a twenty-page letter to Mary dated Monday, November 16th, 3:30 a.m., which revealed her agitated, manic state:

> Mariechen, dear, I think it will amuse thee to know why I write to thee at this awfully solemn hour—I simply can't sleep on account of—Botticelli!!!!! Such a plunge as I made all day yesterday! Of course no one ever looks at a picture even attributed to Botticelli without receiving a very decided impression, and there is no other painter to whom I have given so much time. I went twice to the Academy + devoted myself to the *Primavera* + the *Coronation* and had made one special visit to the Uffizi.
>
> But yesterday—I did more than look or visit—I grafted on. It is really equal to a surgical operation this standing and sitting before the pictures of Botticelli (or anyone else in fact, except that his are so particularly emphatic and tortuous) and trying to scale the impossible wall of mannerisms. In Botticelli they obtrude to such a ridiculous and exasperating degree that I have felt like shouting "Will you ever moderate and leave me and Botticelli in peace!" For after all, it is very much like the confronting of a new personality with the determination of eating his very soul, while he insists on protruding his most studied affectations. Nothing in the world will ever convince me, I believe, that all this mannerism of Botticelli was spontaneous or unconscious—if it were, it could never offend as it does—it is a pulling off from nature as much as if the actual skin of the body were carefully drawn from the flesh and the muscles and veins—aye even the very nerves—were triumphantly revealed in most symmetrical designs! What a hard time the dear human blood has twisting through those con-

torted channels! Only occasionally one face comes clear—un-marred—and appeals with direct inspiration. Then what ear-nestness, what refined vigor—what joy, in spite of Doom! Take for example the young angel in the *Coronation* at the Academy, who is fastening the ermine. He is at the extreme right of the throne in the background of the painting, but really he is very near the throne in the treasure house of my memory.

I think it was at half past three o'clock yesterday after-noon in the little Sala di Lorenzo Monaco that I suddenly felt liberated. It was before Botticelli's *Adoration of the Magi* that the chains of prejudice and opposition fell with a clang to the floor. There was only one other creature present at the supreme moment of the trial—but he was tall red-haired Scotchman of decorous middle-age who was studious and devout, and from certain indefinable indications I think he may have been somewhat deaf—that is to Botticelli—and of course, only the initiated could have heard the spiritual sound of those chains as they severed and fell.

I had determined that I would find those special ador-ing angels of Fra Angelico that everyone knows, if they were to be found in Florence. So when I entered the room, I expe-rienced the satisfaction of having finally pounced upon this prey—Well, then I turned slightly on my red velvet stool (the red-haired decorous middle-aged Scotchman close at my side. Heavens bless him for keeping so still + not having brought some chattering female!) And I beheld for the first time in my life Botticelli's *Venus* landing on the impossible earth of ordi-nary man.

Now—(how I like to hurl this bomb!) I acknowledge at once that I much prefer [...] the Landing of Columbus on our American bank notes!! Ha-ha-hi! [Here she drew a laughing little triangle man running away]. To begin with, he was de-cently dressed and wasn't a prude. No mystic interpretations are to satisfy me. To be sure, I dive down into those symbolic little wavelets and rise transfigured with holy emblems. Is it the consciousness of sensuality which degrades animal passion? Venus cherishing her charms approaches the earth with apprehension. A maiden, sober-minded—with a whole heart, + a fine intuition of the sanctity of Love—comes to meet the Goddess and envelops her in the safe mantel of chastity.* [In left margin, lengthwise: *Haven't read Ruskin or anybody— this only common sense] How beautiful and how marvelous! How revolting and overstrained. It is a lie. Goodbye Venus!

Poor dear Botticelli! Was he having a hard time? (Sensitive natures dislike disapproval, thou knowest, even if the disapproval comes from an ignorant nonentity) No—Botticelli's spirit came nearer to me than ever. That outburst of honesty was the compact of the most delightful intimacy. His invisible hand unlocked the door at once. I had scaled the wall at a bound, and turning, worshipped with the Magi.

Now all along through these insistent attacks of mine, Botticelli and I had a very enjoyable sympathy in regard to clothes. (He has given me the most delicious suggestion in regard to "come out elbows," to which I will refer farther on).* [in left margin, length-wise: * Henceforth I can always be economically artistic in regard to elbows, however poor. Indeed I shall be eager for holes!] I think he liked my intense appreciation of his details in trimming and stitching, and all manner of ornamentation (except flowers), for he kept continually showing me new treasures and finer beauty. So he touched me, especially as he knew perfectly well that not one flutter of his drapery or a single sweep of his musical curves escaped me. "Thou shalt love me a little," he whispered, "but thou must hate me, knowingly, first." So I kept true to my own instincts, in spite of everything, loving what seemed natural and passionately refined, and hating the rest with frank and solid hatred.

But that was the moment of the conquest—the moment I turned away from *Venus* + looked upon the *Adoration*. I used my opera glasses—for without them I find I lose everything but the grouping. I must tell thee exactly the spot which captivated me. It is as if it were there, the perfect flame of sympathy sprang to life. It was the group in the foreground, to the right of the center: a figure in white, embroidered with gold, + two men standing with arms interlaced. When thou goest to see the picture—think of me lovingly when thy eyes fall upon these people. I staid and staid (I and the silent, straight-backed Scotchman) and I actually didn't care that the infant Christ was an outrage to childhood—there was so much positive enjoyment elsewhere in the picture my eyes wandered ecstatically +forgave and forgot.

As to the *Primavera*, the Graces are cameos. It is so obvious to see their marvelous beauty that I do not care to write out my impressions. The figure of Flora I do not care for—+ right here I wish to say that Botticelli's roses in Flora's arms are ridiculous as the wavelets in the *V[enus]*. Moreover I was really surprised that he did not represent the flowers in his textures more accurately. What with his persistence of display of sepals, petals, stamens, pistils (I did not notice any pollen), I should think he would have tried at least to have the flowers woven or embroidered +represented as part of the material. As it is they are sprinkled in the drapery as sugar on a cake + are hard + unyielding, viz: Dress of Flora in *Primavera* + mantle +dress of right hand of figure in the *Birth of Venus*. That Botticelli could have done better is more than evident from his dexterous management of transparent fabrics. Perhaps it was a convention* but whatever the cause, it is a pity and disappointment. [*along left margin, lengthwise: perhaps he meant them to be real flowers applied—suggestively—for of course certain sprays about the waist represent real flowers.]

When I said goodbye to the *Primavera*, Mercury looked back at me in that wistful way of his, and I almost wondered if he knew how sincerely I had spent my life before him. I felt that same mute attachment that I am always conscious of feeling when leaving a room in which I have been much alone. It is the memory of silent communion and of perfect sincerity. There is however a difference. The room weds the memory of self + the Invisible + the life of introspection—but with the picture there is more than solitude, for there is individuality and a silence full of speech.

In three hours Gertrude had written sixteen pages. Next, she addressed her own sadly confused situation:

> And now it is almost half-past six. I was going to visit a Kindergarten this morning, but I shall probably have to stay in bed as I shall have some watching [of the children] to do this evening.—Miss Bliss is going to the theater with her Venetian-Americans. I really do not know when I shall leave Florence. I have a lingering, fluttering weak-hearted little hope that perhaps I may still be here when thou wilt be back again. Do not stay one day longer in Vienna than is necessary, if I am actually here after the 1st of December.

Here she expressed her longing for Mary's friendship, perhaps her strongest incentive for coming to Europe. Gertrude was humiliated by her own physical weakness, fearing it might be mistaken for a feebleness of spirit or intellect, while Mary and Berenson enjoyed vigorous health, passionate love and compelling research. For above all things, Gertrude prized self-control and independence:

> Individually my one + chief pleasure in coming to Europe was the chance of seeing thee. Really there is much I want to have from thee before I return across the sea. When dost thou think of returning to England in the spring? If I sail in June, have I no hope of seeing you there? O Mariechen, it is hard!

But she found it too painful to end the letter with such a raw confession, and added a gently self-deprecating, comradely postscript:

When I came home yesterday (I had been in the gal-leries the whole day—imagine my fatigue) I was startled, perplexed, amused to see that Harold positively had a fam-ily resemblance to Botticelli's Madonnas + that Arnold, even Arnold, was decidedly like one of the angels. Then I looked at the two other children in the room to assure myself that it was not some sort of incipient Botticelli Insanity—but no, they had no resemblance whatever—it was only my children that could boast of that mystic distinction. Were not my eyes sensi-tive to every minute resemblance after such hours + hours of Botticelli's lines?! I hugged the boys + laughed, and thought of thee + Bernhard, and how thoroughly you would under-stand my picture-tired eyes!

Thines, once more, and finally, Gertrude

Mary answered immediately, and Gertrude's reply to her, on Wednesday morning, November 25, 1891, expressed even more openly the pain of defeat, despair, and dependence. She had failed to achieve her goals of self-reliance and self-control. Her self-image was shattered. She was lonely, tired, and ill. She needed affection and care. Yet, she leavened her anguish with self-irony:

Mariechen, dear, thy letter has come. Few things could be sweeter to me than thy sympathy. I am so very glad to hear that the Botticelli Letter was hailed with such appreciative joy—Several of the recommendations urged upon me with such dear enthusiasm I have already looked at carefully and enjoyed in varying degrees.

But not of pictures just now—I may return to them by and bye.

… It is really <u>very</u> pleasant to me to know that thou findest anything I write really <u>delightful</u>. I live constantly now with such a sense of <u>insufficient accomplishment</u>, that to know that anything—even a hastily scrawled letter—is thought to be well done is a very delicious comfort indeed.

...Ah, Mariechen, thou cans't not know what a solitary life I live. But indeed I have not the strength to meet new people and to hear the irritation of "tinkling brass." And thou knowest I can only be with my children when at my best— they only rest me when I <u>am rested</u>.

It is all so strange—this being forced to acknowledge <u>defeat</u>. I have always felt—in years that have gone—singularly sure of my power of self-control. And indeed, I know—and thou must know, and all those who used to know and love me must know—that my present weakness is of the body and not the spirit.

A loving hand could do so much for me. This I feel with the same wondering simplicity that a child lost in some unknown path—dazed and tired—will trust anyone with a kindly voice. This is why thy sympathy and any word of appreciation brighten my days with such a tender sense of blessing.

She described still unresolved practical matters and the desire, if possible, to share in their mission:

We may leave Florence day after tomorrow, or if the Doctor lets me, I shall stay until the 15th of December. I await his final word of command and shall send thee one of the green [post cards] as soon as I know or do something positively. If I stay, dear, it will be with joyous feet and eager eyes that I shall seek all thou hast asked me to see. I think that even if thou and Bernhard were here I should wish to do my studying alone—and then talk over the pictures together afterwards. I think it will please Bernhard to know that almost without exception I have liked best the things which he likes best. I did not take his letter with me until my very last farewell visit, and was almost surprised to see how frequently we had agreed.

With aching self-awareness, she reflected on her own ways of seeing art, her dramatic bent, and, most profoundly, her respect for technical excellence, self-control, "masterly execution"—her passion for perfection:

> One thing I know that I am apt to insist upon—and it is not only in painting and sculpture, but in music + manners as much as in the deeper + more subtle expressions of character in individuals, and that is <u>masterly execution</u>. That is the dramatic spirit creeping through me everywhere—there must be no weakness, no uncertainty, no apparent self-consciousness—but always perfect poise—the spirit beautiful, + whole and sound, +ripe + sweet. So, of course, I have liked Donatello and Giorgione—and Andrea del Sarto (the ease of del Sarto is rest and joy to me always)—By the bye, when thou seest the Giorgione pictures in the Uffizi, please remember how much impressed I was with the <u>positive</u> value + beauty of his use of <u>black</u>…O the face of Giorgione's Knight!!! When I go to heaven I shall turn against all the existing rules and <u>insist</u> on marrying him.
>
> …Thank thee Mariechen for saying that thou wilt really try and see me again. It is what I want most earnestly. I shall certainly tell thee of every movement that I make…

On December 13, Mary finally arrived from London, accompanied by Ray and Karin. She found Gertrude in her rooms at the Pension Pendini, recovering from the acute collapse prefigured in her letters' feverish effusions.

# CHAPTER 13

## *A Fully Declared Case*

GERTRUDE'S PROVEN CAPACITY FOR DENIAL FORTIFIED HER TRUST IN the power of mind over matter. In a letter to her mother, she described her recent emotional and physical crisis "as a very peculiar attack of pneumonia, preceded by three days of hemorrhages." She explained that "the hemorrhages were not directly from the lungs but from the adjoining capillaries, and although more copious, were of the same nature as the one I had in West Newton." She assured her mother that she was receiving the best care possible from "well-trained nurses, one Scots." During the worst of the illness, Dr. Baldwin looked in twice a day for a week, and later, once a day. Then, Mary had been on hand to attend her, so, she promised her mother, "… in sum, I have been ill under the most favorable conditions…I am now considered well, over all the difficulty with the lungs, and sit up every day, and walk about my room."

She thanked her mother for the Christmas check, as "every little helps me at a time like this when the expenses are so heavy." The children were well, except for slight colds; she hoped her mother's eye troubles were better; and she asked indulgence for her clumsy handwriting, owing to her "stiff neck and rather trembling hand."

In closing, she reported that "… I have passed through this illness in a most extraordinarily favorable manner, and the doctor himself says it is almost unheard of that the fever should have kept so low—and that I should have been kept so entirely free of pain and discomfort."

Yet, despite this deceptively positive report, Gertrude's fevers and coughing, exhaustion and frayed nerves, persisted.

Mary's mother, Hannah Whitall Smith, arrived in Florence on December 29th and stayed for over a month in the rented family apartment on via Principe Amadeo. She was content to look after Mary's and Gertrude's children, with the help of a nurse. She arranged for the Burton boys, now six and three, and the Costelloe girls, five and three, to be photographed together in their holiday clothes. Arnold's smooth, Prince Valiant pageboy coiffure contrasted sweetly with Harold's still babyish wisps and Ray and Karin's thick, short, curly locks. Hannah departed on February 6th, taking the girls with her, after trying unsuccessfully to convince Mary to return to England. Ray and Karin had required more attention than Mary had expected.

Gertrude's health worsened, with continuing hemorrhages and severe fatigue, during a dismal, rainy January. By the 10th, the situation had become critical. Alarmed, Mary accompanied Gertrude to the neighboring Blue Nuns' convalescent home where nurses honored the Blessed Virgin by wearing white linen habits with pale blue veils. On January 21st, after consulting with Gertrude's doctor, Mary wrote to Burton and Jane Hitz with shocking news, but she withheld the truth from Gertrude, as Baldwin deemed best:

> Gertrude's physician, Dr. Baldwin, has asked me to write and tell you about her illness, as he is anxious to keep her real state from her—for fear of making her worse—and yet thinks at the same time that her relatives in America ought to know...
>
> The doctor sent her sputa to be examined under the microscope and the result...confirm[s] his fear that there is tubercular disease—that consumption has begun...she is very much an invalid, requiring most careful nursing, and at any

moment more serious complications might arise. He thinks, however, if all goes on as it has begun, since she went to the nursing home, that by April or May she will be able to go to the south of Italy and a little later to come home and go to the Adirondacks. He says that would be much better than Switzerland…

I think that she has at present no idea of the real trouble, and that she feels comparatively happy at the Home. The doctor goes to see her every day and watches her temperature carefully…If she grows worse, I will write and tell you—or wire, if it seems better…

The same day, Mrs. Alexander Graham Bell, who was touring in England, France, and Italy with her daughters, cabled the news from Florence to John Hitz in Washington. Hitz was overcome after reading her distressing report regarding Gertrude's condition. He noted that he "thought much about Florence, Mrs. Bell and especially Gertrude. The emotions are not to be noted down. And yet how much of one's life [one's emotions] do constitute—they are largely the life."

Disjointedly, he also recorded in his diary:

Gertrude's account of her removal to Sisterhood Home…stating that she had hemorrhages. Putting as cheery a face on the circumstances as possible—speaking of the kindness of Dr. Baldwin etc. But it looks serious unless some change for the better can be effected. She must weaken… weaken—letter from Mr. Burton—Wrote to Gertrude…

Standard medical texts from 1881 listed the causes of tuberculosis as "hereditary disposition, unfavorable climate, a sedentary indoor life, defective ventilation, and deficiency of light and depressing emotions." But in 1882, German physician and microbiologist Robert Koch published his eagerly anticipated findings on the disease, identifying the causative agent to be, instead, the slow-growing *Mycobacterium tuberculosis*. His later discovery, that tuberculosis was contagious (for which he won the 1905 Nobel Prize), was a turning point in medicine. Even so, Koch could offer no effective treatment for victims besides "cheerful surroundings, isolation from stress, a healthy diet, exercise and rest, and travel to a better climate." Gertrude would have recognized that consumption was incurable.

※

During her stay in Florence, Mabel Bell visited Gertrude as often as she could. On January 24th she declared to her husband, who was preparing to join his family in Europe, "I must confess I am rather afraid to call on [Gertrude] for fear she may think I interfered unwarrantably in her affairs, but I wrote Dr. Baldwin that her father was in your employ, and that if he wanted him to come on, you would be the proper person to apply."

※

Alexander Graham Bell visited Gertrude before returning to Washington. He gave her $500, the equivalent of $10,000 today, in place of the lesser sum of 500 francs her father had asked him to leave with her, should she need it. And later, Bell extended even more generous help, presenting John Hitz with seven shares of International Bell Telephone Co., worth $100.00 each. "What a man!" Hitz wrote in his diary.

Surely by this time, Gertrude must have suspected consumption. Early symptoms, it was now known, sometimes included joint pain and weakness, which would explain Gertrude's mysterious knee trouble a decade earlier. What did she feel when she learned the whole truth? Did she blame herself for want of willpower or "masterly execution?" We don't know what she confided to Mary as she came to grips with this second, and even more certain, death sentence, or what details she shared with her mother, her husband, her father, or Bliss Carman.

❧

Mrs. Bell stayed on in Italy. On March 8th she remarked to her husband,

> I went to call on Mrs. Burton, and Alec, dear, I am shocked at the change; she had a relapse just after you saw her, and now cannot speak or see anyone. I saw her for a few minutes, but she said she could not see anyone, even Miss Bliss, who has charge of her children. Miss Bliss says she [Gertrude] is very nervous; she looked absolutely colorless, and I think her face is thinner, too.

The illness fluctuated: On March 10th, the doctor pronounced Gertrude better. On the 19th, feeling stronger, Gertrude sent a note hoping to see Mrs. Bell. But on April 8th, when Mrs. Bell inquired from Rome about Gertrude's condition, Mary replied:

> I cannot say that the doctor has been <u>explicit</u> with me in regard to Mrs. Burton's case, but he said he felt <u>much less</u> hopeful than at first. All winter he has been fighting against the increase of the tubercular trouble, but in spite of his efforts, it has advanced. He cannot at all say how it will end. She may be able to throw it off, but I fear that he thinks the chances are not favorable, owing to the nervous complications. She is growing steadily weaker, but he seems to regard it as a good symptom that she has not lost flesh. He asked me, or rather acquiesced when I suggested it, to write to her husband and tell him she was weaker. He says she probably cannot leave Italy this summer. It is now a fully declared case of consumption, and while the cure is possible it is by no means certain.
>
> It is so good of you to ask what you can do. I know the flowers you have been sending have been a great pleasure.

Perhaps when you go away you could leave word at the florist's to send flowers every now and then for a month, it would be the most welcome thing you could do. She is not able to read much, but she thoroughly enjoys looking at the flowers.

Her children, and the various complications that arise with them, make her very nervous, so as soon as Miss Bliss is gone, I am going to take them with me to Viareggio and keep them there till Mr. Hitz comes. She really needs someone with her now, to shield her from every care...

Gertrude's family made arrangements for her treatment. Miss Bliss was dismissed. Although Mary assumed John Hitz would come over, instead, Burton decided to leave for Italy as soon as possible. Before sailing, he met his father-in-law by chance on a Boston street and supplied additional details of Gertrude's grave condition. Her illness disturbed Hitz "more than he could tell," but he made no plans to travel. As Bell's secretary, he was facing increased responsibilities, primarily planning a new building in Washington to house the Volta Bureau for Research on the Deaf, of which he would become superintendent. Further, during the spring months, Bell had strengthened his professional relationship with the family of Helen Keller, and with her teacher, Ann Sullivan. Bell had begun instructing Helen Keller to speak by a method quite different from that of her previous teachers. John Hitz acted as Bell's go-between with the Keller family, and was enchanted with both Helen and Annie Sullivan, a strong, intelligent woman almost exactly Gertrude's age. He increasingly concerned himself with their welfare. Their relationships became lifelong bonds.

Burton sailed for Italy on the Imperial German and US mail steamship *Werra* on May 7th, and arrived at Genoa on May 19th. Once in Florence, Burton cabled Hitz that Gertrude's condition had improved. He saw to her situation and deliberated with the doctor about her treatment: she needed various atomizers and syrups for hoarseness and coughs, spray solutions, ointments and tablets, powders and lozenges. The three-month bill at Henry Groves English and American Chemists, 15 Via Borgo Ognissanti, totaled 57 Lire, or $9.50—about $190, in today's dollars. Burton took responsibility for his young sons, and settled accounts for childcare, meals, and fees at the Pension Pendini, and for the nursing services of the Blue Nuns, who accepted only donations.

Jane Hitz sprang into action and arrived in Florence in mid-June. She must have been deeply concerned for her daughter and grandsons, for at fifty-five she was not fond of travel and was recovering from serious eye ailments. Her arrival allowed Burton, already in Florence for a month, to leave the children with her while he traveled alone to Rome and Naples. The summer heat had not yet reached its peak, and he welcomed the opportunity. In a large blue album documenting this 1892 trip, he fixed a photograph of the Vatican's cabbage fields and vegetable gardens stretching behind St Peter's Basilica. He also inserted a post card, printed in pencil by six-year-old Arnold, anxious for his father's return and curious about Mt. Vesuvius: "Dear Father, I do want to know, when are you coming? I want to know what you have seen…tell me how high the fire went on the volcano. Good bye Felix Arnold Burton, Florence June 15, 1892."

While Gertrude convalesced quietly with the Blue Nuns, on Burton's return, he, the boys, and Jane Hitz took refuge from the summer heat at Vallombrosa, a forested hill retreat and monastery site in the foothills of the Apennines, about twenty miles east of Florence. The English poet John Milton had made this shady valley famous in his poem *Paradise Lost*, referring to "the autumnal leaves that strow the brooks, in Vallombrosa." The Abbey there was founded in the 11th century by Saint Giovanni Gualberto, the son of a noble Florentine family who underwent a conversion and withdrew into the solitude of the forest. He founded a Benedictine order and was canonized in 1193. At an altitude of 900 feet, Vallombrosa's climate was refreshing, and by 1890 the church and its surrounding woods had become a summer resort with several hotels serving a well-to-do clientele.

During their six weeks' stay, Jane Hitz and the family ate most meals at the well-appointed Grand Hotel Vallombrosa. Burton spent much of his time hiking and sketching: his album contains watercolor drawings of hunters squatting over an open fire, grilling game on long skewers; views of the church and the monastery; and scenes of the small commemorative chapels on the steep Calvary path leading to the Paradisino hermitage, where he and the boys slept in the monks' former cells. Views from there extended over the Abbey and its deep spring-fed water basin, with a large grassy meadow a short distance away. The broad sunny expanse contrasted with the deep, cool pine forests.

By the beginning of August, Dr. Baldwin and the family decided Gertrude might soon be well enough to travel. With some difficulty, they reserved six tickets on the *SS Fulda*, second class, but with first class privileges, for Mrs. Jane Hitz, Mr. and Mrs. Burton, Arnold and Harold, and Eugenie Vuistaz, a Swiss nurse for the children, recently arrived from Lausanne to take the place of the departed Miss Bliss.

The *Fulda* was a four-masted steamer, its two giant engines augmented by sail power. The ship departed from Genoa on August 24th and arrived in New York harbor on September 5th. Although Gertrude was consumptive, she was neither quarantined on arrival nor deported, as she might have been, according to America's Undesirable Persons laws, which were applied chiefly to steerage passengers. After disembarking, the family ferried to Hoboken and from there rode by train to Morristown, New Jersey, where their routes diverged:

Burton returned to Boston to begin the fall term, Jane Hitz to Washington.

Gertrude, the boys, and Eugenie sped west by stagecoach on the final leg of their journey, in the mellow light of a warm September afternoon, to the Oliver boarding house in Mendham, New Jersey. They recovered from the trip among the rolling hills, ponds, and lush foliage east of the village. The Olivers' Mendham establishment was located fifteen miles from Schooley's Mountain, where Gertrude and Alfred Edgar Burton had honeymooned so joyfully, eight years before.

CHAPTER 14

## *So Entirely Not Me*

GERTRUDE RESTED AFTER THE LONG OCEAN VOYAGE. THE OLIVER Cottage was peaceful in early September, when most summer boarders had departed. Mendham's imposing 1765 white Church on the Hill punctuated the rolling contours of the landscape, and enhanced the tranquility of the natural scenery. Some weeks in the country would allow all of them time to prepare for Gertrude's next challenge: treatment at an Adirondack sanatorium. After two weeks aboard ship, the two Burton brothers, seven and four, now had room to run and time to play in this delightful atmosphere. Eugenie began to adjust to the utterly foreign surroundings. She spoke French with the boys, and sometimes, with Arnold, a little Italian.

A week later, on the 12th, John Hitz arrived, eager to reunite with his invalid daughter and grandsons. For over two years he had followed their progress in photographs: before-and-after portraits of six-year-old Arnold's first short haircut; Harold at three, dressed in Swiss *lederhosen;* the boys together with the Costelloe girls in Florence. Finally he could assure himself of the boys' welfare and judge for himself Gertrude's true condition.

Hitz found the group waiting excitedly in her room, Gertrude resting in bed but looking comparatively well. She was relieved and happy to be with him again. After supper, he stayed talking with her until nine. They spent the next day, warm and rainy, on the veranda. Eugenie watched the children while father and daughter "talked over many things—about people and events."

September 14th, John Hitz's sixty-fourth birthday, dawned cloudy after overnight downpours. At eight o'clock Gertrude and her boys invited him to her room for a grand celebration. Arnold and Harold came in, each bearing a salver with "fruit of the place":

> pears and grapes. One was wreathed with goldenrod, the other (Harold's) with field daisies, "… and each child having made for his gift, a card—Harold's with blue ribbon, and worked on paper "Grandfather," with a real edelweiss above—and Arnold's card, a banner in red with the words around it "Happy Birthday" and a Swiss cross…All very touching and beautiful…"

The afternoon turned clear and warm, perfect for sitting outside and enjoying quiet conversation. Hitz read aloud from John Addington Symonds's memoir, *Our Life in the Swiss Highlands*. Symonds was a consumptive English expatriate author who retreated for his health to Davos, the Hitz family's ancestral home, and now a treatment center for tuberculosis victims. A theme of Symonds's works—and the subject that made him famous—was his theory of "sexual inversion." A patron of Walt Whitman, his writings represented one of the first public recognitions of homosexuality, which he ennobled by linking it to Greek origins. Symonds's romanticized reminiscences of earthy peasant life turned the discussion to matters of human sexuality, a recurrent topic of interest. This sunny afternoon was one of the few when Gertrude and her father were able to visit together calmly and quietly.

The following day, young Eugenie became ill and took to her bed. Gertrude and her father drove the Olivers' buggy into Mendham village, about a mile, to make some purchases. After the noon dinner hour, the boys gathered goldenrod with their grandfather in the fields until almost four o'clock. Then John Hitz rested in his room, not feeling well himself, and took supper with Arnold, while Harold stayed with his mother. They put the children to bed in the still ailing Eugenie's room, so they could take tea together in the evening.

As Gertrude rested the next day, Hitz drove Arnold in the buggy to find a nurse to care for Eugenie and look after the boys. Unsuccessful, they finally called in the Mendham doctor, and the next morning continued the search. In Dover, they located a Mrs. Buchanan, engaged her, and drove her back to Oliver Cottage.

Gertrude was up and about when they returned. Bliss Carman had arrived from New York. The two friends had met infrequently, and she eagerly awaited his visit, resolutely resuming a more normal routine. Gertrude and Carman spent most of the afternoon in a sunlit grove where he shared photographs of his mother and father, sister and friends. That night, she wrote to him, touching on his mother's death—and reflecting on her own approaching fate: "And now it is so still—it is very near midnight. How I wish I had the delicacy of truth which would help me to tell the thoughts that drift before me—thoughts of the impenetrable Darkness, and the great unending Calm..."

Hitz and Carman both enjoyed hiking. In the morning they set out for the nearby "mountain," climbing to Legend Rock, the summit's large stone outcrop. From there they beheld Harmony Brook, on one side, and Dismal Brook, on the other, calling to mind complicated sentiments surrounding Gertrude's return. They walked back to the Oliver Cottage in time for the noon meal and, though tired, John Hitz felt better. He spent several balmy, bright, breezy hours with Arnold and Harold. Then, having lost track of time, he left hastily in Mr. Oliver's buggy with other boarders to catch a train from Morristown to New York City. Because of the last-minute confusion of settling his board bills, servants' fees, and carriage rental, John Hitz left without saying goodbye to the children, and was "depressingly affected" for some days following. Not long after Hitz departed, Carman returned to New York. For years afterward, Gertrude cherished the memory of their intimate conversations on those ripe September days.

Gertrude busied herself arranging admission to Dr. Edward Livingston Trudeau's Adirondack Cottage Sanitarium [sic]. At her request, her father copied and sent Dr. Baldwin's letter of diagnosis and recommendations for therapy to Dr. Trudeau. Less than a month later, Gertrude arrived in Saranac Lake on the Mohawk and Malone Rail Road, completed only months before. The health facilities at Saranac Lake were now easily accessible for invalids and tourists—just an overnight train ride from New York City.

Dr. Trudeau, a physician and himself a victim of tuberculosis, had arrived in upstate New York from New York City more than fifteen years earlier, in 1876. He had contracted consumption while nursing his brother through the final stages of the disease. Trudeau partially recovered by adopting "the Adirondack wilderness life." Later, he read Dr. Koch's 1882 report identifying the *tubercle bacillus* and studied the treatment offered in Davos, emphasizing fresh air and a fortifying diet. In 1884, he founded his Adirondack Cottage Sanitarium to help others recover, starting with one small cottage called "Little Red," where two tubercular sisters from New York City became his first patients. More and more consumptives, both the disadvantaged and the celebrated, visited the region hoping for a cure. Trudeau's fame grew. When the town was incorporated in 1892, Dr. Trudeau became village president. Over the next sixty years, beginning in the 1890s, Saranac Lake transformed itself from a backwoods logging center into "the Western Hemisphere's foremost center for the treatment of pulmonary tuberculosis."

More and more, Gertrude communicated with family and friends through the mails. When she arrived in the Adirondacks, she exuberantly described her trip north in a circular letter intended to be passed around among a dozen friends and family:

First, I want you all to know what a comfortable journey we had in our "Palace sleeping car" and how much eager enjoyment there was for the children in the elegance and mysteries of our cushions and berths, and our luxurious meals—and how gorgeous all the country was in the wealth of autumnal coloring. Field after field, each more beautiful than the last, such flaming red, such masses of pure living gold—such ecstasy of clear, pale yellows—I never saw before!

I would lie back upon my seat—looking up into the trees—then far under, into the very heart of mellow silences— then be floated on such a sea of wavering color that I really seemed to be swimming body and soul through some rapturous element of another world. We would exclaim helplessly to one another—and then I would sigh and gasp, yielding to the intoxication which was so keen as to reach the delicious verge of pain. In the morning all the beauty was intensified, for we plunged into the wildness of the mountain districts and the track lay in the midst of the woods.

When they reached Saranac Lake's new railway station, only one vehicle awaited the passengers disembarking in the rain. Although they were amazed by the beauty of the natural surroundings, Gertrude, Arnold, Harold, and Eugenie felt disappointed and perplexed:

We found the station of Saranac Lake a rather picturesque brownish little affair, and entered the only covered vehicle (a great lumbering omnibus), glad enough for shelter against the cold air and drizzling rain. Then began the hunt for the boarding house—(a bumpy ride up and down Saranac Village) and after the unsatisfactory investigation, we went straight to the Ampersand, a very big and expensive hotel, as it was the easiest way of finding our doctor and of making our more permanent arrangements.

The Ampersand is on the shore of Saranac Lake and about a mile and a half from the village. We found ourselves introduced at once to one of the loveliest scenes of the Adirondacks, and the sun came out in most gracious ways that we might know and love the charm of the beautiful little lake. The trees along the shore were rich as gathered sunshine—a wonderful, throbbing treasury of gold—with such deep flashes of bronzing crimson, it seemed as if the trees had gleamed forth all their juices, and that all the summer's wealth of light and heat were poured back into the world in one great flood of flaming color—one final, passionate rapture—the exultance of memory over death!…What endurance—what restraint, what unconquerable dignity I saw pictured there!

It was as though she were describing her own intentions to conquer illness with passion, poise and self-possession.

There, she broke off her composition. The first days "in the wilderness" must have been especially trying for all of them. Gertrude took up her pen again on October 27, 1892, once they had found their boarding house, or "cure cottage," named the St. Bernard.

It is more than ten days since I began to write this letter. We are now firmly established at the "St. Bernard," and Saranac Lake with its inhabitants and various characteristics becomes less and less a mystery.

The "St. Bernard" perhaps suggests a great, lonely stone house, isolated among rocks and almost buried beneath eternal snows. No, my friends, it is a very unpretentious, ordinary wooden structure, with a porch, and two gabled ends, and as it shows its yellowish front through a cluster of friendly trees one would not accuse it of any institutional air whatsoever. It is indeed a modest, homelike house such as any well-to-do farmer often builds. It stands by the roadside, just out of the village, and the gently flowing [Saranac] River runs before my windows, bubbling and foaming a little as it passes under a bridge—then winding reassuringly through the trees, and so on to quiet meadowlands, and Lake Champlain. And indeed the mountains are very beautiful. Even Eugenie fresh from Lausanne and Lake Geneva rejoices in their loveliness, and little Harold exclaims *"N'est-ce pas c'est ravissant?"*

The two rented rooms in the St. Bernard, one for her and one for the children and their nurse, were rustic but comfortable. The house was built in 1875 by one of the town's prominent citizen-developers and bore various names during succeeding decades: Cedar Cottage, then Sunnyside. The clapboard farm house, with a large porch for the occupants' outdoor "curing" sessions, occupied the corner of Bloomingdale Avenue and Depot Street, within easy walking distance of the town center, across the Saranac River, over the Church Street Bridge. Dr. Trudeau's house and laboratory stood nearby, at the corner of Church and Main Streets, opposite the picturesque, pocket-sized, shingled Episcopal Church of St. Luke the Physician.

Her room, Gertrude wrote,

> ... is large—comfortably large—and is remarkably cheerful, having four windows all open to sunshine, and a great corner fireplace besides. The tints of the wallpaper and carpet please me—yellowish-fawnish—inoffensive. When my fire blazes and I lie back on my bed or on my long chair, I am almost <u>too</u> comfortable, am I not? I shall have to have a great black stove—by and by—but meanwhile, dancing flames & the merriest of cheer!
>
> The "Salon" of the St Bernard adjoins my room. It is one of those emphatically gay rooms where each bright colored chair and the flowers of the carpet and the blue vases on the mantel and the looking glass of the bookcase all stare at you separately and seem to exclaim in a jumble of smiles: "Am I not pretty! I am so cheerful!!"

Gertrude's curiosity and unfailing eye for detail—and her desire to entertain her correspondents—mingled with profound sadness:

> The books all have glittering covers and look as if they were on exhibition. Shelley and Browning and Tennyson are there & Whittier very bold in imitation alligator. *The Duchess* also presents herself and Jules Verne and my old, old love *John Halifax* [her father's present to her on her sixteenth birthday]. It is such a medley, with *Felix Holt* and *Jane Eyre* leaning against *Robinson Crusoe* and *That's Her Name*, that I was sorely puzzled at first.
>
> Then one day I take out a volume & see the crimson stamp of a dealer in "dry-goods." The books were advertisements—cheaply distributed—and so the miserable paper and shameful printing and glittering bindings were all explained. Yet Browning sings his brave message and Shelley's skylark soars and soars. The book most used is the volume of Byron's poems. And upon the top shelf, over the books, in front of the mirror, upon a crushed-strawberry China silk handkerchief (hem-stitched) is a bust of Byron. Is my young proprietor Byronic? He is very fair and very modest. His hair and eyebrows and mustache and coat and flannel shirt and cloth cap are all a blending of café-au-lait. He thinks easily and has sensibilities and is an engraver by trade. He is consumptive, but has gained steadily in strength and will probably live here all his life.

To her, the transition to life in the woods of Saranac Lake felt like entering a version of Hans Holbein's *Dance of Death*.

> Everyone in Saranac is consumptive. It is a collection of invalids, from Dr. Trudeau (ruler overall) to the very servants and drivers. Dr. Trudeau himself has only one lung. But he is practically cured and lives a life of great activity and inestimable usefulness. He is tall and dark, eyes sparkling with

energy; voice resonant, determined, genial, teeth strong and white, and a personality commanding instant confidence and respect. Moreover, he wears picturesque clothes, great soft leather gaiters reaching to the knees & fastened with countless little buckles.

But the young assistant physician—ah! He is arrayed in rich brown corduroy and wears creamy flannel shirts—and as he dashes by in his carriage, he waves off his cap with the most graceful sweep of his arm and as he passes on I hear his "Good morning, Mrs. Burton" in tones low and almost reverential—and I am glad that he carries with him everywhere his freshness and beauty and the certain something in his voice that is more than all merely physical charm. But, of course, he is consumptive, or has been…But now it is taken as a matter of course and the mind adapts itself all unconsciously.

Other renters shared the large farm house with Gertrude, her boys, and Eugenie. Directly upstairs, a young man recently graduated from Yale, "Pale as ivory—thin and ghastly, with the look of baffled youth in his eyes." And, "In the room across the hall there lies a young woman (Ah! These are all young—so pitiably young!) She is so ill that her people were telegraphed for last night. Father, Mother, brother all came together this morning."

Elsewhere in the house,

… we have a romance. There came a young Canadian here early in the Fall…He was brought on a stretcher. He gained strength in a short time & was suddenly married. His young wife saw him grow stronger & stronger. They walk a mile or two every day now. They are to stay all winter.

One young man—a slender fellow…always goes to the post office. Had a consultation with the physician a day or two ago. The doctor told him outright that he was doomed. The poor boy came back saying it was all he could do not to break down like a baby and cry in the office.

Another young man with his sister also ill is afraid to consult the physicians here & has decided to rush off to Colorado.

... Yet—yet—it is all like something I <u>watch</u>—like a scene passing before my eyes in which I have no part but that of a silent and sympathetic spectator.

Gertrude was fascinated by their affecting stories, but held herself at a distance. It was a long time before she could acknowledge that the disease had sidelined her, too, from the passionate lifework she had envisioned. She drew some consolation from accounts of consumptives and doctors who fought the good fight, and sometimes won:

> And this new phase of life that is being presented to me—this picture of a perpetual battle without a visible enemy—is indeed rich in lessons. Many, many of the people recover. One hears story after story of apparently wonderful cures...Dr. Trudeau in his exquisite little laboratory works and works with indefatigable zeal—hoping someday, perhaps, to discover that which will destroy the tubercular bacillus without injury to the human system...

But it would be a half-century before the discoveries of the antibiotic streptomycin, in 1944, which would cure most cases of tuberculosis, followed in 1952 by isoniazid. With these powerful drugs came the triumph over tuberculosis, and the demise of Saranac Lake's flourishing economy.

Gertrude followed Dr. Trudeau's prescribed regimen of four hearty meals a day and long periods of rest on the cure cottage's veranda. Very soon she became restless, longing for physical activity and a change of scene. On November 11th, she wrote to her father about buying a horse and carriage. He sent $100 of Bell's stock—about $2000 today—for the purchase, and she responded gratefully,

> It is by driving that one sees the mountains at their best. The soil is so sandy and the carriages are so light that the driving is luxurious. We have taken drives of twelve and fifteen miles, and the air is so invigorating and sustaining that when I came back I had the mingled sense of having been nourished through and through and being most deliciously tired—just as a child is after a long day of play and freedom in the fields.

The pleasures of driving out in the autumn and the obvious joy of her children playing in the open air ("they have never been better since they were born...") compensated partly for Gertrude's withdrawal from the causes she had hoped to pursue.

"... I was born an actor and I love nothing dearer than self-control," she confessed to Bliss Carman. The disease confounded her sense of self, her very identity. This situation created intense feelings of loss—loss of control and loss of the ability to act, to make her mark in the world. She had always pictured herself on stage, as a performer, even a star. Now, in her own eyes she was becoming a bystander, a watcher. She understood, she wrote, what it must be like "to be hidden away in a leper colony, friendless and forgotten by the world."

As early as the end of October, she had declared to Carman:

> No one writes to me. And indeed it is an isolation I never knew before—here in my cheerful room, with the half-living all around me. It is all so entirely Not Me. And it is impossible to revel in solitude with this consciousness of consumptives ev-

erywhere—Of course, this is only one phase. The Sun is going
to Shine, and the superb, bracing weather—the clear, cold,
beautiful days will be here. I was never in a place, however,
where I seemed <u>to have to smile</u> so much. Everyone expects
you to be groaning.

Just after Halloween she assured him, "Every letter that comes
is like a fresh morning to me, dear, and now that I have grown to look
upon death as something familiar—O thy words are more than words
have ever been before—peace, joy, strength! They do indeed give me
added life…I do not exaggerate…postcards will do!" She came to
rely on Carman's letters to connect her with the world—his warm
friendship and epistolary devotion confirmed her feelings about their
time together in Mendham. "—Ah, dear Heart—how sweet thy love
is to me these dreary days! I close my eyes and think of thee, and drift
down the sweet flood of Memories—thou and I together in fadeless
sunshine, soft and still!"

After leaving Mendham, Carman had traveled home to Canada with the poet Richard Hovey to collaborate on a new collection of
poems and visit with friends and relatives. When Carman returned to
New York in late fall, he yearned for deliverance from editorial office
work and managed to arrange for a six months' leave from his post.
He shipped his belongings to Hovey's parents' home in Washington,
DC. Carman was a special favorite of Mother Hovey, who promised
him a comfortable room and a freedom to write.

Gertrude could easily picture him there. During her childhood,
the Hovey family had lived close by the Hitz cottage on Capitol Hill.
As a girl, she had played with Dick Hovey and his brother Fred. Dick's
father, General Charles Edward Hovey, was an old friend to her father. She was astonished to learn that Carman would now inhabit her
old neighborhood: "Thou mayest go to Washington! It is wondrous
strange to think of you there. So many ghosts of me!"

## CHAPTER 15

# *A Masquerade of Death*

A FTER CARMAN'S MOVE TO THE CAPITAL, GERTRUDE REVISITED THE city in her imagination. Through her informants, she again became part of its tightly woven social fabric: "I know thou wert to be in New York. My father met Mrs. Hovey in a street-car and she told him." In 1892, Washington City, with a population of about 230,000, was half the size of Boston, and a quarter of the population of New York or Philadelphia. But most streets were now paved, electric trolleys had succeeded the horse drawn cars, and the first electric streetlights had recently replaced oil and gas lamps along a short stretch of Pennsylvania Avenue, which became magical after dark.

In early December, Carman and Hovey, the two footloose poets, established themselves at 125 Indiana Avenue, NW, the home of Hovey's parents, Brigadier General Charles Edward Hovey and Harriette Farnham Spofford Hovey, cousin to Ainsworth Rand Spofford, the Librarian of Congress.

As soon as Gertrude learned that Carman was living in familiar surroundings, she alerted him to people and places in Washington they could now share. Following her suggestion, Carman became acquainted with Mrs. Kappeler, the Hitz family friend, an attractive, energetic woman, intelligent and warm. She and her children, Freddie and Jessie, had frequently visited John Hitz while he was incarcerated in the Washington Jail in 1886. Later that year, Mrs. Kappeler's husband took his own life, leaving the family in debt. Recovering from the shock of widowhood, in 1890 Dorothy Kappeler earned a degree from the Columbian Medical School (of which Jane Hitz was a board member), becoming one of the school's first female graduates. She later became a dentist and a practitioner of magnetic therapy, the latest treatment for just about any ailment. She was now in her early forties. Freddie was in his first year at Swarthmore College and Jessie, sixteen, was developing into a talented singer and a striking beauty.

Gertrude encouraged Carman to visit the family:

> Yes, I would like thee to see Mrs. Kappeler—and per-haps Jessie—thou shall look upon her as one in a dream—as a vision in my own heart. Dear Mrs. Kappeler has the richest emotional nature of any woman I know. Of course you will talk about the weather—but in very truth thou couldst go & lay thy heart bare & bleeding in her hand and she would give her own life-blood to bless & soothe thee. Her address is 1331 L Street, N.W. & do go alone. I have been in the house—but it was when I was so ill—my mind almost gone—just before I was taken to the Portland Hospital.

Much of Washington's bourgeoisie lived a mobile existence at the end of the nineteenth century, exchanging rooms, boarding hous-es and homes with startling frequency. Regarding the Hoveys' address Gertrude commented:

> 125 Indiana Avenue? Thou knowest the row of brown houses on the south side? I lived there once—it was the house next to the last in, walking from 3rd Street, or the second house in, coming from the City Hall. My brother [William] was born there [in 1872]. My brother is at Harvard, by the way. And this white court-house is the one where my father's trial was held and where I lived through all those dramatic scenes—which are now but an episode in my strange life-history.

At a distance she played Carman's expert guide:

... Thou art all mixed up about localities in Washington. One might as well be accurate even in sentimentalizing. The house the Hovey's lived in when I used to play with the boys is an entirely different place. I lived on Capitol Hill—(the dear old cottage is torn down now)—at the time. I knew the Hovey's & they lived on B St. opposite the Capitol grounds.

She suggested visits to several other personally significant settings in her "strange life-history:"

For my sake, go up to the Capitol & walk all around the Western Terrace. It must be at sunset. When I was a girl there was no balustrade of any kind, & it seemed almost like walking off into the sky. I have been there so much—alone for the long, long thoughts, & there is much of romance lived there too.

She was glad that Carman, who had enjoyed walks with her father in Mendham, might come to know her family better. "It is good of thee to look up my father. A note addressed 917 R Street N.W. will find him." John Hitz had moved again, too.

Gertrude and Carman's correspondence revolved around shared acquaintances, his poems, her medical condition and family problems, and his tendency to depression. Recently Carman's childhood sweetheart had broken their nine-year "understanding" and married another. He was overwhelmed with regret and further saddened by deaths of other friends and family members. He began a flurry of flirtations and impulsive behavior in Washington. His letters to Gertrude now brimmed with references to the Kappeler family and their doings at 1331 L Street. Carman's tendency to idealize women—and romantic love generally—led easily to infatuation and poetic effusions.

At first, Gertrude welcomed his enthusiasm for her friends with amused, kind-hearted caution, saying, "Bliss, how can I thank thee for this letter...O my comrade there is such warmth of tenderness when there can be sympathy over another human heart. And their hearts are beautiful....O that ride in the front seat of the [electric] car!!...How well I understand thee Blisskin." But she didn't really understand.

She confessed that she responded with tears in her eyes after reading one particularly entertaining description of escapades with the Kappelers, *mère et fille*. Carman misinterpreted her reaction, believing his letter had made her sad, or jealous. She mocked his presumptuousness, playing with variations on his name, and personifying herself as the spear-carrying Valkyrie of Nordic mythology and Wagnerian opera:

> Now Blisskin Bumptious, thou hast entirely misunderstood about that "weeping"! Flatter thyself no longer. Thy knowledge of WOMAN is restricted to generalities. Why, my dear boy I wept because I was so glad—so thankful! If it had been a beautiful picture that I had loved off there in the Italian galleries, if it had been some lovely mountain and a Swiss lake—and thou hadst seen them with the same perfect sympathy, I would have rejoiced immeasurably—but when it is a beautiful child [Jessie]—the most beautiful child I have ever looked upon—and she is woman grown and thou seest her and at a glance know her beauty as I know it—why I wept—because my heart was full to overflowing—Faint-hearted!!! I would like to shake thee!!! What an insult to the Valkyr!

Gertrude sympathetically, but realistically, assessed Jessie's youthful beauty, strengths and weaknesses, and Carman's fears for her feminine vulnerability: "... all thou sayest about that blessed child is so full of interest to me—all thy impressions are so dear to me—Yes, Bliss, she is joyous as a sun angel—Yes, I tremble. But surely such life as hers must bring rich fruit. Even if she suffers bitterly—bitterly—she cannot lose the divine power of turning anguish to sweet and noble ends." Gertrude dreamed that if she herself were "very, very, very rich" she would arrange for a glorious college-bred woman as tutor for Jessie, whose beauty, charm and talent deserved the foundation of an education such as Jessie's brother Freddie was enjoying at Swarthmore.

She was slow to recognize that Carman had fallen in love with the lovely Jessie, half his age.

With Burton, Gertrude continued agreeable exchanges. They met regularly on holidays, together with their boys. The true nature of their marriage remains ambiguous, but they were indeed friends. Gertrude had relied on his help during her crisis in Italy and continued to depend on him for support. Her fragile, unpredictable physical condition, concern for the children's welfare, and attempts to keep up with correspondents "on the outside" consumed her energy. Burton remained deeply engaged in his career at Tech, a world apart from her invalid universe, but by attending to her and the children, he fulfilled their vows of shared responsibility.

On Thanksgiving afternoon, as Gertrude was writing to Carman, she described Burton's holiday visit: "I received a telegram an hour or so ago—announcing that my Burton would be here tonight. My watch tells me the train is probably here—and at any moment now I may hear his steps on the porch." She often referred to her husband as Mr. Burton, and with an ironic touch, sometimes as "my Burton" or "his Lordship."

For Gertrude in the Adirondack winter's darkness, Carman's letters became more and more "as sunlight—they are indeed the life of life." To Carman she could express her neediest, most pessimistic thoughts. On December 13th, she tried to describe her sense of approaching catastrophe:

This has been a hard day for me—almost the hardest since I have been here. Comforting cheer was never so much needed. Indeed, beloved, it is a stern and awful battle. Let me tell thee a little, may I?

Have I told thee of the overwhelming Gloom—have I told thee that life here in Saranac is nothing but a masquerade of Death; have I told thee how the sense of Doom hovers like a shadow everywhere? And then I have had worries—for Eugenie continues ill, and O, the expense weighs me down sometimes so that I have a desperate crushing feeling in the top of my head; and I have to ask for money again and again—But of these last things we will not speak. They are not poetic—The Spirit of Death is enough. Let me keep to that.

She longed for the silence, order, and predictability of her hospital stays:

I really cannot bring myself to tell thee how keen, how oppressive this insistence of illness is to me. If the people were only in beautiful white beds, if there was the silence, the perfect routine, the immaculate cleanliness, the peaceful relaxation of hospital life! What a haven of rest—how sweet the memory of those days in Portland!

She longed to be cared for, and cared about. Illness now isolated her from a caring family and stimulating social networks. The life of action she had once desired, the "short life in the saddle," seemed all too short, and now, among her fellow patients, a pitiful self-delusion:

Here the invalids walk about, rush in carriages, sit on the porches—smile and look ghastly—It is a bitter mockery of a summer holiday....One day a gentleman goes to order some furniture and in a week—the same furniture dealer, who is also the undertaker, comes to take his measure for a coffin and that is the end. The disease is so deceptive. They all hope to live even though the doctors swear they cannot. Every shopkeeper, every coachman, every servant—everybody, everybody—each and all are here because they are diseased. And perhaps what is saddest is that the majority are young men and women. Enough—

One December night she opened her window before turning down her light. The clear mountain air and bracing temperatures helped improve her agitated state of mind. Seeing the bright stars against the black sky, her "heart leapt and the ache vanished for an instant." Her thoughts turned to springtime, nearly three years before. She recalled writing her first letter to Bliss Carman, in the parlor at Green Street, and her joy when his response provided a reprieve from deepest pain. Now too, his sympathetic, amusing letters and poems helped preserve her courage while she endured overwhelming nervousness, and extreme sensitivity to sounds. She constantly dreaded exceeding her physical and emotional limits.

Six days later she experienced another major collapse:

> Now I must tell thee I am in the midst of one of my most painful breakdowns. It is a nervous explosion almost equal to the horrible time I had in the convent in Florence. The chief difficulty lies in the most abnormal sensitiveness to sound—I shriek and groan at the slightest noise if it is at all sudden or unexpected—And thou who hast never seen me all undone will now realize how it is that I weep so easily—it is sheer weakness from long overstrain. The first great breakdown was when I went to the Hospital in Portland—And it is because I was born an actress and because I love self-mastery above all virtues, that I say so little, dear, of all this

horror.....In a few days more I hope to have passed through the agony but if I do not send a word for Christmas thou wilt understand—

Nevertheless, after the holidays she reported that the family Christmas celebration had been a lovely success, and that she and the nursemaid Eugenie felt proud. "It was a Festival in very truth."

After his Christmas visit to Saranac Lake, Burton returned to Boston to enroll seven-year-old Arnold as a boarder at the Allen School in West Newton. Gertrude had misgivings about sending him away, but she hoped life would be less stressful for him there, and simpler for her, with only Harold to care for. She still hoped to mother Arnold from a distance. Before they left, Gertrude sent a letter that would greet him when he arrived at the school:

My dear Arnold, You will think it strange that this letter has reached West Newton before you, and lies waiting to say a word of welcome. It started before you did!! That is the secret! I hope you are not very, very, very tired, and that you saw many things to interest you on your journey. What a rush and noise there must have been in Boston!

I suppose you will know the names of all the boys, and perhaps you have already seen the little boy who has been round the world. I really do wonder if he speaks any queer languages. And the twins, perhaps you have seen them also. Are they exactly the same size and do they look just alike? And the little boy who is younger than you? You can make believe he is Harold and be very gentle to him. But I suppose he wears trousers. How funny it will be when Harold wears trousers! I hope you will sleep beautifully and have the most beautiful dreams, or empty dreams, which are the best kind of all for a tired boy. Please be a good boy every day and all the time, and

say good night to Miss [Sarah] Allen for me. And one huge enormous gigantic kiss on your nose from
Mother!

ఈ

When Carman inquired about Burton's whereabouts, Gertrude explained that he and Arnold had departed on December 28: "There is no such thing as a Christmas Holiday at the Institute of Technology. Plod, plod, plod 'til Summer time, then almost four whole months of freedom. So it is the old address, 54 Waltham St." Burton's rooms were in Boston's South End, within walking distance of Tech on Boylston Street.

ఈ

In contrast to her husband's nose-to-the-grindstone existence, Gertrude's vaster, subtler, poetic reality became evident in her letters to Carman:

The most glorious day imaginable. Just back from an almost twelve miles sleigh ride—and immediately after dinner shall be out again for three hours. The sky is absolutely cloudless and of the tenderest blue…

What do you think of delicate grasses peering above the snow, and what do you think of their shadows beneath them? What do you think of wide stretches of sparkling snow—absolutely smooth and unbroken save by a simple line—the track of some wild creature left in the silence of the night?

# CHAPTER 16

## *Greenery Green*

THE DAILY POST BECAME GERTRUDE'S LIFELINE TO FAMILY AND friends, connecting her with wider social, artistic, and intellectual worlds. She kept up with "her Burton;" Arnold; her brother William at Harvard; her mother, father and Mrs. Kappeler in Washington; and many women friends, including Mary Costelloe and Senda Berenson. She remained attuned to the changing directions of the women's movements, which were focusing on women's suffrage, and replacing efforts to transform morality with political activism.

But while Gertrude cultivated an extensive network of correspondents, she remained removed from the daily delights and disappointments of their lives. Gertrude's situation drew her closer to art and literature. In her "sea of uncertainty," she clung to her life preserver: a passion for beauty. Two and three times a week she responded to Carman's lively letters and commented on his obscure poems.

Rare moments of drama, or farce, sometimes occurred. Once, Carman wreaked havoc by sending along a set of photographs (humiliating evidence of Gertrude's four-meals-a-day girth) to Burton, who was hosting his mother, Martha Jane, and his sister, Mary Agnes, instead of giving them to her brother William. When she discovered his disastrous mistake, she scolded,

> Heavens! Bliss Carman what shall I do with thee!!…I
> told thee or asked thee to please leave those photographs with
> my brother, and gave thee his address in Cambridge, and told
> thee I would send him an address that he might send the col-
> lection on its journey.…There was only one place on earth

that I positively did not want to have those photographs go. That place was 54 Waltham Street ! ! ! ! ! ! ! ! ! ! !

Before crushing thee to an impalpable jelly, however, I will be lenient enough to stop and ask if thou didst place them in my Burton's own hands? If they went directly from thy hands to his hands it is better, but it is still bad.

The simple state of the case is that Mrs. Burton Mother, and especially Miss Burton Sister, have long believed me to be a pious-fraud. From the very beginning I was distrusted and considered an amiable and extravagant exaggeration. Now—Matters are worse than ever: My Burton only makes my illness respectably serious by insisting that I am near death's door etc.—and I never even dared send him one of those photographs for fear of that Argus-eyed Sister. Even under lock & key those unsympathetic eyes would discover my super-abundant immensity! When my Burton saw the photographs here—he exclaimed again and again—"O Gertrude Whatever you do—don't ever allow those pictures to be seen in Waltham St! Whatever you do—don't, don't— allow them by any possible chance to reach My Mother and Sister!"

And Now, great Blissmagog thou—What hast thou done?! Thou hast undone everything—All the careful fabric of tactfully chosen words, all the softening of time and silence and absence and approaching death—all—all flung to the earth!—I am not only a fraud—but a MONSTROUS fraud! Ah me! Ah me! Poor me! Miserable Hugeness that I am!

During this period, Gertrude found common ground with her own mother through their interest in women's issues and political developments. Jane Hitz now shared an apartment at 1109 K Street, NW with Dr. Grace Roberts, a homeopathic physician born in Wales and trained at Howard University. Years before, they had founded the Homeopathic Free Dispensary together, with other Washington Moral Education Society women.

By the early 1890s the Moral Education Society had ceased publishing its national monthly newsletter, the *ALPHA*. The national purity movement, and with it, the Moral Education Society, shifted focus from idealistic social revolution to pragmatic political concerns. Women were gaining greater influence by joining forces with the Women's Christian Temperance Union, the Women's Education and Industrial Union, and the National Woman Suffrage Association. Jane Hitz continued to advocate for women's rights. In letters to Gertrude, she enclosed articles from Washington newspapers regarding efforts to liberalize divorce laws; raise the age of consent; promote voluntary motherhood, temperance, dress reform and employment for women; and press for the right to vote. Gertrude relied on her mother's bulletins to stay connected with the mission that had first inspired her. She was grateful to her mother for subscriptions to *Scribner's Magazine* and *The Century*. Through her mother's undertakings she glimpsed what her own life might have been, if illness had not forced her to the sidelines.

That spring, Gertrude also kept an eye on her father's accomplishments, as he occupied himself with completing plans for Bell's Egyptian-temple-inspired Volta Bureau for Research on the Deaf, under construction at the corner of Q and 34th Street, in Georgetown. Helen Keller turned the first shovelful of sod at the groundbreaking ceremony on May 9th, flanked by her teacher Anne Sullivan and her "foster father" John Hitz. Gertrude missed sharing his success. Her pride in her father's recovery since his imprisonment five years before was mixed with frustration over her own disappointments.

From afar, Gertrude also traced Mary Costelloe's and Bernhard Berenson's travels in Europe. Mary had sworn that she would never return to her husband. However, Frank would not consider a divorce, and demanded a separation agreement that limited Mary's visits with Ray and Karin. The document also prevented her from "interfering" with the girls' upbringing in the Catholic Church. This upset Mary and her Quaker mother deeply—not only because they rejected Catholicism, but also because English law so deliberately upheld Frank's parental rights and disregarded hers, as a wife and mother. But unlike Gertrude, Mary possessed health, confidence, and means. She was able to leave her children, practically and psychologically, and begin a new life with Berenson. Gertrude must have felt some mute pangs of jealousy, even as she cheered her friends' revolt against convention.

Gertrude and Burton continued to share responsibility for their children, but the heaviest emotional burdens weighed on Gertrude, because of her self-imposed, exacting standards for motherhood, stubborn desire for autonomy, and her illness. Burton was reticent by nature, and his side of the story remains a mystery—almost no letters survive. Once, decades later, when his son Harold achieved political success, his father sent him belated congratulations, confessing that "One of your dad's eccentricities is that when he is feeling the most about things, he never says much." Burton's friends and acquaintances, his Tech students, and young family members described him as thoughtful, imaginative, humorous, and gentle, but the relations between Burton and Gertrude, for long periods, and particularly during her time in the Adirondacks, remain a puzzle.

Gertrude kept close track of Carman who, after months in Washington, resigned his position at *The Independent* in New York City and returned to Boston with Richard Hovey. There they rejoined old friends from their Harvard days, now in their late twenties and early thirties. They formed a select literary set, calling themselves the Visionists. Among them were architects Ralph Adams Cram and Bertram Goodhue, photographer and art connoisseur F. Holland Day, publisher Herbert Copeland, photographer and printer Francis Watt Lee, and two female members or "frequent guests," the poets Alice Brown and Louise Imogen Guiney. Cram called Guiney "the most influential voice in the group."

The Visionists cultivated a relatively innocent decadence, laced with humor and rowdy comradeship. They explored mysticism, medieval arts and crafts, aestheticism, and esoteric rituals. In his exhaustive book, *Boston Bohemia: Ralph Adams Cram: Life and Architecture (Volume 1—1881-1900)*, author Douglas Shand-Tucci maintains that they were parlor-Bohemians, with "a light-hearted subtext of homosexuality and drugs."

In April, 1892 the Visionists founded a quarterly review they named *The Knight Errant*. They intended the journal as an aesthetic call to arms, an iconoclastic battle cry for idealism and imagination, a protest against Gilded Age materialism. They also envisioned *The Knight Errant* as a model of typography and the printer's art, enhanced by handmade paper, a beautiful font, and a supremely "decorative and symbolical" cover, inspired by the bookbinding imagination of William Morris.

The first edition's poem of salutation, Guiney's "Knight Errant" (Volume I, Number 1), proclaimed the crusading spirit of their post-Civil War generation and announced a credo of "men against an Epoch." They represented one phase in what Shand-Tucci calls "the progression from Pre-Raphaelitism to Aestheticism to Decadence to Modernism."

*The Knight Errant* conceived a contemporary Quest—in loyal service to Beauty—as a rescue mission to save American culture from the Gilded Age's "dragons of greed" and philistinism. The poem's errant (and sometimes, erring) knight values "a short life in the saddle" more than "a long one by the fire." Questing becomes ennobling and praiseworthy, and as important as attaining any ultimate goal: "The passion of perfection/ Redeem my faulty way."

*The Knight Errant's* October 1892 issue (Volume I, Number 3) included Bernhard Berenson's article, "Some Comments on Correggio in Connection with his Pictures in Dresden;" Ernest Fenellosa's contributions on Oriental Art; Cram's article, "On Ave Maria of Arcadelt," and other features; and Bliss Carman's sassy poem, "In the Wayland Willows:"

> Once I met a soncy maid,
> Soncy maid, soncy maid,
> Once I met a soncy maid
> In the Wayland willows.
>
> All her hair was goldy brown,
> Goldy brown, goldy brown,
> In the sun a single braid
> To her waist hung down.
>
> Honey bees, honey bees,
> You are roving fellows!
> Idly went the doxy wind
> In the Wayland willows.
>
> There I caught her eye a-dance,
> Through the catkins downy.
> "Heigho, Brownie-pate," said I;
> "Heigho," said my Brownie.
>
> Then I kissed my soncy maid,
> Soncy maid, soncy maid,
> Kissed and kissed my soncy maid
> In the Wayland willows.
>
> Goldy eyes and goldy hair,
> And little gypsy bosom,
> Chin and lip and shoulder tip,
> Blossom after blossom!

Hand in hand and cheek by cheek
All the morning weather!
How the yellow butterflies
Danced and winked together!

Till the day went down the hill
Where the shadows waded.
"Heigho, Soncy!" "Heigho, me!"
Then I did as day did.

All her tousled beauty bright
And teasing as before,
I left her there in sweet despair,
A soncy maid no more.

The Visionists' hideout was located at 3 Province Court, an alley around the corner from Cornhill, Boston's publishing district, in what Cram described as a "decadent, disreputable building mostly occupied by locksmiths, cobblers, and other modest practitioners of divers sorts of hand labor." Gertrude recognized the place from her early years in Boston. She wrote to Carman: "Province Court is well known to me. I know it all from its old Colonial history down to its present jumble of queerness, signs, & scrappiness. I have been in several of the houses & the Italian painter man is a familiar person to me." And she recalled "the Rat Hole...the subterranean passage at the end of Province Court that leads to Washington St..."

Once again, she pictured Carman in a city setting she knew from happier days. As she monitored his Boston life, Gertrude felt delight mixed with longing, just as she had when he was in Washington. She savored his descriptions of the Visionists' collective readings, impromptu musicals, and costume parties in their tapestried and pillowed den. Their third-floor, incense-scented, Oriental-carpeted retreat was decorated with images of the Egyptian goddess Isis. Gertrude could picture Cram's boarding house on Beacon Hill, too; The Bell in Hand, in Pi Alley, so like an eighteenth century London pub; and Marliave's "French" bistro, where the wine resembled red ink and diners smoked between courses. She imagined Carman and his friends in the friendly bars of the Parker House and Thorndike hotels.

From the Adirondacks, and with a sometimes skeptical eye, Gertrude appraised the Visionists' literary experiments and intellectual disputes. Questing was not men's privilege alone. Louise Imogen Guiney, Mary Smith Costelloe, and Gertrude Hitz Burton envisioned women, too, as intrepid combatants for Beauty. They shared, in part, the men's Pre-Raphaelite sympathies for bygone times, yet also envisioned a new, egalitarian social order, though Gertrude now had to observe society's changes from the margins.

Over the winter months, Gertrude focused on liberating herself from the dead and dying who haunted the St. Bernard cure cottage. Three young men had breathed their last in the downstairs front room she had left behind when she moved upstairs. She called it the "Death Chamber." To make matters worse, in January her landlord overcharged her for rent. Although she remained under Dr. Trudeau's care, she wanted to move as far as possible from Saranac Lake's gloom, and hoped to find lodgings spacious enough to invite her family and summer visitors: her mother, brother William, and several close friends—Senda Berenson, the Kappelers, and Bliss Carman—especially Carman.

Gertrude's prolonged search turned up a five-room farmhouse with a large front porch in the village of North Elba, near the neighboring town of Lake Placid. Although the house was not beautiful, it was clean, run by "the most obliging man on the face of the globe, with the exception of my father," and staffed by a young housekeeper–cook. The house's exterior, painted a vivid green, was a drawback at first, but later Gertrude and Harold came to appreciate its vibrant hue. They christened their new home "Greenery Green" and completed the move on April 3rd. The new house symbolized renewed life and energy.

William spent Harvard's spring break there with his sister, and Jane Hitz visited for two weeks in early June. Carman was invited for the summer, an extended holiday that turned out to be his final visit with Gertrude. Berenson's sister Senda, who had completed her Normal School of Gymnastics studies and become director of the Gymnasium and Instructor of Physical Culture at Smith College, came for a while in August.

Mrs. Kappeler was unable to come away, but Jessie Kappeler arrived, alone, for the entire month of August. Gertrude arranged a group portrait, including herself, Senda, Carman, and Jessie. Her growing bulk—lamented in the "matter of the photographs"—distinguished her from her slim, stylish friends. Yet she treasured the photo as a memento of summer 1893, when she regained a sense of belonging in the world.

Carman arrived in June and stayed until late August, living on the property in a separate small cottage, with a mountain view framed by yellow curtains ("as dainty as a girl"). His flirtatious affair with Jessie Kappeler, begun the preceding fall in Washington, blossomed. Jessie's fresh beauty inspired verses about moonbeams and sea foam, flowers and hills. She became "Seaborn" to his "Hillborn." To judge from the final stanza of one of these poems, later published as XLIII in Carman's collection *Songs of the Sea Children*, Jessie's green eyes and chestnut hair stirred in him more than purely aesthetic desires:

> ......
> Berrybrown, Berrybrown, give me your mouth,
> Till all is done 'twixt a breath and a breath!
> Naught shall undo the one joy-deed forever,
> God made desire before He made death.

By summer's end their obvious infatuation had frayed Carman's friendship with Gertrude, who no doubt felt a twinge of possessiveness, along with amazement. Although she had long loved Mrs. Kappeler and her children, Gertrude expressed sincere doubts that Jessie could prove a true intellectual and spiritual companion for Carman. She chided Carman for his naïve poetic portrayals of women: his Romantic ideals and sensibilities collided with her deeply held convictions. She deplored his blindness to the trials of contemporary heroines and accused his verses of worshipping Beauty to the point of ignoring women's continual struggles against society's unjust norms:

> The Norns and witches help thee! Another emotional creature with a mysterious tragedy, I imagine. Thy [poems'] women are all hearts with poetical labels. They are neither intellectual nor self-sustaining. Feudal creatures all....I must send thee [John Stuart] Mill's *Subjection of Women*. Thou art a feeble singer of womankind until thou canst realize more forcibly the crushing yoke which chains their minds to traditions & weakness. (This is serious, Blissmugog!)

Gertrude had first begun to sense Carman's fascination with Jessie in January.

> O Bliss, dear heart—... Didst know, I never really thought thy heart or imagination or sensibilities or whatever part of thee it is that yields to infatuation—I never really thought that child's laughter had reached thee—Thee—Thee—the real personal thee that quivers & asks and suffers! Blisskin, I fear I have not understood thee, and I am sorry. I shall let it all rest until I see thee. Here I have been thinking I would like

to have you two children here in the June weather—& watch your frolic like a dear old sympathetic grandmother that I am—& now—now—I must see thee—wait and see thee to understand. (January 17, 1893)

Near the end of the Adirondack idyll, Gertrude tried to explain her opposition to Carman's notion of marrying Jessie, comparing her own experience of passionate love, with what she knew of Jessie's feelings:

> … It is natural that you should hold your view and I mine, but I found an explanation which for the moment, certainly, satisfies me.
>
> I who know what passionate love is, would be unwilling to marry anyone without such love. The child who does not know by experience what such love is, thinks her love sufficient, but <u>different</u> from thine. She is, therefore, true to thee in giving thee as much as she can and knows. When with me, she describes her love as she feels it—and I interpret it in a different way…Her youth and inexperience excuse all things. She is willing to marry with a milder love than I would be, and having said this I have said all….(August 22, 1893)

Gertrude must have been dismayed to find herself, again, a third party in a romantic relationship between two of her closest friends, just as she had with Mary and Bernhard. Though she agonized over the situation, she nevertheless told Carman that she felt nearer to him than ever, "because I have never touched thee at so vital a point." She was moved, she said, by the "sense of intimate comradeship" their talks had created, and felt tenderness at "having seen thee as thou art, of appreciating thy suffering, and the real beauty and humility of thy spirit." Their honest speaking had touched "the core of things," and outweighed her distress. She may have been jealous, but she did not want to lose his friendship.

Predictably, Mrs. Kappeler forbade an engagement. Her own early marriage had proven disastrous, and her experience as a single mother, struggling to support two children, led her to reject the penniless poet as a serious suitor for her beautiful young daughter. After two further tension-filled years, the mother eventually prevailed. Jessie, wooed by a beau her own age, finally terminated the affair in 1895.

Meanwhile, Gertrude's and Carman's long-distance friendship survived. Through their continuing correspondence she overcame her disappointment and salvaged the situation. She commiserated with his frustrations, scolded and cheered him, and reviewed his work. They debated poetry and art and laughed at each other's jokes. She shared stories and poems of her own, asking for his expert advice. They celebrated his numerous publishing successes, beginning in 1893 with the appearance of his collection, *Low Tide on Grand Pré*, and continuing in 1894 with the popular triumph of *Songs from Vagabondia*, his collaboration with Richard Hovey and designer Thomas Meteyard.

During the summer of 1893, Burton arranged for his MIT surveying course to meet in the Adirondacks, near Keeseville, New York, about thirty miles from Lake Placid. He visited on weekends, and when the program ended, he moved to Greenery Green, uniting the family again. In early September, he returned to Boston with Arnold. Now eight, the boy was still among the Allen School's youngest boarders, and received special attention from his teacher, Miss Sarah Allen, daughter of the school's founder, who sent regular reports to Gertrude. Burton visited frequently and took him on occasional out-ings, while his mother wrote cheery letters and filled packages with small gifts.

At Greenery Green, finding a nursemaid for Harold became urgent: Eugenie had taken ill again after Christmas and returned to Switzerland. During the spring and summer months, Gertrude searched for a governess. Finally, in October, she hired Helen King Spofford. Miss Spofford was four years older than Gertrude, the daughter of a prominent physician in Groveland, Massachusetts, and distantly related both to both Richard Hovey's mother, Harriette Spofford Hovey, and the Librarian of Congress, Ainsworth Rand Spofford. Helen had graduated from the Robinson Female Seminary in Exeter, New Hampshire in 1879. When she was nineteen, her father died, and she began supporting herself and her mother as a teacher. She published poems and children's stories in *St. Nicholas Magazine*. Miss Spofford proved an imaginative, loyal, and dependable companion to Gertrude and, after initial problems, showed that she was equal to the challenge of caring for Harold, a strong-willed five-year-old.

By Gertrude's second Thanksgiving in the wilderness, life had become both tedious and aggravating. She felt increasingly restless. Her own health, and both sons' wellbeing, worried her. Sarah Allen reported on Arnold's serious bout with whooping cough. At Greenery Green, Harold's spills, fevers, measles, and dog bites required constant vigilance. The unrelenting demands of running a household on a strict budget overwhelmed Gertrude, who was coming to regard her experience in the Adirondacks "as a dismal dream." She began plotting her escape.

# CHAPTER 17

## *A Grant of Days*

RUTTED, MUDDY ROADS AND UNUSUALLY WET FALL WEATHER TRAPPED Gertrude in sleepy North Elba. After a joyous green spring, a rejuvenating summer, and a second colorful autumn, she was now beset with one demand after another: solving housekeeping crises, planning meals, managing wood stoves, and supervising Miss Spofford, as well as tending to Harold's toothaches and Arnold's West Newton mumps. She discovered that Mr. Morse, her untrustworthy landlord at the St. Bernard, was again overcharging to stable her horse. Worst of all, she suffered an attack of shingles, which the local doctor diagnosed dismissively as "erosis"—a neurotic condition, or, as he condescendingly explained, "rheumatic, if you choose to call it so," implying that the agonizing sensitivity to touch and painful blisters, all on her right side, were only in her mind.

Desperate "to be in the world again," she wrestled with her anxieties. Death was always with her. Trying to discern light at the end of this long, dark "Rat Hole," she reasoned she had energy enough for one more journey. Gertrude carefully constructed a case for leaving the northern forest, since she would have to depend on Jane Hitz's generosity to cover rent and apothecary bills, clothing and travel expenses. In a letter, she explained to her mother that Dr. Trudeau "has expressed himself very definitely to Mr. Burton that I have gained all benefits possible under his care," and she enclosed Dr. Trudeau's professional assessment:

Saranac Lake N.Y. February 23. 94

Mrs. Burton has suffered from pulmonary phthisis since 1892. The onset of the disease was violent and the involvement of both lungs considerable when I first saw her in the fall of 1892. There was softening of one apex, I think the left, and a small cavity has since developed there. She has had abundant bacilli in the expectoration throughout her whole illness. The improvement during the first winter spent here was very marked. She gained in weight, lost her fever, except at rare intervals, and the moist sounds in the lungs diminished.

Of late the disease has again been active and she has shown considerable circulatory disturbance with impaired peripheral circulation. I have advised, as the neurasthenic element in her is very marked, that she make a change of climate, but I fear too high an elevation would overtax the already impaired heart power and have advised a moderate altitude only.

E. L. Trudeau, M.D.

Jane Hitz was skeptical. She suspected the plan to abandon the Adirondack sanatorium was a fantasy (and an expensive one), concocted by her daughter and abetted by Dr. Trudeau. While the doctor encouraged a move to California, where outdoor life would be beneficial for circulation and nerves, he warranted that Switzerland might be better for her lungs—if she did not try to settle at too high an altitude. Gertrude argued passionately for Switzerland. She assured her mother that either Mr. Burton or her father would accompany her there, with Harold; Arnold would remain at the Allen School; and Miss Spofford, elated at an opportunity for foreign travel, had agreed to go along "at very reduced wages."

❧

John Hitz proved a willing accomplice, eager to revisit his homeland and enthusiastic about spending time there with his daughter. The two began researching healthful mountain retreats. He sent her a brochure describing Les Avants, located above the town of Montreux on Lake Geneva, not far from the village of Chernex, a beloved vacation spot when the family lived in Lausanne. Gertrude mailed him a pamphlet describing the new Grand Hotel at Leysin, a luxury treatment facility above the nearby village of Aigle. The Grand Hotel was situated on a south-facing terrace overlooking the Rhone valley, with a view of the majestic peaks of the Dents du Midi. Though situated 4000 feet above sea level, an altitude greater than Dr. Trudeau recommended, the Hotel was exactly the kind of well-appointed establishment Gertrude yearned for.

By mid-February Gertrude wrote Bliss Carman that because of her physical condition she was determined to sail for Switzerland sometime in early summer, explaining that, "The lung trouble, though worse, is not enough in itself to account for my loss of strength and quickness of breath. The heart power is impaired and the nervous system is weakened..."

In April she again shared her heightened sense of mortality, of leave-taking from normal life: "I have heard some bird notes and they have touched me as never before. It is these northern winters which make the heart so sensitive to the miracle of Spring....I have grown to look at all things from "the other side"—my life is so truly like an after-life—a looking on—a watching—a grant of days beyond the end—and O so infinitely precious and sweet and solemn!"

Perhaps she guessed she might never return to America.

In contrast to her intimate tone in correspondence with Carman, Gertrude's letters to her mother revealed her embarrassment about requesting money for household expenses and medical bills. Jane Hitz considered Gertrude to be her father's daughter when it came to finances, and while she usually responded to direct appeals, she rarely offered favors. During her illness, Gertrude had become largely dependent on her mother's financial support—a cruel irony, after embracing her mother's model of independence in matters of marriage, motherhood, and career. As a supplicant, she felt genuinely apprehensive: she was frightened of offending. In one letter to her mother she apologized for "anything I might have expressed unsatisfactorily."

Gertrude had already sold her horse at a disadvantage to pay outstanding debts. By early April, recovering from the misery of shingles and hoping to leave the country the following month, she asked for an advance of $300 to cover expected travel expenses and accumulated doctors' bills, in lieu of her mother's monthly allowance checks of $100 for June, July and August.

She prepared an itemized list of necessities, as of April first: expenses for rent and hired help, and bills at the druggist's, the butcher's, and the dressmaker's (for Arnold and Harold). Miss Spofford provided an inventory of household needs and clothes for Harold: stockings, sailor suit, heavy coat, jacket, extra trousers, caps, and flannel for blouses. Gertrude also listed a shawl, underclothes and gloves as necessities for herself. All these expenses totaled $217.16.

With trepidation, Gertrude dared to add, "Of course, my clothes are in pretty poor condition, but I have grown used to this....I need a night wrapper very much to wear in bed—something of light woolen material and very light gray." She also requested material for a new dress, and velvet for her bonnet. She was grateful when her mother's check arrived a week later. Even so, Gertrude required another $200 to cover expenses through their departure, planned for the 12th of May. In late April, Jane Hitz paid a final visit to her daughter at Greenery Green.

John Hitz arranged for staterooms for Gertrude, himself, Harold, and Miss Spofford on the steamer *SS Amsterdam*. He also settled Gertrude's passport application and money matters so they could secure cash on drafts from banks in Paris, Lausanne, and, for his return trip, England. Before they left, his duties at the Volta Bureau and services to the Bell family filled his time. In March Hitz undertook a ten-day trip south to Tuscumbia, Alabama, to visit Helen Keller's family.

During the winter and early spring, Hitz frequently visited the Kappeler house, and where he enjoyed conversations with Bliss Carman, temporarily back in the capital, and at that time still pursuing Jessie Kappeler.

By late April 1894, Carman had found yet another job in Boston, as editor of a new biweekly literary magazine, *The Chap-Book*, one of the "little magazines" of the 1890s, issued by Stone and Kimball, a "kid" publishing house run by Harvard students Herbert Stuart Stone and Ingalls Kimball. Thus, Carman would be unable to see Gertrude's party off in New York. In any case, Gertrude made it clear she preferred avoiding painful goodbyes, writing him on May 3rd, "It is just as well that thou art not in New York, dear Bliss, as far as the sailing goes. I have decided it is wiser to see no one and to avoid all farewells. Perhaps I shall see thee in Switzerland? Ah! There is a hope…"

Despite the distance, she trusted they would remain close, "And when I am away—really across the sea again—do take pity on me and write to me often—charitable little postal cards if the letters do not come easily—dear Bliss—for I am indeed thy comrade ever…."

For Carman, too, their exchanges were profoundly important. He saved her letters and deeply admired her writing:

> My dear Gertrude: The long letter in pencil was a very welcome one. What a thing it is to command words. A chief delight in thy letters is the quality of them—the evident craftsman's delight in English for its own sweet sake.
>
> …Do you know that in your letters you have shown the master hand? Tons of books are put forth every year, incomparably poorer than this accurate sweet prose of yours. It is all a very precious possession, and I often wish I could gather all the…immortal lines into a handful of paper, a sort of private single book for my own selfish delight. Because it is so rare a thing to see anything like perfect expression; and these letters are so sheer a veil of the spirit behind them.

Although Gertrude had encountered Carman rather seldom in person, Burton met him often in Boston. The two men developed a friendly relationship. In the weeks before Gertrude sailed, Carman recounted that "Burton and I had such a funny experience on Sunday morning. He will tell you about it. We sat in different rooms at the Thorndike Hotel for half an hour, waiting for each other. However, we had breakfast together finally." And a week later, "Last night I had an hour [with Burton] at 60 West Newton St. Wish I could go to New York. Think of me in your quiet hours, in that serene white seclusion which often seems as alluring to me as this turmoil of activity does to you."

Just before she sailed, Carman wrote a final farewell:

> ... Last night I saw Burton and had a very delightful evening. We talked and smoked. I asked him to "tell you" good bye.
>
> Think of me as the steamer makes out to sea and the strong sea-winds make in. There are no words, yet very many long thoughts and wishes. I shall have a letter for you in Switzerland soon, dear Gertrude, and—some pens! Also, I shall have a copy of our first *Chap-Book*. I am working hard on it now.
>
> So fare well, and a high heart be with thee forever.

On the day before they sailed, John Hitz found Gertrude in Hoboken, New Jersey, comfortably settled at the Swiss-owned Naegli's Hotel, on the bustling corner of Hudson and Third Street. By 10:30 the next morning, the travelers' baggage was in place on the *SS Amsterdam*. Burton arrived, and Harold and Miss Spofford boarded the ship while father, daughter, and husband lunched together at a nearby café. Afterwards, Gertrude mailed a letter to her mother exclaiming how glad she was to be in the world again. She could not refrain from writing a postscript on the back of the envelope: "A Most Beautiful Day! May 12th."

⁂

Gertrude scanned familiar slopes and buildings as the steamer passed out of New York harbor: Governor's Island, with its antique circular fort; Liberty Island's famous welcoming statue; Ellis Island's huge new immigration station; and the upper anchorage crowded with vessels from all over the world. Brilliant sunshine and a soft breeze. As the ship sailed on, she anticipated the mournful drone of the Robbins Reef bell buoy at Arrochar, at the tip of Staten Island. She strained to hear "the lonely, hopeless calling of the bell buoy on the bar," conjured in Carman's poem "Pulvis et Umbra," written during the summer he had lived nearby. However, in a letter to him she described the buoy's mute farewell that day, and her own silent hope:

> It was such a dim, half visionary thing, and it seemed to me that the sound that must come would indeed be the speech of some fateful spirit. I listened and listened, and waited with the swaying waters between us, but absolutely nothing could be heard. The silence, the restraint of that mournful note seemed to me a wonderful and sweet farewell. For this once, there shall be no sigh, no disquiet, no foreboding. The spirit doomed to speak in sadness closed her lips and let me pass under the benediction of hopeful calm.
>
> … Was it not—going out across the silence of the sea— to ask for strength, to beg for grace, that the long last Silence might not envelop me, that the dear sweet earthly life might still linger for a few precious years? Are these not the thoughts which grace the depths too deep for words? Blessed bell of Arrochar!

Portrait of Bliss Carman, 1889

A.E. Burton sketch, Vallombrosa, Italy 1892

Maine General Hospital

Harold and Arnold Burton with Mary's daughters, Ray and Karin Costelloe, 1892

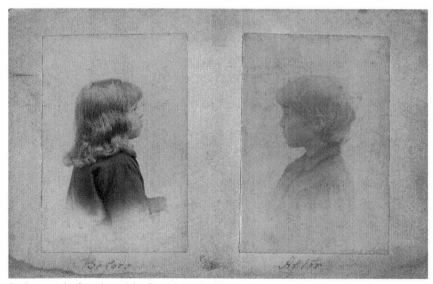

Before and after Arnold's first short haircut

The St. Bernard cure cottage, Saranac Lake, New York (courtesy of the Adirondack Collection, Saranac Free Library, 81 304D 015)

Gertrude's "Miserable Hugeness," 1892

Studio portrait of Gertrude with Senda Berenson (also seated), Bliss Carman, and Jessie Kappeler, Greenery Green, 1893

*The Knight Errant*, Volume One, Number One, April 1892
(courtesy of JSTOR)

# PART III

*The passion of perfection/Redeem my faulty way!*

# CHAPTER 18

## *A Sea of White Clouds*

THE CROSSING, AGAINST STRONG HEAD WINDS, PROVED LONGER THAN
usual. The *SS Amsterdam* took twelve days to reach the coast of
France. One evening, there was dancing to music by a fiddler invited
up from steerage. Another day, a thousand miles out from New York,
an iceberg 60 feet high and 150 feet long passed about one mile to the
south of the steamer, chilling the afternoon air. After high seas and
wet surfaces in the voyage's early days, the weather calmed, and Gertrude was able to spend time in her deck chair from morning to night.
Unlike the others—Harold, Miss Spofford, and even her father—she
suffered no seasickness.

The four disembarked at Boulogne-Sur-Mer about eight a.m.
on May 24th, and reached Paris by dinnertime, on the afternoon
express train. Gertrude sent a postal card to her mother declaring
she was happy to reach land and only a little fatigued. They found
suitable rooms at the Hotel Boston, on Rue Louis le Grand, just steps
from the Place de l'Opera. There, Gertrude was confined to bed
while six-year-old Harold and Miss Spofford took in the Louvre and
other essential Parisian sites, and Hitz attended to shopping and settling practical matters at the bank. After a few days, they continued
by train to Lausanne, where they were enthusiastically received by old
friends. After some weeks' rest at the Pension Clement on the rue du
Grand Chêne, they set out in early July to interview doctors at Weissenburg Bad, a well-reputed watering hole catering to the European
elite, about sixty miles away.

To reach Weissenburg they rode trains via Bern to Thun. An
exhausting carriage ride followed, on narrow, steep, winding roads
through the mountainous terrain surrounding the Simmental valley.

The New Bath Hotel was set amid picturesque woodland paths and fern-bordered streams, and surrounded by steep rocky precipices. It was a large, stylish three-story facility with a glassed-in veranda running the length of the façade. John Hitz was surprised to discover that their destination was situated in what he called a "perfect chasm," and declared, "It could not even be called a gorge." Hitz, Harold, and Miss Spofford found less expensive lodgings higher on the slopes of the deep ravine. Gertrude's father spent days hiking nearby trails, sometimes twenty miles in a day, stopping for a drink of fresh milk offered by farmers or cowherds. In September he would be sixty-seven.

Gertrude was examined by Dr. Gustav Huguenin, a neurological specialist, on arrival and periodically during her five-week stay. He observed that "it was a very serious case," but assured her he could afford relief. A Dr. H. Enderlin concurred that "the danger period was over...but it would be a long and slow process needing care." However, Gertrude felt no real relief. Her energy ebbed and flowed, and soon she grew weary of the mineral baths. She decided to move on to the appealing alternative option, sight unseen: the new sanatorium in Leysin euphemistically named The Grand Hotel.

The four left the Weissenburg valley for Lausanne on July 26th and returned to the Pension Clement. There they attended to practical details: watch-buying, shoe repair, and sundry purchases. On the 28th, with great anticipation, the party set out by train, following the picturesque shores of Lake Geneva, then along the Rhone Valley to Aigle, where lush vineyards surrounded a twelfth-century castle. From Aigle, Gertrude, Miss Spofford, and Harold engaged a two-horse team to drive them up the steep roads leading to the tiny village of Leysin. Their trunks were taken up by a large stagecoach known as a *diligence*. John Hitz walked up the rocky footpaths in two hours, taking a boy along as a guide, and arrived at their destination an hour before the carriage.

About a hundred families inhabited the village of Leysin in the quaint, rather spacious chalets lining the main street, from which several lanes ran perpendicularly farther up the slopes. Most of the local landowners were prosperous, cultivating productive vineyards on the plains of Aigle and Yvornes below, and maintaining extensive pastures for farm animals, principally cows and goats. When Gertrude and the others reached Leysin, Mademoiselle E. Cullaz accommodated them at her Pension du Chalet, the only public inn. After their strenuous travels, Gertrude rested quietly for a day or two, grateful for the Chalet's comfortable furniture, rugs, good beds, and efficient heating system.

The physicians and hoteliers of the Swiss Société Climatérique had established the Grand Hotel just two years earlier, in 1892. They chose to locate their first sanatorium for tuberculosis sufferers at Fedey-sur-Leysin, a still smaller settlement perched on a sunny plateau above Leysin village, where mists and clouds were less common. The sanatorium's developers, Dr. Charles Secretan and hotelier Monsieur Chessex from Montreux, pronounced it an ideal site: the grand setting would attract an affluent clientele, and the invalids would live far enough away from the village to allay local inhabitants' fears.

The gracious five-story Hotel commanded the highest spot above the village, facing south, opposite the molar-like peaks of the Dents du Midi. The Hotel's exterior was freshly stuccoed in white, with green-shuttered windows and awning-shaded balconies for each room. Shortly before Gertrude's arrival, the Hotel had been expanded to accommodate a growing clientele. A separate pavilion was being constructed for guests with contagious diseases, such as scarlet fever. Several nearby villas, named Beau-Site, Soldanelle, Edelweiss, and Paquerette, provided private accommodations. Two years after this, the steadily increasing demand prompted the Société Climatérique to open a second luxury hotel for invalids, the Mont Blanc, on the hillside slightly below the Grand Hotel.

Gertrude's rooms, numbers 96 and 97, were located in the southeast front corner of the Hotel's uppermost floor. Large windows and a balcony afforded panoramic vistas to the east and south. The majestic mountain views reinforced her relief at escaping Weissenburg's dark, narrow chasm.

Downstairs, the grand salon, or winter garden, resembled a palm court, with huge potted palms and marble pillars surrounded by circular banquettes upholstered in tufted leather. Graceful groupings of tables, chairs, and sofas scattered about the parquet floor invited card parties, tea, and conversation. The elaborately carved woodwork was painted white and gold. A large oval mirror hung over the sumptuously decorated mantelpiece. From the ceiling hung Art Nouveau chandeliers, whose petal-like shades camouflaged the electric bulbs that illuminated the tastefully opulent room.

Double French doors opened from the salon to numerous corridors. One led through the large dining room to the building's main entrée with its grand marble staircase. From there, using the strength of his arms, a muscular *liftier* transported guests and their belongings to the upper floors in a cable elevator. Such luxury would have been unthinkable in America, but the basic cost in Swiss francs, covered largely by Jane Hitz's assets, was reasonable. Accommodation for Gertrude, Harold, and Miss Spofford cost twenty-three francs a day, excluding heat or the services of a special nurse.

In Weissenburg, Gertrude had asked her father to see her through to Leysin, although John Hitz had planned to return earlier. She seemed pleased, though wearied, finally to have arrived at her destination. Hitz felt sure she would be well cared for. On July 31st he prepared to travel first to Bern and then London, having secured a berth on the *SS Madura* to Halifax, Nova Scotia, where he would join Alexander Graham Bell's family at their summer home in Baddeck.

The evening before he left, Hitz recorded that father and daughter "talked considerable together about things near to our hearts, in a becoming manner." The following day, when he came to say goodbye, Gertrude was sitting on her balcony, "not so bright as usual, but content." There she delivered the unexpected news that Burton would soon travel to Hamburg, and then visit her in Leysin. That afternoon, Hitz left by stagecoach. He wrote in his diary, "Saying goodbye most hard to do…waved handkerchiefs to each other as far as the stage could be seen from her balcony."

In mid-July, Burton had received an unexpected request from the Boston law firm of Shattuck and Munroe, which represented the owners of estates on the northerly side of Beacon Street in the Back Bay. Boston developers wanted to determine whether the estuary of the Charles River could be transformed into a safe, beneficial fresh water basin by means similar to Hamburg's Alter River dredging project. They proposed that Burton travel to Germany to find out more. For this professional service they offered him a ticket and the sum of $300. Burton jumped at the opportunity and booked passage a week later, on the *SS Rhaetia,* leaving July 21st. When he completed his official duties, he planned to stop at several other cities and then visit Gertrude and Harold in their new surroundings.

After a month's tour of Hamburg, Berlin, Dresden, Munich, Landau, and Zurich, Burton arrived in Leysin at the beginning of September, and put up at the Pension du Chalet. Both Gertrude and he were pleased with the Grand Hotel's new physician, Dr. Burnier, who, like all her previous doctors, assured them she would benefit from his care. Gertrude recommended treatments with accustomed medications, including a strong, distasteful mixture of creosote and whiskey. But, she noted dryly in a letter, "in much smaller doses than on the other side of the Alps." Burton remained for a week, then was called away earlier than expected, on September 10, and sailed home from Antwerp on September 15th.

❧

After her husband's departure, Gertrude sent him a set of ten photographs capturing the spectacular scenery of her "Magic Mountain" world, and cataloguing the Grand Hotel's inhabitants. The candid shots were snapped by the Comte de Forestier, with whom Burton had made an excursion to the nearby peaks of the Tour d'Ai during his visit. The Comte's young son, Jacques, and one of Dr. Burnier's sons had become Harold's playmates. Forestier also photographed this gang of boys running down the low-slung roof of a chalet and hanging off the railing of the hotel's lower veranda.

Gertrude explained the photos of the hotel, village and surrounding peaks. One pictured

> ... a portion of the view directly in front of the hotel (at 1540 meters), and the sea of clouds which frequently covers the Valley of the Rhone; as shown in the picture it is at about one-half the height of the mountains that rise above it. The highest Mt, whose broad summit is broken into many small peaks, in the center of the picture, is the famous Dents du Midi—the whole range shown in the photograph is covered with a deep cape of snow. It is between the Dents du Midi and the next peak toward the left, that one of the summits of Mont Blanc can be seen. The young trees at the extreme right are on the edge of the hotel terrace.

Gertrude delighted in observing the Grand Hotel's European clientele, mostly French-speaking, as if casting them in a play or imagining them in a novel, predating Thomas Mann's classic saga. Some were grouped in an impromptu photo as they picnicked in one of the Hotel's sun galleries. She annotated the image:

Beginning on the right—

Robert de Cultures, here for his health

The young Viscount of Mousilly—his mother American, deliciously garrulous about all her private affairs at *table d'hôte*. The Viscount's father supposedly dead. The Viscount himself has charming manners (also a new astrakhan-lined coat—newly purchased, which the doctor won't let him wear). Said to be entirely cured. He is not yet twenty-one and carried on a violent flirtation with

Mademoiselle de Cultures, the young girl at his side, sister of Robert. Mademoiselle has now been removed to a Parisian convent

Monsieur Peticari (?), French Jew, an invalid

Mr. Alfred Mowat—nearly cured—very polite, not inclined to frivolity, worthy young man!

A young Frenchman whose name we don't know…in outward manners inoffensive.

Madame de Cultures, very vivacious, supposedly a widow, mother of the flirtatious young girl and of Robert, and the most escorted woman of the hotel.

Madame Peticari Beautiful hair and complexion, better profile than full face, always dresses in black, is very graceful, but the impression of her personality is not altogether agreeable.

An invalid no longer here, and whose name we have forgotten…

And finally,

Jacques de Forestier

Harold Burton

Mademoiselle Cecile Reinbold, ex-governess to Jacques, very kind to Harold

The Grand Hotel, its guests, and its sublime, sunny setting contrasted starkly with Gertrude's nightmarish Adirondack experience.

Before she became ill, she said, she had never imagined so solitary a life as she had found there, in the northern wilderness, with only small comforts, and surrounded by the dying, cheated by her landlord, and saddled with enormous responsibilities. Finally, she had reached the transcendent "white" place she had imagined as a girl. She was grateful every day for the crystalline air, the vast mountain silences, and the sea of clouds ebbing and flowing beneath her balcony.

## CHAPTER 19

# *The Triumph of Nothing*

GERTRUDE DEVISED ELABORATE CELEBRATIONS FOR BIRTHDAYS, whether the children's or George Washington's, using whatever materials came to hand—a paper doily purloined from a dessert plate, magazine illustrations, ribbons, wildflowers. Holidays and other noteworthy dates became formal occasions. She became skilled at creating festive invitations, party favors, costumes, and eats from "nothing."

At the Grand Hotel, Gertrude's spirits remained high, even though her purse was empty. In October 1894, she devised an event to commemorate Helen Spofford's birthday, on the 15th. She combined the birthday festivities with the one-year anniversary of Miss Spofford's arrival at Greenery Green and, belatedly, with St. Helen's feast day, August 18th. The elaborate ceremony—almost a masque—celebrated Womanhood's powers and paradoxes, honoring the beauty of women's souls, satirizing their foibles, and applauding their impact on mankind's moral development. She called her allegorical entertainment *The Triumph of Nothing.* The script and props revealed Gertrude's theatrical imagination, ironic sense of humor, ideological commitments, and awareness of current trends—as well as her limited financial resources.

The imaginary spectacle began with *The Announcement,* penned in Gertrude's best script on creamy paper, slipped into a matching envelope:

### The Announcement

"How shall it be done? Shall I indeed lay aside my cherished plan—the dream of many months? Shall I discipline myself as far as this? Not spend a centime for this anniversary?"—"Yes, even this," whispers Economy, "even this shall be required of you." "But how?" I answer, where are my materials?—"Ah, be of good cheer, says a firm, decided voice, I am Necessity and I will send you my daughter."

Scarcely are the words uttered when Invention herself appears with eager and fearless gaze.—"Mother, dear!" she exclaims. "I really must have a companion for this undertaking, and you know whom I like best."—"An excellent idea, my child, of course, of course that precious friend of yours has been at Mrs. Woodbury's (*note 1) almost constantly, and may be spared a few days, especially for this particular occasion."

And so it is that bright-eyed Humor comes, trippingly and free, "Gladly, oh gladly will I help," she cries: "What shall it be?"

Then the stern old mother smiled. "What must it be my pretty one? What does custom ordain? Is it not first a bouquet, then a cake? Are not these the two columns of convention upon which all further elaboration is sustained? Yes, a bouquet and a cake there must be, but since you are witches both—both partake of the magician's temperament—let me suggest that the flowers of this bouquet be immortal and that they be plucked by a friendly hand, and that both Switzerland and America unite for its perfection. As for the cake, let it be simple and chaste—not too sweet, nor too soft—let it have some "snap."—

"But other gifts," exclaims the daughter, "where shall we find them?"—

"That is for you to discover my child; but I impose three conditions. One gift must relate to the physical side of life; the second must relate to the sentiments, or emotional nature, while the third must touch the region of the infinite progres-

sion—must relate to the spiritual."
What happened? Look and see.—

### The Bouquet

Inside another envelope, pressed between two sheets of writing paper and protected by a square of white shirt cardboard, rests *The Bouquet*—a spray of seven white edelweiss, tied with delicate white silk cords, which in an earlier incarnation may have adorned an undergarment, or nightgown.

### The Cake

A tiny *Cake* nestles inside a dainty round container, only 2 ¾ inches in diameter, its sides and snug top tinted a lovely lavender, wreathed with dainty purple blossoms and delicate golden leaves. Handwritten in the center of the circular lid: *"De La Grande Confiserie de Leysin, Cinquieme Avenue 97, Feydey* (alluding to Miss Spofford's room number, 97, on the fifth floor). Inside, the miniature box is lined with a tiny, lacey doily, upon which rests a chaste yet spicy ginger snap, cushioned in soft white cotton. Encircling the cookie, faded and almost invisible over a century later, is a sugary, leafy border. And inside the border, so faint as to be easily missed on first glance, is written the name *Helen*, surmounted by a tiny *fleur-de-lis*—the lily, a symbol of purity and the "Art for Art's Sake" emblem of the Aesthetic Movement.

❧

Invention and Humor devised other gifts to fulfill Mother Necessity's three conditions: first, "relating to the temporal," a small handmade pouch of white linen, embroidered with another *fleur-de-lis* in miniscule white stitches, and threaded through with a rather coarse linen drawstring. Next, "relating to the sentiments," a tiny box carefully wrapped in paper, with the words *Concerns the Affections and Explains Itself* written on the top. And third, "relating to the spiritual," a larger, flat, square *Gift*.

*Relating to the Temporal*

A tiny envelope contains a message *Relating to the Temporal*—*or Material*. It accompanies the small linen bag and is written in lightly penciled script, best read with a magnifying glass:

"Know you not the scraps of linen and the hempen string?"

"But why transformed for me," you ask, "with in-wrought fleurs-de-lis?"

"Why?! Oh, questioning mortal, these are money bags!! They come to you with sweet anticipation; they are drawn to you by the subtle laws of possible chance. Do you not remember the prudence of Mrs. Toodles (*note 2), dear Mrs. Toodles of fame dramatic—she was very fond of attending auction sales and made it an invariable practice to buy something on every occasion. But once, she surpassed herself, and returning, confided her ingenious investment—outwitting, perhaps, the very secrets of Fate. "Do you know, she cried, I have bought a door-plate, a solid silver door-plate. It bears the name of Smith—think of it, the name of Smith. It suddenly flashed upon me—if we should be blessed with offspring, if we should have a daughter, if she should marry a Mr. Smith, how singularly appropriate! It must be an inspiration!"

—And if door-plates, why not money-bags?

"The socialists may be nearer victory than we know, some utterly unknown relative may leave you a fortune (and no really unexpected fortune was expected before it came), or like the daughter unborn, you may have a Mr. Smith, a wealthy Mr. Smith shall be as your own. Await the propitious day! The bags will be ready for the overflow—that which cannot be clasped in purses—that which remains after all desires are satisfied!"

*Relating to the Sentiments*

The little box marked *Concerns the Affections, and Explains Itself* is neatly wrapped in cream colored paper. Within is a diminutive hinged box about 2 x 1 ¼ inches, its sides decorated in iridescent gold paper covered with dainty pink flowers. On the top is inscribed *Worth its weight in gold.* Inside, fluffy white cotton, top and bottom, surrounding a miniscule picture of a heart-shaped locket, cut from a magazine advertisement. The text reads, *Trilby's Heart,* (*note 3).

### Relating to the Spiritual

The flat, square *Gift,* also wrapped in stationery, is tied with a narrow blue satin ribbon. The *Gift* is a reproduction, cut from *Scribner's Magazine* and mounted on cardboard, of a young, calm and beautiful girl, Beatrice, seen in a round, low-relief profile (*note 4). A *fleur-de-lis* is placed to the left of her head. Beatrice is accompanied by Gertrude's penciled note, *Concerning the Spiritual*:

> One day glancing through the "slave-book" (*note 5), a lily spoke to me. "Send me to her—Beatrice will tell the message—"
>
> Women have always been loved by men, but the historians of Humanity, the biologist, the sociologist, the literary critic all agree that love is a term of variable meaning, according to the age which may be considered. And then I remember one clear voice that sings forth, that Beatrice—she of the unspotted soul—stands forever before all women as the symbol of aspiring and spiritual affection.

Gertrude further explained,

> Dante's worship of Beatrice merely suggests the adoration of the heart and soul of woman, + is the passionate revolt against the grossness of idealized sexuality. It is Dante who lighted the flame of modern love + set it aloft in poetry. For centuries Beatrice is a mythical being, cold and unreal, but she wins, and slowly she is loved again in human forms—the something that is more than physical charm—the something

divine which leads steadily on. And as the years advance she is no longer so severe and distant; the artist shows her smiling—and so she comes to you this day out of her mediaeval world into yours, with the glad hope upon her lips, the sweet assurance that Love grows, as the soul grows, more and more beautiful as the race ripens toward higher standards.

ঙ৬

At this point in her elaborate creation, Gertrude's energy and physical strength waned, and she suffered a setback. In a final tiny envelope she offered

*Apologies and Explanations: Greeting and Wishes!*
We deeply regret the insignificance of our results—the scribe has been so severely afflicted that she must flee from pen to pencil, fearing even now that our messages may not find expression.

Moreover, we had scarcely begun when a preemptive telegram arrived from Alexander Graham Bell insisting on an immediate personal interview with Invention herself, as he was inextricably involved in some aerial problem, and could neither sleep nor stay awake. Invention felt obliged to leave, but sent me one of her assistants who, although extremely "willing" was evidently an undergraduate of immature abilities.

Humor felt so lonely that she only half-sparkled, and when, after two or three days she kept receiving importunate messages from Mrs. Woodbury, she came to me very winningly and said, "You won't mind if I skip, will you, because you know Mrs. Woodbury does love me so very much—we seem to belong to each other—but I will send you my second cousin. She is very gentle and just suitable for an invalid."

And so the second cousin came, a timid, rather vapid Humorosity who begs forgiveness for anything she does or says.

The flowers which had to be immortal did almost come from the skies, and were gathered by friendly hands (Nurse Aeschbacher's). Switzerland gave her own chosen favorite, and America—America gave the creamy silken cords. Do you not recognize them? Do they not suggest intimate relations— have they not served to adorn the hidden places? Judged by American standards, they may be treasured as antiques...."

Abruptly, the *Triumph of Nothing* ends.

As she adapted to illness and isolation, and as she relinquished her youthful ambitions and almost all material possessions, Gertrude held to her belief in humankind's persistent, if uneven, progress.

Notes on *The Triumph of Nothing*
(1) Mrs. Woodbury (Josephine Curtis Woodbury) converted to Christian Science in 1879 and became a flamboyant preacher, advocating sexual abstinence. However, in June 1890, she produced a child, whom she inventively proclaimed had been conceived by Immaculate Conception. She baptized the child "Prince of Peace," but was barred from the church. After the scandal quieted in 1892, Mrs. Woodbury was admitted on probation to a reorganized Christian Science Church, but in 1896 the Mother Church excommunicated her forever.

(2) Mrs. Toodles: a character in the English play, *The Toodles*, first performed in America in 1889. Mrs. Toodles is mad about auctions and always manages to find treasures that, if not useful now, will certainly come in handy in the future, if circumstances are right.

(3) Trilby: the hapless victim of the fictional hypnotist Svengali in the 1894 novel *Trilby* by George du Maurier, published serially in *Harper's Weekly*, and then as a book, in 1895.

(4) This portrait of Dante's beloved Beatrice is credited to A. Apolloni, then a well-known contemporary Italian sculptor who had exhibited a work at the 1893 Chicago Exposition featuring a telephone, as a symbol of American progress.

(5) Slave book: a reference to the Bible by Margaret Fuller in her book, *Nineteenth Century Woman*, who wrote: "There exists in the minds of men a tone of feeling toward women as toward slaves." See similar references in *The Subjection of Women* by John Stuart Mill, and in *The Woman's Bible* (1895) by Elizabeth Cady Stanton: "The Bible and the Church have been the greatest stumbling blocks in the way of women's emancipation," quoted in *Free Thought Magazine* (1896).

# CHAPTER 20

## *George Eliot's Heroines*

OVER THE COURSE OF THE WINTER OF 1894-95, GERTRUDE'S PHYSIcal strength declined. She often dictated letters, with Miss Spofford as scribe, but she wrote to Carman in her own hand as often as she could. On his birthday, April 15th, she recounted a vision.

> … Night before last a poet appeared to me in a dream. He was about to start on a journey and had come to make me a visit of two or three days. He was clad in familiar gray homespun, but lo! His hair was the color of flame! I was much amazed and then the poet bent down his head, and shook it slightly, and I saw that on top there was a goodly mixture of gray. "Ashes and flame!" I exclaimed. Then the poet lifted his head, and tossing it back, smiled gaily but the shadow of melancholy was in his eyes. "Flame and ashes!"

In early May, Carman replied from Washington, "… the post card with the dream was a welcome thing and laid its hand on my heart. 'Ashes and flame' is too true! Flame of desire, aspiration, hope. Ashes of achievement, failure, depression."

All winter he had been, as he put it, "rather gay and vagrant at heart," but with the coming on of spring, he now truly felt "the perfection of the world." The day before his birthday, he and Jessie Kappeler had looked down on the earth from the Capitol dome. They had gone up to the Congressional Library to look up some books on dancing, and then "had the freak to climb the stairs, round and round and up and up." They met only one or two people; mostly, "the place was deserted as a ruin." From the outer balcony at the top they "looked down on the soft green well of city at noon. It was a day of soft mist, warm and sunlit, though damp as fog to the face; and the mood of spring was melting, not strenuous nor assertive any more, but subdued and tolerant."

The following week he hoped to go to New York City and on to Boston. All was unsettled and he had no prospects. Yet, he assured Gertrude, "My heart is full to-night. Do you not feel it? There must be a pulse of it in thy mountains surely. Do you not feel it? The peace of Spring, night and all the stars, keep thy sleep, dear Gertrude, and the greatness of the world support us…"

But by the end of April, Carman had broken off the secret engagement with fickle Jessie Kappeler, and once again he experienced the ashes of failure and depression. Despondent, he wrote to Gertrude: "I see my life slipping like water through my fingers and cannot make it stay. All my affairs go wrong, so sadly wrong, and I often doubt the worth-while-ness."

Nevertheless, he had succeeded in completing a new collection of poems titled *Behind the Arras, A Book of the Unseen*. He dedicated the book to Gertrude, and wrote to her: "I have sent a book in to the publishers to try and have it out by the fall. But, O Gertrude, I have no heart in it, none at all…when I pass out of this 'penumbra' (!!) I shall write again."

She responded, "… I thank thee tenderly for writing to me in the penumbral moment. It made me feel myself precious to have another spirit near to me in the hour of shadow. 'I love you' twenty times over would not have been so sweet and satisfactory. And I can assure thee of a kind sympathy. I think I understand the exact shade of thy shadow…"

She received his sad letter while on a rare holiday in the small village of Chernex-sur-Montreux. Gertrude and Miss Spofford had delayed their departure from Leysin until May 20th, detained by late spring snowfalls. Eight inches were already on the ground on the day they finally left. Even so, the carriage made a smooth ride and they arrived, without undue anxiety or problems, surrounded by fields carpeted with wild yellow narcissi, at the Pension Dufour-Cochard, where the Hitz family had spent spring holidays in Gertrude's childhood. The air was warmer at the lower altitude and Gertrude hoped she would soon be able to take excursions in her rolling chair. When Harold arrived later from Lausanne, where he was living with Madame Morf and attending kindergarten, he would accompany her on foot, gathering flowers and no doubt chattering incessantly.

Gertrude's doctor forbade all exercise, owing to her tendency to feverishness, and ordered her to pass her days reclining quietly, *tranquillement étendue,* in the garden. In the mornings, she sat by the side of a hedge of laurel, beneath a lilac tree in full bloom. On days when the dampness of the ground prevented her from spending time in the garden, she was carried to a terrace beautifully garlanded with delicate and luxurious wisteria. She wished she could describe to her mother "the exquisite loveliness and color of its filmy russet-green leaves and masses of flowers in all the tints of lavender and purple" that Jane Hitz loved so well. Gertrude thought the garden "seemed to have grown exactly according to [her mother's] taste, like something [her] spirit might have planned and created."

She was deeply grateful for her mother's support and wrote to her each Tuesday, lying almost flat on her steamer chair. She wrapped herself in a new camel's hair shawl ordered from Geneva, purchased with her mother's birthday check. It was "a very light, soft brown in color and surprisingly warm for its weight."

In fine weather Gertrude read on the terrace—a biography of John Addington Symonds, Washington Irving's *Sketchbook*, and Dickens' *American Notes*. Both she and Jane Hitz were readers, and books provided a recurrent topic in their exchanges. Gertrude's favorite was Mrs. Gaskell's *Cranford*: "I find my taste is far more for biography and such delicious books as *Cranford* than for novels…" Nonetheless, that spring Gertrude was also reading Charlotte Bronte's books, *The Professor* and *Villette* ("rather tedious"); Jane Austen's *Pride and Prejudice*; George Eliot's *Silas Marner*, and a volume of Eliot's writings, *Essays and Leaves from a Notebook.* Mother and daughter especially admired George Eliot. Gertrude remarked that "… the characters in George Eliot are far more complex and one feels the pressure of heredity, of circumstance and environment to a degree that Austen and Bronte never suggest."

When she read the closing words of Eliot's *Middlemarch*, regarding the death and legacy of Dorothea Brooke, Gertrude may have reflected on her own now "hidden life," with hope that her efforts might produce similar "diffuse effects for Good in the world." She certainly perceived, as the contemporary American critic Abba Gould Woolson had observed, that for George Eliot's heroines, "Individuals must make their best efforts toward a worthy end, but it is the effort toward a goal rather than the achievement of it, that makes us who we are." Gertrude was focused now on remaining loyal to her ideals while meeting her illness with all the self-possession she could muster—for her own sake, and for her sons'.

Harold arrived in Chernex with newly shorn hair. At nearly seven years old, he had had his first boyish haircut. Gertrude reported wryly that she was "pleasantly disappointed in the effect." She also noticed affectionately that, since Christmas, Harold's English had become "Frenchy in construction and accent…" In the garden, reading George Eliot's *Romola*, Miss Spofford sat near her and Harold, who talked to himself as he played.

On June 18th, three acquaintances of Gertrude's English friend in Lausanne, Fanny Byse, arrived at the Pension. Mrs. James C. Geddes and her two daughters came with the express goal of visiting with Gertrude. Mrs. Byse, the wife of professor Charles Byse, had encouraged their call because Mrs. Geddes had been a friend of George Eliot's, and Fanny Byse knew that Gertrude admired the late author's remarkable works.

On arriving, Mrs. Geddes penciled on her delicately engraved calling card, in response to Gertrude's inquiry: "I am George Eliot's

Mrs. Geddes! Will you allow me to come and thank you for your kindness to us?" She was referring to the small bouquets Harold had gathered and placed in the visitors' rooms.

Although old enough to be Gertrude's mother, Mrs. Geddes was in no sense an old lady, and she appeared much younger than Gertrude had anticipated. Gertrude described her to Jane Hitz: "She was of medium height and build, with a rather florid complexion, a turned-up nose, unmistakably English, but with a remarkably frank, decided expression that lifted her at once beyond the merely ordinary woman." It was the "clear sparkle of her pale gray eyes" that Gertrude noticed most vividly—and perhaps

> ... also a certain quick way of shutting her mouth at the
> close of a sentence. She was very simply dressed in black when
> she first appeared, wearing a surplice waist with soft *crêpe-lisse*
> at her neck and sleeves. She wore a round locket around her
> neck made of black enamel surrounded with a single row of
> pearls which hung from a black velvet band. In the center was
> a delicate monogram in gold. There was an air of neatness
> and precision about her: her manners were very simple and
> direct, her voice soft and kindly.

The visitors stayed from Tuesday until Saturday. Gertrude sat with them in the garden on her steamer chair within the shade of a high wall, with Miss Spofford nearby on the other side of a little iron table. Their conversations for an hour or two each day brought George Eliot nearer, and invited Gertrude into her world.

Mrs. Geddes' father, Dr. Berry, had attended George Eliot's father in his final illness. The doctor was impressed by the nursing skills of his patient's daughter, Marian [Mary Anne] Evans. Dr. Berry took his own young daughters—Mrs. Geddes and her sister, now Mrs. Congreve—to meet her, so their friendship began in the simplest and most neighborly fashion, long before Mary Anne Evans became known as the author George Eliot. Still a child then, Mrs. Geddes was asked to accompany George Eliot and her partner Mr. Lewes ("pronounced Lewis," Gertrude noted) during walks in the countryside, as a guide to local roads. Once, she remembered, George Eliot sat on a bench with her, while Lewes searched the ponds for his "little beasts." Laying her hand on the girl's, George Eliot counseled her earnestly, "Remember always that it is the near relations—the people by whom you are naturally surrounded—that should occupy your affections."

Perhaps Gertrude took this advice to heart, and wished also to impart it to her mother. In a letter to Jane Hitz she enclosed the visiting card autographed by Mrs. Geddes, imagining that her mother would use it as a bookmark in her own copy of Eliot's *Life and Letters*.

Mrs. James C. Geddes. One–Oak, Reddington Road, Hampstead

Gertrude was happy to provide the details she knew would interest her mother intensely: that George Eliot's head scarves were generally of white lace, rarely black; that Mr. Lewes took charge of the house entirely, doing the marketing and ordering the dinner so that George Eliot's morning might be altogether free for writing. Their life was most systematically regular. After breakfast, each retired to a separate study and worked until the dinner hour. The afternoon was devoted to a walk. They were always together—George Eliot was never seen alone—never—not even in a shop. Lewes even accompanied her to the dressmaker's. The dresses were always made short, as Lewes abominated trains, saying they tripped him up.

Mrs. Geddes also freely shared her adverse opinion of Mr. John Cross, George Eliot's second husband, twenty years younger than she, whom she married after Lewes' death. On their Venice honeymoon, Cross scandalously had leapt in a panic from their hotel window into a canal, but survived.

Mrs. Geddes was an ardent Positivist and, along with her husband James, she was one of the original members of the London Positivist Society. Other members included her sister's husband,

Richard Congreve; George Eliot's Mr. Lewes; and the influential sociologist Herbert Spencer, whose Social Darwinist ideas Gertrude and her parents admired. Spencer had extended the theory of evolution into the realms of sociology and ethics, confident of progressive development in the physical world, biological organisms, the human mind, and human societies, and even asserting that behavioral traits acquired by the previous generation can be inherited by their successors. This implied the possibility of infinite human progress, through eugenics and social engineering, an idea that resonated with Gertrude and her parents, too, who believed that humankind could be morally and spiritually improved through mindful, scientific choices.

Gertrude sent Mrs. Geddes a note before she departed, enclosing "as a kiss" a quotation from one of her own Boston lectures: "The glory of man is to educate all elemental forces to the dignity of powers, which shall persistently ennoble and refine the race."

For Harold's seventh birthday, on the 22nd of June, Gertrude ordered bundles of birthday gifts sent up to Chernex from Montreux. She had never seen her younger son happier or more charming. White packages tied with blue ribbon surrounded a fresh garland of pink eglantines arranged in the center of the table. His cake with seven little candles was a great success ("the *chef-d'oeuvre* of a Montreux *confiseur*") and large enough to supply a piece for everyone in the house—seven guests and five servants. Adèle, the innkeeper's daughter and Harold's bosom friend, had a generous portion, and after supper, the village children were invited to play games. Each one was made happy with a five-centime paper *cornet* of mixed candies.

To Gertrude, best of all was Harold's sweetness and delight. Before he went to bed he exclaimed, "O, Mother, I can hardly look at you I love you so much!"

# CHAPTER 21

## *Our Taste of Beauty and of Pain*

GERTRUDE RETURNED TO LEYSIN FROM CHERNEX IN EARLY JULY 1895, just before Burton and Arnold arrived from America for the summer holidays. She summoned the energy to write to Carman, back in Boston again, writing and editing for *The Atlantic* magazine. With a new lease on life, he replied to her long letter:

> This note is brief and scrappy, but I have a full heart and life grows richer every day, and I feel as if I might yet learn to grow young gracefully…
>
> From thee as from none other have I learned something of the art of living well. The winter is over and passed. The sermons of spring are gone. It is full summer.
>
> I send you all my love, and may the great mountains comfort thee and tell thee tales of one far away who is happy if he can be ever and ever thy tender loving and durable
>
> Bliss.
>
> P.S. I missed Burton here, as I was much at the sea shore. Love to him.

She answered him in the final letter written in her own hand, full of news of her stay in Chernex, and expressing joy simply at being alive, with optimism about the future, if not about her own immediate prospects:

> When one's heart is very grateful, surely the poor bodily hand should be eager to do its service—but it is so strangely hard for me to write—something somewhere in the essential

mechanism refuses and rebels so violently that I force myself even to say thank you.

The fourth letter came a day or two ago....Thank thee, belovèd. I want thee to feel how this kindness has gladdened me not only because of the faith—the larger + surer trust which it brings to the ardent, ever-hoping spirit. This is the solemn part of all individual human relations—this subtle inevitable tendency to add or detract something which reaches to the core of one's beliefs and generalizations. How keenly, how passionately George Eliot realized this effect!

I have been hearing a great deal about George Eliot lately. I had the great pleasure of making the acquaintance of Mrs. Geddes a week or so ago. She is a friend of a friend of mine and came to Chernex. But best of all she was an intimate friend of George Eliot. How we talked! And then too we harmonized deliciously on many points + parted as if we had known each other from childhood. But apart from this meeting, + the fact that my living expenses were decidedly diminished—the weeks at Chernex were disappointing, and I was very glad to come back to the heights again a few days ago. I notice the change of altitude however, much more than when I first came here last summer, and must keep my mouth tightly shut when out of doors.

But how exquisitely sweet to be alive! Talk of resignation! One is resigned because it is infinitely more comfortable than fussing + fretting. I lie here in my chair in a luxury of quiet ease—glad, so glad that my sight is not denied me—that I can look upon the village roofs + the dear quaint little church, and see the wide blue sky and the tops of the great snow mountains + watch the swaying branches here close by. And it is all such a precious marvelous world—this one tiny speck which turns among the millions in the great whirl we condense in our one word—universe! "Without Haste! Without Rest!" was perhaps the most comprehensive phrase Goethe has left us.

She closed her letter with a testament to the scientific laws and transcendental faith that sustained her, and explained her apparent composure in the face of approaching death:

> ... there is something that stirs me...deeply, as I think of the grave and the dead human being lying in the silence of its mystery. It is the simple law of the indestructibility of matter. From this, what hopes, what changes, what boundless wonders, what ineffable trust! All the cruelty, all the vexed problems, all the small individual cares, how they fade within the conception of such a law! For if we can comprehend a law like this, believe it, accept it—surely the vastness of eternity need not cause dismay. Why should we fear? What can we fear? We all go down the same dark way—each living thing alone. What we all do, must be done. In the end, freshness must come—must come, as certainly as dawn follows night. What if we know it or do not know it? We have had our taste of beauty and of pain, + if consciousness be not ours again, surely what will be, will be orderly and subject to laws quite as marvelous + inevitable.
>
> Χαίρε, beloved, And thy hand!
> Gertrude

She signed with their special Greek greeting, Χαίρε, "peace and joy."

Bliss Carman answered immediately:

> Ah, for thy beautiful words sent on paper! Dear Comrade!
> The mood is gone now and I am glad again of the dear world; I even tolerate myself. It is well. But most of all I am fortified and rejoiced of thy letter—O a thousand thanks! I shall try to learn some of thy serenity....I am impatient to have my next book to send you, dear Gertrude, for it has some things I want you to like. And it is more impersonal than the others so far.

Now I must go to my work, but with what gladness—because from thy white solitude came these divinely clear messages.

Burton and Arnold were expected soon, and Gertrude had taken rooms at the Pension du Chalet for them all. They were less expensive than her accommodations at the Grand Hotel, and the Chalet could accommodate the whole family. When Gertrude first saw her elder son, she lamented his pale face and pinched expression. She exclaimed with irony in a letter to her mother about his preoccupations with soldiers and battles: "Military interests still supreme! I console myself that it is inevitable—a passing epoch corresponding to racial development." She was referring to the educational theories of Herbert Spencer, G. Stanley Hall, and Ernst Haeckel ("ontogeny recapitulates phylogeny"). Her words recalled Richard Bucke's comment at the long-ago Sunday dinner with Walt Whitman, at Mary's Philadelphia home, that all boys pass through a "natural and inevitable" period during which they dislike and avoid girls.

The brothers, seven and ten years old, were delighted to be together again. They often played charades after dinner, under Miss Spofford's direction. Their elation charmed Gertrude but also strained her nerves. Her coughs and fevers persisted. She described her dilemma to her mother, "It is the most delicious enjoyment... Such naïveté! Such abandon! [but] I have to restrict myself to certain hours—to be much alone and very quiet, for the presence of so many [people] taxes my strength to the utmost, unless everything is managed with great care and regularity...."

As she rested, she found ways to amuse herself, reading magazines and playing word games. At one sitting, using only the letters in her mother's name, *Jane Catherine*, she created an impressive one hundred and forty words: from *antic* to *jar*, and *recant* to *Teheran*.

Burton soon set out on sketching expeditions: "Mr. Burton is off on a second tramp. This time, he has gone to Gruyères, which is not far from here, and which apart from its cheesy fame is a most picturesque little village with a marvelously well-preserved feudal castle and all the quaintness of walls and gargoyles that make a sketcher's delight."

Dr. Burnier examined Gertrude when he returned from his summer holiday, and found her in about the same condition as before, although he thought she had lost flesh, which she "knew to be perfectly true." Her cough had worsened, although she found some relief from her sore throat in a new menthol prescription for the respirator. But she did not "feel herself," and began to wake again at three o'clock each morning. The doctor promised new remedies which had had phenomenal success in Germany. She was skeptical, but the experiment gave her a new interest, at any rate. She confided to her mother that "I find it much harder to keep a 'stiff upper lip' (as you say) this year than last. But, *Quandmême* (as you and Sarah [Allen] say). I shall battle on against body and mind."

During his stay, Burton arranged for both Arnold and Harold to attend school at the Collège Gaillard in Lausanne during the fall term. They each would live with old friends, Harold staying on with the Morf family at the Villa Marguerite on the Boulevard Grancy, and Arnold with Madame Morf's daughter, Madame Carrard, at Villa Le Muguet, on the rue du Grand Roche. In a September letter Burton assured his own mother that the Swiss school was "much better than the Allen School in Newton, and certainly less expensive."

He reported, too, without commenting further, that Dr. Burnier was discouraged, and "did not believe Gertrude would live more than through the winter—and if she would do that was doubtful." The doctor made provisions to keep Burton informed during the coming months, and promised to cable if there were any sudden changes. Miss Spofford agreed to remain with Gertrude until Burton could come over again in the spring. Then, after settling the boys in their new surroundings, Burton made his way to France, sailing home on the *SS Spaarndam* from Boulogne. Gertrude and Miss Spofford reclaimed their rooms in the Grand Hotel.

By October, Harold and Arnold were established in Lausanne. Gertrude pictured her two sons in the setting of her own childhood, treading "the very stones" she had trod as a nine-year-old. She imagined them following her route uphill from the train station toward the Place St. Francois, emerging into the Rue du Grand-Chêne by way of the Rue du Petit-Chêne. She recalled the day of her sister Pauline's birth, October 3rd, twenty-five years earlier, when she had brought her mother an offering of flowers. Daughter and mother were bound by those memories in Lausanne, and by Pauline's death in Washington, when Gertrude was fifteen. In one of her final letters to her mother, Gertrude commemorated Pauline's birthday by enclosing a spray of wild myrtle.

By early December, Gertrude was no longer able to write. Miss Spofford warned Bliss Carman that Mrs. Burton was "far more ill than she knows, suffering much with high fever and great weariness… Let your messages come soon."

# CHAPTER 22

## *Nothing Material Truly Perishes*

Miss Spofford also sent news of Gertrude's failing health to John Hitz and Jane Hitz in Washington, and to Mary Costelloe, who was in England for Christmas. Jane Hitz was suffering a severe eye inflammation; William had dropped out of Harvard and was living with his mother in Washington. Dr. Burnier was "hopeless of any gain," he cabled in his report to Burton, in Boston. Burton felt he could not abandon his academic duties. He asked Hitz to go over to Gertrude in his place. After a flurry of preparations, Hitz booked passage on the steamship *SS Normandie* with funds contributed by Jane Hitz and Alexander Graham Bell. He sailed on December 6th.

The voyage was relatively calm for a December crossing, and on the ninth day, at seven a.m., he sighted houses on the coast of France. Because of delays, Hitz did not arrive in Paris until three o'clock the following morning. After some hours of rest at the Terminus Hotel, he traveled by train to Lausanne, on to Aigle, and finally, by stagecoach, to the Grand Hotel in Fedey-sur-Leysin.

Gertrude was lying in bed, emaciated and very feeble, when John Hitz arrived on the afternoon of December 17th. He talked with her softly for a long time. After supper, with Dr. Burnier's approval, they agreed to arrange a consultation with Dr. Huguenin, the specialist from Zurich who had examined her the year before at Weissenburg. Her father noted that Gertrude seemed "to desire to do everything she could—was willing to submit to any treatment—and if all should prove fruitless, did not seem to shrink from her Heavenly Father's call."

Days before, Gertrude had communicated with Mary, who was visiting her parents' Sussex estate:

> Thou knowest now to be sure (Miss Spofford's letter must have reached thee) that I am not in constant agony— only constant discomfort—that there is hardly ever a minute or two when I am not teased by some sort of malaise, my cough or my bones being the chief tormenters. For I have grown very thin and now that I am confined to my bed and can only occupy one or two positions and am so weak, I grow very stiff and sore and so, *viola*!
>
> The fever is about the same.
>
> I was so much touched and thrilled by that outburst in thy first letter about the continuance of life…I have felt no such positive assurance—I have only the general laws of the persistence of forces and that nothing material truly perishes. For the rest I cannot tell thee how humble I feel '*en face de l'Univers!*' What is, must and will be, and I have absolutely no fear…

The next day, after consulting with Dr. Burnier, she wrote again, asking Mary to visit Leysin before returning to Italy:

> … The doctor last night told me he did not feel sure I would live through the Spring—it depended on 'a certain turn' in the malady. I do not accept this as prophecy, but it is enough to make me feel I will not be too selfish in asking thee to try surely to come and see me on thy return from England, or as soon as convenient.…This announcement stimulates me—I feel: I <u>will</u> live! And I mean to try all I can.

In the weeks leading up to the Christmas holidays, her father looked after her, sitting quietly in her room. Gertrude remained almost entirely silent, her throat so irritated she could only whisper. The weather sparkled. Through the French doors to her balcony the views of the mountains to the south, beyond the Rhone Valley, were spectacular—whether crystalline or cloud-shrouded. Sometimes only the jagged snow-covered peaks thrust above the sea of white clouds that filled the valley below.

Her father left for Zurich to locate Dr. Huguenin, who promised to visit Gertrude soon. Hitz returned from his mission on the misty afternoon of December 21st and found Gertrude "tolerable—and brighter after tea." She did not hesitate to make plans for her end of life. She expressed her wishes about the disposition of her body, if should she pass away: she wanted to be buried at Leysin, the children should not see her corpse, and everything connected with the final rites should be very simple. She directed that her wedding ring be given to Arnold, and her edelweiss pin to Harold. Each token symbolized important prenatal events connected with the conception of each child, but she was too weak to explain to her father exactly what these were. She also wanted each boy to have a gold chain she had chosen herself, to be worn always around their necks as a symbol of her love. To her father, she communicated that she did not fear death, and although she was not Christian, she comforted him by saying that she accepted many of his New Church (Swedenborgian) beliefs, in regard to the separation of the soul from the body.

John Hitz recorded in his diary that, during their conversations she spoke frankly about her still raw feelings toward Burton: "... of the Absence of Soul and heart in Mr. B., whose conduct first brought on the existing nervous trouble, and his utter lack, last Summer, to appreciate her condition and show an improved heart & Soul." Hitz was glad he had come over in Burton's place.

His diary records, too, that Gertrude spoke of her troubled relationship with Jane Hitz, "Of...her Mother's great kindness on the one hand, and her rigid disregard of her [situation], in providing only what means was absolutely required—and after being asked—in place of voluntarily placing an ample sum at her disposition..." To Gertrude's relief, her father assured her that, although he needed to be economical, "the Bell family had placed him virtually beyond anxiety in regard to funds." But when her restless nights, weakness and severe coughing spells required regular morphine injections, she asked her father to write her mother's lawyer requesting an additional $200 for a night nurse, until the following May, and $100 for Miss Spofford, who had agreed to stay until April.

The holidays required a great deal of planning: the days before Christmas were busy with preparations for Arnold and Harold's arrival on Monday the 23rd. St. Nicholas would arrive the following evening, according to European custom. Their grandfather bought ice skates at the Bazaar so they might be used Christmas Day. Gertrude desired a small tree to be lit in the boys' room, so Hitz trudged up the mountain in the snow and cut a fir, leaving it with the carpenter to be put on a stand.

On Christmas Eve, Miss Spofford decorated the tree and lit the candles while the children were downstairs with their grandfather. The Hotel's Christmas dinner, with a large tree in the dining room, was a very orderly affair, but there was also much hilarity. The children enjoyed it greatly, although their grandfather would have preferred to be elsewhere. When they all returned upstairs to the rooms, the boys were surprised and delighted with their own tree and presents.

The children slept in Miss Spofford's room, adjoining Gertrude's, while Hitz moved to the Pension du Chalet and Miss Spofford took his guest room at the Hotel. Gertrude dictated a letter, and had an envelope inscribed "To My Boys!" placed on their bed:

> My precious boys,
> It is sweet to me to have a little glimpse of your room and to see where you sleep all the long quiet night. I would

like to cover all the walls with my love and leave beautiful and loving messages everywhere to whisper in your ears when you least expect them.

I would like to pack your pillows full of the most beautiful and wondrous dreams and to watch over you in the still night-time and to fill your hearts full of good things for all the hours of the day.

I would like to kiss your eyes open in the morning and always to sleep with you in some sort of tremendous bed that nobody ever heard of!

And I would like to do a thousand things more, "SUPPOSING" that I could; but most of all, I would like you to feel me near you always and to help you like a sweet voice in your hearts always whispering 'Remember!' 'Be good! Be good! Make others happy!...'"

To John Hitz's relief, Dr. Huguenin telegraphed he would soon arrive for consultations. After careful examination, in the presence of Hitz and Dr. Burnier, the doctor concluded that Gertrude's condition was very deplorable—her left lung almost entirely gone and the right affected at the upper end. She had been ill too long in America, he stated, to recover here. They would continue the morphine and other soothing medicines, but he did not think it possible she would recover. She might survive yet one or two more months, but a catastrophe or complete collapse from which she could not rally might occur any day. The bracing air that now sustained her would lessen with the approaching spring, and the end must be expected. He counseled against any removal to other facilities at Davos or Arosa, as she had better treatment at the Grand Hotel than she could get at those, or similar, places. The best thing to do was to alleviate her suffering and calmly await the outcome.

Dr. Huguenin visited her room to bid Gertrude goodbye. John Hitz accompanied him to Leysin and paid his fee of 300 francs, as well as expenses to and from Aigle. Later, after a quiet afternoon,

Gertrude and her father talked the situation through. She seemed truly grateful to have had Dr. Huguenin's counsel, and was resigned to his conclusion. Hitz mailed letters to Mr. Burton and to the Bell family giving an account of the doctor's opinion.

The next day, Arnold and Harold left for Lausanne by stagecoach with their grandfather. Parting from their mother was quiet, as if on any ordinary morning. John Hitz left the children with Madame Morf and then engaged a room at the nearby Pension Clement before going to the bank, and shopping for gold necklace samples, velvet and pillows, and a purse for Gertrude. The next afternoon he returned to the Grand Hotel and remained with her until eleven p.m., when the night nurse arrived.

A beautiful, bright morning greeted the New Year 1896. The mountains were covered with a fresh mantle of snow. Hitz noted that "the Sun rose in all its splendors from a deep blue firmament and the play of clouds beneath the mountain summits was very fine." The nurse reported, however, that Gertrude had had a trying night. Hitz remained with her throughout that day, and she seemed to cough less, but was less disposed to read or speak, from sheer weakness. She became nervous at times.

Day after day, John Hitz sat with her, wrote letters, shopped for necessities, visited the pharmacy, and took an occasional tramp to get some fresh air. Sometimes Gertrude was able to sit up and converse. More often, her restless nights caused daytime exhaustion. Morphine and belladonna by hypodermic injection gave her the prospect of resting more quietly. Occasionally she would suffer a severe and painful stitch in her chest, and became unable to take a full breath for hours at a time, but then she might rally and quiet down, becoming herself for a brief period, and able to look at magazines.

Worries over money plagued Gertrude still. One afternoon, she tried to draw checks and disburse remittances, but was unable to complete the task—and in any case, the funds were not sufficient to cover her expenditures. She was two weeks in arrears. Finally, she was able to make out three checks to pay part of the Hotel bill, the doctor, and the pharmacy. Hitz could not refrain from commenting in his diary that he could not "understand the penurious way her mother has of doling out the pittance she sends her at such a time—in comparison to her own actual income."

Gertrude's nervous spells, faintness, and sensitivity to touch often made her father feel utterly useless as a nurse. Increasingly, she would smile and talk to herself incoherently, so that neither he nor Miss Spofford could understand. When she could communicate, she would pencil certain requests or remarks on slips of paper. For example, she wanted a new photograph of Nike, the *Winged Victory of Samothrace,* for her room. She asked that, in the event of her death, her corpse might be taken to the church and set aside there overnight. Later, however, when Hitz inquired, Pastor Louis Favez explained that it was not permitted. The church could not be used for funeral services, which took place in a designated room at the Grand Hotel. Burial would be in the cemetery.

When Gertrude was restless but not suffering, she requested that her father read aloud. He often chose excerpts from the writings of Swedenborg, about death and resurrection, and from the Bible— psalms, as well as verses from the Book of John, when Jesus reveals himself, saying, "Peace unto you."

Now Gertrude was constantly under the influence of morphine, but seemed not to have lost appetite, often dispatching her meals with relish. After eating heartily, there was trouble at every movement of the bowels, and both her father and Miss Spofford felt unequal to those nursing tasks. She could no longer lie down but sat upright in bed, propped with pillows, or she leaned over, with her head bent down. The windows had to be opened wide and the heat shut off to prevent difficulty in breathing. Even so, she suffered from oppressive spells. Sometimes she dreamed she was dying.

# CHAPTER 23

## *A Quite Simple, Natural Phase*

GERTRUDE'S NIGHTS BECAME MORE RESTFUL, WITH ALMOST PAIN-free spells during the day. It snowed beautifully during the early weeks of January. White Chasselas grapes arrived from Zurich. One afternoon with her father, as they were looking quietly at photos sent by Arnold, she penciled a note: "Oh, beautiful! Why, this is actually a moment of simple quiet and delight! How my heart sings within me! Let us be thankful, let us be glad—now in the sweet afternoon light—when body and spirit have this little holiday of peace. Ah! If I could sing what sweet music it <u>would</u> be!"

She hoped to accomplish many things before the end. To finish them, she enlisted Miss Spofford's help, as well as her father's and, finally, Mary's. She particularly wanted her brother William to understand fully the reasons for the hostility between their mother and father, though she knew they would never reconcile. Family discord had affected her own relationship with her brother, which she had wanted to rebuild. She hoped he would seek out Walter Davidge, the respected Washington lawyer who had represented Hitz's co-defendant, bank treasurer C.E. Prentiss, during the trials. She began writing, in pencil, but she was unable to complete the note: "My dear brother, every day may bring the end now, and I have a special request to make of you…" She recruited Miss Spofford to take up the important task (in ink, with a worn, fraying pen point):

22 January 1896
My dear Mr. Hitz,
Your sister has been hoping and trying to write to you
for many days about a matter that is especially close and inti-

251

mate between you. But her increasing weakness has prevented her from doing so,—or at least from finishing any attempts and so she has entrusted the messages to me.

As soon as the doctor made known to Mrs. Burton that she might have but a short time to live, she made arrangements for an interview between you and Mr. Davidge who could satisfactorily explain to you her father's position in the failure of the banks and the complications which followed. She chose Mr. Davidge because she was anxious that the person who discussed the subject with you should be someone who thoroughly knew the facts and yet had no close personal relations with her father.

… though at first reluctant to undertake the matter… Mr. Davidge realized his own suitability for the purpose and consented to have the interview with you if you would seek it.

Your sister feels that she is not leaving this life quite loyally unless she does her utmost to secure to you a presentation of facts which she feels unequal to doing herself.—And so now when nothing can affect your future relations with your sister, she requests you to ask Mr. Davidge for an interview at his office or residence. Walter D. Davidge, 17th and H Sts, Washington.

Gertrude often seemed "in a dazed, absent-minded condition—not suffering, but pitiful," according to her father. Hitz tried to engage the exclusive services of Nurse Aeschbacher, but Dr. Burnier refused to allow her to overtire herself or abandon other patients. "Gertrude took it calmly and said Miss A. might find a friend from Aigle who could come as a special nurse." Gertrude's mind was greatly eased when her mother agreed to send the funds needed to settle accounts.

Flowers arrived from friends in Zurich.

A packet of letters for Hitz was forwarded from Washington, including one written by Gertrude herself, two months before, "most affectionate and spiritually beautiful." He knew it was the final letter he would receive from her, and prayed that the Lord might strengthen him to do His will.

Although a dense sea of clouds covered Lake Geneva and all the villages and towns on its shores, hiding the Rhone valley 1500 feet below the Grand Hotel, "the sun frequently [shone] in Feydey-sur-Leysin, from a cloudless firmament, and the mountains glisten[ed] in their vestments of snow." On clear days, Hitz often walked to the overlook called the "Eagle's Nest," where he could see the river flowing north into Lake Geneva. One day, he walked the mile and a half to the village cemetery. On the way back to the Hotel, he stopped to admire a balsam fir standing alone on the hillside. At waist height its trunk—formed by twenty intertwined shoots, each a tree in itself—measured 540 centimeters, or nearly six yards, in diameter—an emblem of endurance and survival.

But as Hitz waited and watched, his daughter's life force was fading away. Gertrude was extremely weakened. On January 23rd, he telegraphed Mary Costelloe in England, who was about to travel back to Italy to rejoin Bernhard. Mary arrived the next afternoon, and Hitz again ceded the guest room he occupied at the Hotel, relocating to the Pension du Chalet. Mary could see Gertrude only briefly that day, for at four o'clock the doctor ordered morphine. But the following day, Gertrude and Mary had a long visit, and Gertrude was able "to give instructions for diverse messages to be relayed and directions in regard to matters she wanted done." She asked Mariechen to send a farewell letter to her mother:

Feydey sur Leysin le 25 January 1896

Dear Mrs. Hitz,

… It seems she cannot live for many days. She knows this, and would not be sorry for the end to come soon, for she is very weary. Nevertheless, I find in her, weary as she is, the same <u>timbre</u> of character, if I can use the expression, which has always been such a delight to her friends.

She is intensely interested in this new experience, which is without terror for her, as it seems so simple and natural as any part of human existence. Without certainty that her conscious personality will continue, she is waiting to see if it will, and is prepared to enjoy it, if it does. All the great renunciations of things dear to people in this life have been made by her some time ago—she does not feel torn from an existence full of clinging attachments, but passing quietly from a sphere where she could do no more.

…She is thin and weak, but the beauty of many lines of her face asserts itself only the more strongly. She has the same smile she always had. They are taking good care of her, and giving her morphine to relieve her pain. She hopes to die in sleep.

Believe me, Yours sincerely, Mary Costelloe

Indeed, during the course of this relentless illness Gertrude had gradually, not always easily, let go of all the places and people she had held dear.

At Gertrude's request, Mary also wrote to Bliss Carman, enclosing several white edelweiss flowers along with an exquisitely bound book of Matthew Arnold's poetry, inscribed

To Bliss Carman
From Gertrude Hitz Burton,
January 25, 1896, Leysin-sur-Aigle

In December, Miss Spofford had written him: "Let your messages come soon." Carman replied then that he was sorry Gertrude would not have his latest book of poems, *Behind the Arras*, before Christmas, and explained to her that:

> I have been anxious for it to come into your hands, since for you chiefly it was put together. And in fitting it out piece by piece, I have smiled to think it would please you. Some of the lines are old ones we have read together; others are new; and I have wanted them all to be connected to our enduring friendship. Accept them as the very smallest mark of that sentiment which has kept fresh all these years now—so unalterable.

The book, *Behind the Arras, A Book of the Unseen*, arrived on January 3rd. Carman dedicated it

To G.H.B.
I shut myself in with my soul / and the shapes come eddying forth

In his letter, he explained the epigraph: "The little couplet on the page of dedication is a fragment from Rossetti—no more was ever written. It is fitting, I think…I hope you will like my heart's words as they come to you in print…"

Miss Spofford answered him that although Gertrude "wanted to acknowledge his thought of her in the new book, everything else must go unsaid, although she would like to say so much."

Mary and Gertrude separated letters to be burned from letters to be returned to her correspondents, which included Carman's. She

asked Mary to read aloud favorite excerpts from Whitman's *Leaves of Grass*, the poems they had shared over the past decade, including Number 48, which includes the line, "No Array of terms can say how much I am at peace about God and about death."

During the afternoon of January 25th, Mary walked with John Hitz to the "Eagle's Nest" lookout to view Lake Geneva. She expressed to him what a privilege it was to be with them at this time, and remarked that Gertrude's "attitude to death is what one would wish for one's self."

At six o'clock her father bade Gertrude goodnight, and she gave him her usual adieu-smile, "with evident sympathy and seeming pain."

That night, his sleep was restless. Soon after five o'clock the next morning the nurse summoned him from the Chalet to Gertrude's bedside. Gertrude was sitting up in bed, her head slightly bent forward and to the right side. She was already unconscious when he arrived, and the doctor said that it was the end. Her breathing continued gently, long after the pulse died away. Hitz described the scene:

> At 6:45 Sunday morning, the stars still shining in through the open windows, the last of the breathing was heard. Almost at the same moment the flame of the lamp on the table went gently out, for want of air. Sitting with her were the assistant nurse, with Mrs. Costelloe, Miss Spofford, and her father. It was a trying, very trying day.

He cabled to Mr. Burton: "Gertrude this morning gently passed away. Inform her Mother and Professor Bell."

Mary Costelloe departed for Italy that afternoon at three

o'clock. Days later, she described in her diary Gertrude's "release" as peacefully sublime:

> Tuesday, January 28, 1896 I reached Florence at 11 and Bernhard met me...
>
> I had been with Gertrude at Leysin and she died early Sunday morning, her father and I with her, holding her hands...She was unconscious and death was very easy: we had talked so much about it the day before and she said it seemed to her a quite simple, natural phase of life and one in which she was intensely interested. She was not sure it would lead anywhere but if it did, so much the better.
>
> I quoted our dear Walt to her (she first made me read him): "No array of words can say how much I am at peace about life and death," and she smiled at me to say that was her own attitude.
>
> Her old father, a Swedenborgian, really triumphed in her release—though the tears were dropping out of his eyes and hanging on his long white beard at the loss of her whom he described to me as his "dearest idol." Dawn was flushing the mountains as she died, but the stars were still bright and the air that came in the open window was fresh and still. It was very noble and poetic.

The simple casket arrived on Monday. It was made of oak and ash in natural color with a stained margin. After midnight, John Hitz could not sleep. He arose just after three a.m. and succeeded in writing a few letters. He read in Luke: 24 and John: 20 in regard to the resurrection, and prayed fervently beside Gertrude's casket in her room. He placed his pocket edition of the psalms on her bosom, with lilies of the valley and a white rose. He put violets in her hand, and laid a palm frond diagonally inside the coffin.

The casket—well fastened and covered with a fringed black cloth—was taken down from Fedey to Leysin at half past seven, on a sled drawn by two strong horses. Dr. Burnier, J. A. Bassi, director of the Grand Hotel, Pastor Louis Favez of the village church, and three others walked alongside. Madame LeComte, from Lausanne, the wife of Hitz's friend Colonel Ferdinand LeComte, Miss Spofford, Nurse Aeschbacher, and Hitz rode in a closed carriage. The interment service was held in French, at the cemetery about a mile and a half away, as the sun was lighting up the monumental Dents du Midi like a vast altar. John Hitz prayed that his daughter's resurrection in the spiritual world would mirror the sun's brilliant ascent. In the evening, he and Miss Spofford walked to the overlook to view the sunset.

The next day, the two rode again to the cemetery to lay two wreaths—one was of violets and water lilies, sent from Zurich. The headstone would be of pure, smooth white marble, with a gracefully rounded shape. Hitz arranged for a villager to care for the grave for years to come, tending to weeds and keeping it neat. Telegrams were sent and received: Jane Hitz and Job Barnard, her lawyer; the Bell family; Burton; Hitz's friends, Major Kloss of Bern and Reverend Frank Sewall of the Swedenborgian Church in Washington. Questions were asked and answered, travel plans arranged, flowers ordered. Accounts were settled, and more letters and cards sent, acknowledging bouquets, gifts and condolences. Hitz prepared the announcement for the Lausanne newspaper:

M. **John HITZ**, ancien Consul général aux Etats-Unis, à Lausanne;
Madame **Jane C. HITZ**, à Washington;
M. le professeur **Alfred Burton** allié **Hitz**, à Boston, Mass.;
MM. **Arnold** et **Harold BURTON**, à Lausanne
ont la douleur de faire part à leurs amis et connaissances
de la mort de leur chère fille, femme, mère:

## Madame Gertrude BURTON née HITZ
décédée à Leysin le 26 janvier 1896, à l'âge de 35 ans,
après une longue maladie.
*Peace be unto you.* St-John XX, 19.

He was unable to write or accomplish anything beyond these painful responsibilities.

All the necessary letter writing, sorting, and packing began before Arnold and Harold learned of their mother's death. Hitz and Miss Spofford waited four days, until Thursday afternoon, the 30th of January, to break the news to her boys at Madame Morf's home in Lausanne. The children wept when their grandfather presented the gold chains that Gertrude had chosen as her *adieu* gifts. Hitz solemnly requested they "wear them continuously, as long as they lived, in memory of their mother."

There was still much to be done in February, before returning to America: accounts, letters, and the stonecutter for Gertrude's gravestone; visits to friends in Lucerne, Geneva, Basel, and Bern. There were nagging money worries. Hitz, Madame Morf, and Madame Carrard decided the children would remain in school in Lausanne, living with their host families. It would be best for them if their father came to accompany them home in June, when the boys', and Tech's, school years ended.

Suddenly, Burton cabled that he was coming over. Hitz responded: "No need your coming. Await my letter posted 13th. All well." The next day, another cable arrived: Burton would leave on Wednesday. Extremely annoyed, Hitz considered this proposal "stupid," and telegraphed immediately: "Stay home. Utterly useless your coming. Await letters posted the 13th and yesterday. All right here."

Burton remained in Boston.

A bank draft arrived from Jane Hitz, via her lawyer, for funds to cover Gertrude's outstanding expenses at the Grand Hotel, as well as payments to the Morf and Carrard families. Hitz booked first class passages for Miss Spofford and himself on the *SS Gascoigne* sailing from Le Havre on February 29th.

After an uneventful crossing, they docked in New York on March 8th. John Hitz accompanied Miss Spofford and her baggage to Grand Central Station, and arranged her journey to her mother's home in Groveland, Massachusetts. Then he boarded a night train to Washington, arriving at 7:30 the next morning. Though deeply fatigued, he was relieved to be home.

In the first days, he was still profoundly affected and "indisposed to talk or to be entertained." He withdrew from friends, yet longed long to speak with them about Gertrude, who remained present for him every day, in memory and in his dreams.

# CHAPTER 24

## *Family Epilogue*

GERTRUDE, LIKE GEORGE ELIOT'S NARRATOR IN *MIDDLEMARCH*, BE-lieved that human progress, "the growing good of the world," depends partly on the "unhistoric acts" of anonymous individuals. Yet, she also yearned for a public recognition, and struggled with this inner contradiction. Largely because of her illness, Gertrude played only a minor role as a teacher, lecturer, and author in the Gilded Age movement for women's equality. But as a living exemplar of loyalty, passion, and courage, she profoundly affected the lives of her friends and family. Through them, her influence—like Dorothea Brooke's in *Middlemarch*—became "incalculably diffusive." Her integrity and commitment directly and indirectly inspired her father, mother, brother, and husband, Alfred Edgar Burton. Her memory guided the lives of her sons, Arnold and Harold.

To commemorate Gertrude's death, John Hitz published her pamphlet "Story of a Fern," delicately printed and tied with a ribbon, for Christmas 1896. In a short preface, he praised "the inimitable manner in which she taught to her own...and other children the most profound truths of creation. She held there is nothing in sexuality which forbids a fearless and open search for the highest truth concerning it; the real shame lies in neglecting this matter..."

Her father lived and worked in his Volta Bureau library quarters, where Gertrude's life-sized portrait, painted from a photograph, hung on the wall. He collected her correspondence and bound the letters to her sons in leather volumes, to preserve "a mother's legacy such as few are blessed to have."

Without a close family circle, Hitz deepened his professional and personal relationships with the Bell family. Hitz's surrogate daughter, Helen Keller, called him *Phlegevater*—her "foster father," and she and her teacher, Anne Sullivan, regularly welcomed him for summer sojourns at their home in Wrentham, Massachusetts. To Helen, he imparted Emmanuel Swedenborg's philosophy of "usefulness"—the idea that the truest form of religious devotion is the service we offer each other—which guided Helen Keller's lifelong humanitarian work.

John Hitz tended to New Church and civic affairs while continuing to serve as Superintendent of the Volta Bureau. At eighty, in March 1908, he collapsed of heart failure at Washington's new Union Station, awaiting the train carrying Helen Keller and her mother from Alabama. Helen honored him with a published homage, *John Hitz as I Knew Him*. She described him to the overflowing crowd at his memorial service, held in the Volta Bureau's great hall, as "...a wise, good man [who] has lived among us as a benediction..." She appreciated especially John Hitz's encouragement of women's "independent, fearless thought and reflection."

On the day of the ceremony, The *Washington Evening Star* reported that

> The portico of [the Volta Bureau] was draped in black, and there were black and purple hangings on the wall before which the coffin was placed. A bust of Mr. Hitz draped in the Swiss flag stood at its head, flanked by palms. Great quantities of beautiful flowers lay on and about the bier....Many unable to gain entrance stood outside on the broad steps in the rain. Among those present were Miss Clara Barton...Helen Keller and her mother, Mr. and Mrs. Macey (Anne Sullivan Macey, Helen's Teacher), President Gallaudet...Mr. Alexander Graham Bell and Mr. Charles J Bell.

Reverend Frank Sewall eulogized, "His personality, sweet by the discipline of trial, radiated the gentle influence of true friendship toward all whom he could benefit." Overlooking the troubles of thirty years before, the Swiss Minister, Leo Vogel, paid tribute to Hitz's love for his native country and his compatriots.

John Hitz directed the executors of his small estate to erect a plain monument in the family plot in the Congressional Cemetery, to the memory of his children, parents, grandparents, and other relatives, "adding thereto also the name of my daughter Gertrude, with date of death in Switzerland," and his own name and date of death.

Jane Hitz summered every year at the cottage on Deer Isle. Arnold and Harold often joined her there, with their Uncle Will. Their grandmother remained imperious and lonely, according to Miss Spofford, who visited her in her later years. However, she helped finance her grandsons' educations and remained, emotionally as well as financially, connected with them. Her self-published book of poems, *Deer Isle Days*, revealed her feelings of loss and isolation as she grew older, recalling Gertrude's death and witnessing her grandsons growth from boys to men.

*Burning Letters* by Jane Hitz

How oft within this chimney nook
Has gleamed the ruddy household fire;
And often too this hearth has been
A sacrificial pyre.

Ah! Many a letter, sad or gay.
Has smouldered into ashes here,
Some freighted rich with words of love,
Some pale with words of fear.

The first rude, stumbling letters traced
By boyhood's childish pen,
Whose authors tread these chambers now
With heavy steps of men;

A poet's letters here were brought
And offered up in flame
When she to whom he wrote them slept
'Neath a stone which bears her name.

In that far Alpine graveyard where
The snows lie half the year,
Till, trembling through their pallid pall,
The first faint flowers appear.

And letters too from friend and foe,
The cruel and the kind,
Here found alike their graves, and spread
Their ashes on the wind.

Crowned with the ashen crown which Time
Has set upon my head,
These other ashes at my feet,
I sit among the Dead.

Jane Catherine Shanks Hitz died suddenly, in June 1909, in her Washington apartment building, The Ontario, to which she had recently moved. She was seventy-two.

Gertrude hoped that her brother William, who was twenty-four when she died, would reconcile with their father. Honoring her wishes, William consulted Mr. Davidge, and reestablished cordial relations with his father. Later, in 1908, he offered to fund a voyage to Switzerland, but John Hitz died before he could make that final journey.

William Henry Hitz attended Harvard College, Class of 1896, and earned an LL.B. from the Georgetown School of Law in 1900. At thirty, in private practice in Washington, he married Esther Porter of Baltimore, a thirty-four-year-old Goucher College graduate as intelligent and independent-minded as his mother. William and Esther had two sons, Frederick Porter Hitz (born 1905) and William Jr. (born 1909).

Their uncle William remained a great favorite with his nephews, Arnold and Harold, who loved fishing and sailing with him in Maine on their boat, *Flicka*. Jane Hitz bequeathed the cottage at Hitz Point to her son and two grandsons. The brothers eventually sold their share to their uncle. Five generations of Hitz descendants have returned each summer to the Deer Isle cottage.

In 1916, President Woodrow Wilson appointed William Hitz an associate justice on the Supreme Court for the District of Columbia (now the United States District Court for the District of Columbia). In 1931, President Herbert Hoover appointed him a federal judge on the United States Court of Appeals for the DC Circuit. William Hitz gained national renown as presiding judge in the trial known as the Teapot Dome Scandal. In 1929 Judge Hitz sentenced Albert Fall, a former Secretary of the Interior, to serve a year in jail and pay a fine of $100,000, the amount of the bribe he was convicted for accepting from Edward L. Doheny to secure western oil production rights, without competitive bidding. Hitz's decision struck a blow against government corruption and cronyism, marking the first time a Cabinet member had received a felon's sentence.

A newspaper profile described William Hitz as "a nonconventional type of judge" who appeared the picture of authority on the bench, with flowing black robe, graying hair, and steel-rimmed spectacles, "ruling over the courtroom with an iron hand." Yet he emerged, after adjournment, "as a witty, small-sized, well-dressed man who leans slightly forward when he walks, and enjoys human society and the company of old friends." He was sixty-three when he died in 1935.

⳹

Alfred Edgar Burton also died in 1935, at seventy-eight. In Gertrude's words, he truly "accomplished much with the least amount of noise," both personally and professionally. The year Gertrude died, 1896, Burton rose to the rank of full professor at MIT. He took a leave of absence from teaching that spring to join his old roommate Robert E. Peary on an expedition to Greenland. Their goal was to retrieve the two-hundred-ton Cape York meteorite and deliver it to the American Museum of Natural History in New York City. Burton did much of the preparatory scientific work for the trip and also collected valuable data. In subsequent years, Burton headed Tech expeditions, to Georgia in 1900, and to the interior of Sumatra the following year, to observe the total eclipse of the sun. In 1902, he was appointed the first Dean for Student Affairs at the Massachusetts Institute of Technology. He remained in that position, beloved and respected by generations of students, until he retired in 1922. MIT named an undergraduate dormitory, Burton-Conner, for him.

In 1905, on a walking tour in France, Burton met Lena Yates, an Englishwoman fifteen years his junior. In July 1906 he sent news to Jane Hitz outlining his plans to marry Lena and bring his new wife and her mother to live in Boston. "I am to be married next week," he wrote, to "the only other woman except Gertrude that I have ever loved."

Lena Yates Burton developed artistic and literary aspirations during fifteen years as a faculty wife and suburban mother to three young children. As an author and poet, she changed her name, first to Lena Dalkeith, and later to Jeanne D'Orge. Feeling stifled in Boston, and unhappy in her marriage, she moved across the country to California, taking their children, Christine, Virginia Lee, and Alexander Ross, with her.

Burton retired from MIT in 1922 to join them, and the family eventually settled in Carmel-by-the-Sea. There, Jeanne D'Orge fell in love with Carl Cherry, an eccentric inventor fifteen years younger than she, and thirty years younger than Burton, who had once been his professor at MIT. When Jeanne D'Orge left the house late one night to live with Cherry, the family was irreparably fragmented. The children, aged sixteen, fourteen, and ten, found temporary homes with friends and relatives. Alfred Edgar returned to Boston in 1925 and began working with the Harry E. Burroughs Newsboys Foundation, providing education, vocational training, and life opportunities for poor, mostly immigrant, boys.

His artistically talented daughter, Virginia, joined him in Boston in 1929. She "kept house" for her father at 36 Joy Street, on Beacon Hill, around the corner from Myrtle Street, where Burton and Gertrude had lived forty years earlier. Twenty-year-old Virginia studied design, taught art, and illustrated drama and dance reviews for the *Boston Evening Transcript*. In 1931, she married George Demetrios, a sculptor who was teaching drawing at the Boston Museum School. Virginia Lee Burton founded the Folly Cove Designers collective and became a Caldecott Medal winning author–illustrator of children's books, including the classics *Mike Mulligan and his Steam Shovel* and *The Little House*.

Alfred Edgar Burton loved and lost two ambitious, uncompromising women, and fathered exceptional children. He died of a heart attack on a visit to Virginia's home at Folly Cove, Gloucester, Massachusetts. His son Arnold designed his elegant gravestone in the Evergreen Cemetery, Portland, Maine, inscribed with lines from Leigh Hunt's poem, *Abou Ben Adhem*, which was found in Burton's pocket when he died: "I pray thee, then, / Write me as one that loves his fellow men."

When his father died, Felix Arnold Burton was married and living in a small house of his own design in Waban, Massachusetts. He and his wife, Helen, settled less than two miles from the Allen School and the familiar surroundings of his Newton boyhood. Despite his sunny name, Arnold endured more than his share of ill health. Gertrude had correctly predicted in 1889 that of her two sons he was "the one whose soul will suffer more." As a child, he fell victim not only to "an ill-fated experiment with poison ivy," but to most other common maladies, and many more serious conditions.

After he and Harold returned to America from Lausanne, Arnold grew to be an artistically gifted young man. He graduated from the Allen School, then from Bowdoin College, his father's alma mater, in 1907. He decided on a career in architecture, earning a bachelor's and master's degree from MIT's School of Architecture. In 1911, he married Helen Lancaster Eaton, whose family lived near his grandmother's house in Brunswick, Maine. Their daughter Alice was born in 1915.

During their European honeymoon, Arnold and Helen managed a nostalgic visit to Lausanne and Leysin. Arnold produced a portfolio of exquisite architectural watercolors capturing each of their other stops across the continent. In 1918, after World War I ended, he returned to Europe as a civilian attached to the Army Quartermaster Corps, documenting damage to artworks and buildings. Some of the ruins were the very monuments and churches he had sketched before the war.

Arnold's young family settled in Boston in 1920. He joined the well-known architecture firm of Allen and Collens, and later established his own office at 234 Boylston Street. Arnold Burton became well known for residential designs and historic renovations, college campus facilities (for example, at Bowdoin and Reed colleges), and public buildings in the then popular neo-Colonial and Georgian styles. His designs' classical proportions and graceful, historical details produced pleasing domestic and public spaces, as though Arnold were creating the calm, home-like surroundings he had missed, living in boarding schools and with surrogate families.

Arnold closed his practice in 1943. Rheumatoid arthritis eventually made drawing, letter writing, and even typewriting daunting tasks. He later succumbed to non-Hodgkin's lymphoma, after years of "therapeutic" X-ray treatments. He died in Boston in 1949, at age sixty-four, and is buried in the Pine Grove Cemetery in Brunswick, Maine with his wife, Helen, her parents, and their daughter Alice, all with graceful grave markers of his design.

At the time of Arnold's death Harold wrote affectionately to his niece Alice, "Your father and I grew up unusually close together because of the early loss of our mother. He therefore felt a greater responsibility for me than usually would be the case, and I have no doubt that I was a considerable trial to him…He lived a constructive life full of courage and helpfulness."

The gold chains Gertrude had given her sons bound them to her memory and to each other. As adults, they researched Gertrude's life and contacted many of her acquaintances, curious to know and understand the mother who died so young. They each visited her grave in Leysin, and over the course of their lives brought children and grandchildren there to connect them to her and to Switzerland. It seems as though each of her sons tried to follow Gertrude's admonition to "Remember! Be good! Be good! Make others happy!"

Gertrude's influence on Harold—"more serene…and more exuberantly glad"—was especially strong: they shared daily life until he was seven years old. In 1927, Harold returned to Leysin for the first time after leaving the Grand Hotel in 1896. It was a tender homecoming. He wrote in his diary, "I am glad mother's grave is here…it is great and grand and pure and high and full of peace…Mother and I have lived again together and I am glad I have more time to live the life I should and that God has offered."

If Arnold's life personified Gertrude's aesthetic sensitivity and nurturing qualities, Harold's embodied her idealism and passionate, reserved drive to make a difference in the world. After their mother's death and his return to the Allen School, Harold attended Newton High School during his senior year. There he encountered a poised classmate, Selma Florence Smith. The two became devoted during their college days at Wellesley and at Bowdoin. Harold went on to earn his LL.B. at Harvard Law School, and immediately after he graduated in June 1912, the couple married in West Newton, at the newly built First Unitarian church, designed by Ralph Adams Cram, Bliss Carman's "Visionist" colleague.

Harold and Selma moved to Cleveland, Ohio where he began practicing law. When America entered World War I, Harold enlisted in the infantry and saw heavy fighting in Belgium and France, rising to the rank of captain and earning the Belgian *Croix de Guerre*. After the Armistice, he resumed his law practice and the family grew. Four children were born between 1913 and 1921: Barbara, William, my mother Deborah, and Robert.

In the late 1920s, Harold Burton decided to enter politics. After serving briefly in the Ohio House of Representatives, he became law director for the city of Cleveland. In 1935, the year his father died, he was elected Cleveland's mayor and reelected twice, by wide margins. The newspapers called him "the Boy Scout Mayor" for his exemplary personal life and effective opposition to organized crime.

Harold was elected to the US Senate in 1940, where he encountered fellow Senator Harry S. Truman. He served on Truman's "Special Committee to Investigate the National Defense Program," which monitored the US war effort during World War II, and he also co-sponsored the Hill–Burton Act, legislation that established hospitals nationwide.

Harry Truman became President in 1945, upon the death of Franklin D. Roosevelt. As a bipartisan gesture, Democrat Truman appointed Republican Harold Hitz Burton to fill a vacancy on the United States Supreme Court. He was confirmed unanimously, and took his seat on the Court the next day, serving as associate justice until his retirement on October 13, 1958. In his later years, Harold suffered from Parkinson's disease. He died on October 28, 1964, in Washington, and is buried in Cleveland's Highland Park Cemetery, with his wife Selma and their children.

Before he stepped down from the Court, the *New York Times* ran a Burton profile headlined "The Quiet Arbiter" (October 7, 1958). It began: "A pleasant, soft-spoken gentleman who has moved quietly through American public life for twenty-nine years is about to move quietly out of it." On the Supreme Court, Harold gained a reputation as "moderately conservative, moderately liberal"—making "little noise" while promoting the "growing good of the world," through his conscientious efforts. According to Chief Justice Earl Warren, Harold Hitz Burton played an important role in uniting his fellow justices in the 1954 landmark case *Brown v. Board of Education,* when the court ruled unanimously that racial segregation of public schools was unconstitutional.

Harold Burton's public career in Washington brought one chapter in the Hitz family story full circle. The majestic, white-columned Supreme Court building stands next to the Library of Congress, at the former intersection of A and First Streets. Directly opposite, within the grounds of today's Capitol Visitors Center, stood the original Hitz family home, at 29 A Street, SE, where Harold's mother, Anna Gertrude Hitz was born, much sooner than expected.

The Grand Hotel's promotional postcard

The Grand Hotel, high on the slope above Leysin village

The sea of white clouds above the Rhone River, with the Dents du Midi in the background

Some of the Grand Hotel's guests, in a sun gallery, with Harold on the steps

Harold and his playmates on the
veranda of the Grand Hotel

Publicity poster for Bliss Carman's
book, *Behind the Arras, A Book of the
Unseen*, 1895 (courtesy of Houghton
Library, Harvard University, p Typ
970 00 7084 #99)

Gertrude's grave, with wreath, 1896

Volta Bureau library, about 1900

Portrait of John Hitz about 1900

Portrait of Jane Catherine Shanks
Hitz, about 1899

Jane Hitz, William Hitz, Harold and Arnold at Hitz Point, Deer Isle, about 1899

Portrait of Dean Alfred Edgar Burton, about 1930

Felix Arnold Burton passport photo, about 1918

Portrait of Honorable
Harold Hitz Burton,
Associate Justice of the
US Supreme Court,
about 1956

The view from
Gertrude's room
in 2014

# *Afterword*

ARLY IN THE WRITING PROCESS, A FRIEND ASKED ME WHAT THIS BOOK
was about.

"Sex and death," I joked.

And so it turned out: sex and death, but also love and birth, along with ambition and self-discipline, longings and regrets, family loyalties, warm friendships, and a haunting illness. Gertrude's three-part life story resonates today: the radical idealism of her early twenties, guided by "humanity's star;" her "short life in the saddle," searching for self-fulfillment; and finally, her efforts to reconcile "faulty ways," and accept mortality with curiosity and grace.

Gertrude's belief in gender equality and companionate marriage, her advocacy of voluntary motherhood, which we call reproductive rights, her convictions about mind–body connections, which we recognize as holistic medicine, and her tolerance for homosexual love all prefigured contemporary feminist movements. She embraced revolutionary means toward goals of personal autonomy and societal progress. Yet, at the same time, Gertrude prized order, calm, and predictably lofty models of integrity and principled conduct. As I learned more, this complicated Victorian woman, born two centuries ago, became someone I wanted to get to know, through conversations over many cups of tea.

Though most women's lives remain hidden from those who come after, I have been privileged to follow Gertrude's journey of noble aspirations and endeavors. Like the Knight Errant's passionate dragon-quest in a favorite poem, Gertrude's quest proved imperfect and incomplete, but nevertheless eloquent and inspiring.

❧

Have little care that life is brief/And less that art is long.
Success is in the silences/Though fame is in the song.
—BLISS CARMAN, *Songs from Vagabondia*, 1894

# *Acknowledgements*

MANY PEOPLE AND INSTITUTIONS CONTRIBUTED TO MY RESEARCH and writing process. Thanks first to my fellow Cumberland Writers—Barb Desmarais, Deb Gould, Judy Maloney, Lisa Schinhofen, Pam Burr Smith, and Amy Waterman—for their support and helpful commentary all along the way. Also, thanks to readers whose invaluable notes and thoughtful suggestions helped me envision Gertrude's story with fresh eyes, especially Jane Brox, Ann De Forest, Linda Docherty, and Jeff Fischer; Beth Borgerhoff, Tiffany Johnston, and Deanne Urmy.

In addition to the trove of family records, the internet often made it easy to locate resources. Archival research in libraries yielded deeper insights into Gertrude's relationships with colleagues and fleshed out her social context. Thanks go to the helpful librarians in the collections at Bowdoin College (Special Collections); Harvard University (Houghton Library); Dartmouth College (Rauner Library); Smith College (Sophia Smith Collection); Wilson College; Queen's University, Kingston, Ontario (University Archives, Bliss Carman fonds, correspondence series, Locator 2070, Box 6, folders 1 and 2, and Box 16, folders 1-9 ); University of New Brunswick, Fredericton, NB; the Wisconsin State Historical Society; Maine Medical Center Archives; the Library of the National Institutes of Health, Bethesda, MD; the US National Archives, Washington, DC; and the Villa I Tatti, Harvard Center for Renaissance Studies, Florence, Italy (the Berenson Archive).

I also appreciated the help of dedicated volunteers in several local libraries and historical societies: in Maine, the Curtis Memorial Library and the Pejepscot Historical Society (Brunswick), and the

Boothbay Region Historical Society; in Massachusetts, the Medway Historical Society; and in New York, the Saranac Lake Free Library and Adirondack Research Center. I am grateful, too, for information from the Volta Bureau and the Swiss Club of Washington, DC, and the online archives of the Washington, DC Congressional Cemetery, and the Library of Congress.

The Bowdoin College Faculty Development Fund supported research and travel. Noma Petroff, theater and dance department coordinator, expertly prepared many photographs. Helpful, cheerful Bowdoin work–study students transcribed diaries and letters.

I am deeply grateful to the generations of family who guarded the materials that inspired—and enabled—me to tell Gertrude's story. And to my generous parents, sisters, cousins, aunts, and uncles, who shared their own albums and files. Most of all, I thank my sons, Ben and Nick, and especially, my husband David, for their enthusiasm, encouragement, and patience.

## *About the author*

J UNE ADLER VAIL FOUNDED BOWDOIN COLLEGE'S DANCE PROGRAM
and, as professor, chaired the department of Theater and Dance
for many years. Her courses ranged from choreography to dance eth-
nography and history. She was dance critic for the *Maine Times*, wrote
numerous articles, academic papers and book chapters, and authored
a previous book, *Cultural Choreographies*. She lives in Brunswick, Maine.

Visit her website at: www.junevail.com